TAX REFORM
AND THE ALLIANCE FOR PROGRESS

Latin American Monographs, No. 4
Institute of Latin American Studies
The University of Texas

TAX REFORM
AND THE ALLIANCE FOR PROGRESS

by Raynard M. Sommerfeld

Published for the INSTITUTE OF LATIN AMERICAN STUDIES
by the UNIVERSITY OF TEXAS PRESS, Austin & London

Library of Congress Catalog Card No. 65–21300
Copyright © 1966 by Raynard M. Sommerfeld

Printed in the United States of America
by the Printing Division of the University of Texas, Austin
Bound by Universal Bookbindery, Inc., San Antonio

To Barb

PREFACE

International economic aid can never be anything but a temporary and marginal form of financial assistance. When such aid is extended to a country that is normally an economically advanced nation—but which is experiencing a temporary setback—the aid generally need not be conditional. Under these circumstances the recipient country will tend to assimilate the aid in a manner permitting the country to return to its normal status as promptly as possible. However, when aid is granted to an economically less well developed country—in an effort to stimulate economic development—then the reasons for placing conditions upon the aid are imperative. Under these circumstances, if major internal reforms are not promulgated the aid will expire long before the desired objective is achieved.

The financial aid promised in the Alliance for Progress is intended to hasten the economic and social development of nineteen Latin American republics. If the Alliance is to achieve its stated objectives, numerous difficult and far-reaching reforms must be initiated by the recipient countries. This book deals specifically with the tax reforms that may well determine the difference between the success and the failure of the Alliance-for-Progress venture.

Like almost every book, this study could not have been completed without the assistance and encouragement of many people. While no attempt will be made to name each of the individuals who contributed, the following persons deserve a special acknowledgment: Professor Walter Krause, of the University of Iowa, who read the original manuscript in its entirety and who offered numerous valuable suggestions for its improvement; and Mrs. Carol Ritter, who patiently typed the manuscript through its various stages. The author also gratefully acknowledges the permission to quote granted by numerous publishing companies, and the financial assistance extended by the College of Business Administration Research Program, The University of Texas.

Finally, I must thank my wife, Barb, and daughters, Andrea and Kristin, for lengthening my days during the preparation of this manuscript by excusing me from family obligations on numerous occasions.

Austin, Texas

TABLE OF CONTENTS

LIST OF TABLES

LIST OF ILLUSTRATIONS

. . . we must insist that the Latin American leaders plan to act with us to use aid in combination with the energies and resources of their respective countries to build sinews, rather than symbols, of modern progress.

The New York Times Magazine
December 4, 1960

TAX REFORM
AND THE ALLIANCE FOR PROGRESS

1. An Introduction

Perhaps no other problem is as crucial to the world today as that of satisfying the increasingly vocal demands made by the vast majority of the world's inhabitants living in the underdeveloped countries. Their demands for economic betterment, human dignity, and political freedom are growing with rapid intensity. The ability and rapidity with which their demands are met will have significant repercussions on the history of the last half of this twentieth century.

This monograph is concerned with only one small part of the "Great Awakening"[1] of rising expectations, in only one geographical area of the world. It is specifically concerned with the role of tax reform in the Alliance-for-Progress program. The Alliance is a concrete proposal intended to help the peoples of Latin America realize their ambitions for economic development. It is a proposal that the United States of America join nineteen republics of Latin America in a pooling of financial and technical resources to make possible, for the poorest of these republics, a "take-off" from the vicious cycle of poverty and economic stagnation, and to permit a more rapid, continued development for those republics already started on their "drive to maturity."[2]

THE ALLIANCE FOR PROGRESS

The Alliance for Progress was first proposed by John F. Kennedy, President of the United States, before a group of Latin American diplomats meeting at the White House on March 13, 1961. In making his proposal, President Kennedy suggested "a vast cooperative effort, un-

---

[1] This term is adopted from Gunnar Myrdal. See his *Rich Lands and Poor,* pp. 7–8.

[2] The "take-off" and the "drive to maturity" are two early stages on the road to economic development, according to W. W. Rostow *(The Stages of Economic Growth: A Non-Communist Manifesto).*

paralleled in magnitude and nobility of purpose, to satisfy the basic
needs of the American people for homes, work and land, health and
schools."[3] The same plan was presented to the U.S. Congress in March
1961. As is true with every major government program, an interesting
history antedates it.

History

It has been suggested that the history of the Alliance for Progress dates
at least from the time then-Vice President Richard Nixon made a much
heralded trip to Latin America in 1958. His reception of stones, brick-
bats, and human saliva caused a "Great Awakening" in the United
States. It awakened the U.S. government to the fact that although Latin
America was still a physical neighbor, she was no longer willing to sit
idly by and watch the gap between the standards of living of the two
peoples widen still farther.

Then, in the Republic of Cuba, a boisterous Fidel Castro overthrew
the Batista regime and eventually introduced world communism to the
Western Hemisphere—introduced communism within ninety miles of
the continental limits of the U.S.A.! The time for action had clearly
arrived. It came in the form of the Act of Bogota, ratified at the third
meeting of the Special Council of the Organization of American States
To Study the Formulation of New Measures for Economic Cooperation, called at Bogota, Colombia, September 5–13, 1960.

The Act of Bogota

The Act of Bogota openly recognized that more than continued private
foreign-investment capital flows were necessary for the realization of
economic development aspirations in Latin America. President Dwight
Eisenhower promised that the United States would make available to
the Latin American governments some $500 million in foreign aid.
The aid was to be administered through the auspices of the Inter-
American Development Bank on rather flexible terms. Especially at-
tractive were provisions for "soft loans" (those repayable in local
currency) and the relending of funds repaid to the special fund for
social development.

But much more important than the limited, external, public aid,
were the provisions for self-help. The Special Council recommended

[3] The complete text of the Presidential address is reported in the *Department
of State Bulletin,* XLIV (April 3, 1961), 471–478.

to the Council of the Organization of American States that numerous ambitious programs for social improvement be enacted. These programs included measures for the improvement of conditions of rural living and land use; measures for the improvement of housing and community facilities; measures for the improvement of educational systems and training facilities; measures for the improvement of public health; and measures for the mobilization of domestic resources.

The Act of Bogota provides that, to the extent possible, the social improvement programs are to be accomplished through the utilization of domestic savings and improved fiscal and financial practices.[4] It suggests that additional revenues can be realized through improvements in assessment practices and collection procedures. In addition to the increase in revenues allocated to the social development projects, the suggested reforms would provide greater equity in the existing systems.

Other provisions of the Act of Bogota called for more long-term, low-interest lending, and for commodity price stabilization. It recommended consultative meetings of the signatory members and a special high-level meeting to be called by the Council of the Organization of American States. Yet, most importantly, it emphasized and re-emphasized that the success of the program depended upon the self-help efforts and, "in many cases, the improvement of existing institutions and practices, particularly in the fields of taxation, the ownership and use of land, education and training, health and housing."[5]

The Presidential Meeting

Before the Act of Bogota could become a reality, the executive branch of the U.S. government changed hands. It was up to President Kennedy to implement the aid promises initiated by former President Eisenhower. Mr. Kennedy did more than that! In proposing the Alliance for Progress, he proposed a ten-year master plan intended to make each American republic "the master of its own revolution and its own hope for progress." He suggested that the United States contribute not $500 million but the better part of $20 billion in aid.

The U.S. government was to provide $12.5 billion in public loans

---

[4] The Act of Bogota, Title I, Measures for Social Improvement, paragraph E, Measures for the Mobilization of Domestic Resources. The text of the Act of Bogota is reproduced in the *Department of State Bulletin*, XLIII (October 3, 1960), 537–540.

[5] *Ibid.*, p. 538.

and grants over the next ten years. Secretary of the Treasury Douglas Dillon estimated the annual U.S. contribution would come from the following sources: the Export-Import Bank, $400 million; the Food-for-Peace Program, $150 million; the technical-assistance program, $75 million; and the Development Loan Fund, $75 million. Even this unheard of "big-money" program was admitted to be but the marginal effort necessary to attain the stipulated objectives. However, the marginal aid promised was enough to secure agreement among the leaders of nineteen republics meeting at Punta del Este, Uruguay, in August 1961.

The Charter of Punta del Este

As José A. Mora, Secretary General of the Organization of American States, stated, the meeting at Punta del Este was concrete expression of "the call to action" of the Alliance. The purpose of the meeting was "to deliberate and resolve on a common strategy" for economic growth.[6] The formal results of the meeting were a Declaration to the Peoples of America and a document entitled the Charter of Punta del Este. All the Latin American republics, except Castro's Cuba, became signatory nations to this Charter.

The Setting

Before examining the objectives of the Alliance for Progress, as set forth in the Charter of Punta del Este, it should be helpful to make even the briefest examination of the setting for this vast, new effort. Latin America includes twenty independent countries of widely varying degrees of development, natural endowment, social heritage, and institutional arrangements. Therefore average statistics for the area as a whole are atypical of each individual country of the area. Nevertheless, in economics, we frequently find resort to such a non-entity average (think, for example, of the "economic man") an extremely helpful device in understanding some general proposition. In this sense, the author believes average statistics will be helpful in understanding the Alliance for Progress.

While obviously not exhaustive, the following statistics suggest the setting that the Alliance for Progress is expected to alter:

[6] José A. Mora, "Note of the Secretary General," in *Planning for Economic and Social Development for Latin America*, p. v.

1. Average per capita gross national product is approximately $300 (ranging from a low of $55 to a high of $1,060; the U.S. average is approximately $2,700). Incidentally, increased per capita GNP is made doubly difficult by the fact that population growth—the fastest in the world—is expected to average 29 percent in the next ten years (the estimate for the United States is 13 percent).

2. Of the 190–200 million inhabitants, 80 percent live in substandard housing.

3. Average life expectancy is 46 years (compared to 70 years for the U.S.).

4. The infant mortality rate is 110 per 1,000 live births (compared to 26 per 1,000 in the U.S.).

5. There are 340 hospital beds per 100,000 population (compared to 910 per 100,000 U.S. inhabitants).

6. There are 54 physicians per 100,000 patients (compared to 135 per 100,000 in the U.S.).

A comparative table of some of these statistics for six of the large Latin American countries is suggestive of the wide variance between individual countries (see Table 1). While the precision of the statistics may be subject to great debate, no reasonable person could argue the necessity of an economic development program intended to attack poverty, illiteracy, substandard housing, and disease in the area depicted. This, then, is the setting for the Alliance for Progress.

TABLE 1

Selected Statistics for Six Latin American Countries

Country	Average Per Capita Income	Annual Population Growth	Literacy Rate	Life Expectancy
Venezuela	$1,062	3.2%	51%	. . . years
Chile	492	2.5	80	52
Argentina	376	2.0	86	59
Mexico	296	3.0	56	38
Brazil	216	2.4	49	45
Peru	156	2.4	50	46

Source: Senate Document Number 80, *Special Report on Latin America,* 87th Congress, 2nd Session, p. 12.

The Objectives

The Charter of Punta del Este stipulates the following goals, or objectives, for member nations:[7]

1. Per capita income growth of not less than 2.5 percent per year;

2. A more equitable distribution of income concurrent with an increased percentage of the national product devoted to investment;

3. A more balanced economy—especially freedom from dependence upon a single export commodity;

4. Increased industrialization;

5. Increased agricultural productivity and output;

6. Land reform—including distribution of ownership rights to the man who works the land;

7. Decreased illiteracy—with a minimum goal of six years of primary education for all children by 1970;

8. Improved health—with a minimum goal of increasing life expectancy by five years; decreasing the infant mortality rate to one half the present rate; and eradicating those illnesses for which effective cures are known;

9. Increased construction of low-cost housing;

10. Maintenance of reasonable price stability;

11. Strengthening the economic integration of the Latin American area through common market arrangements;

12. Stabilization of commodity prices to avoid the disasters associated with wide fluctuations in foreign exchange earnings.

The attainment of these goals presents a truly Herculean task. As in any area inhabited by approximately 200 million people, there is both great pressure for, and great resistance to, change. The eventual success or failure of the venture depends primarily on indigenous leadership, resources, and skills. Title II, Chapter I, of the Charter of Punta del Este, states that "the American republics recognize that to achieve the foregoing goals it will be necessary":[8]

1. That well-conceived development programs be initiated;

2. "That national programs of economic and social development be

___

[7] This list is a brief paraphrasing of Title I, Objectives of the Alliance for Progress, The Charter of Punta del Este. The complete text of the Charter is reproduced in the *Department of State Bulletin*, XLV (September 11, 1961), 463–469.

[8] *Ibid.*, p. 464.

based on the principles of self-help—as established in the Act of Bogota—and the maximum use of domestic resources, taking into account
the special conditions of each country";

3. That women be given equality of treatment with men;

4. That external aid be provided on flexible terms "to supplement
domestic capital formation and reinforce their import capacity; and
that, in support of well-conceived programs, including the necessary
structural reforms and measures for the mobilization of internal resources" $20 billion be provided in the next ten years;

5. That institutional reforms be accomplished to permit a fair distribution of the fruits of economic progress.

Organization and Procedure

The actual operations of the Alliance for Progress are to be conducted
primarily by a panel of nine high-level experts chosen freely from any
country. The appointed (for a three-year, renewable term) panel is attached to the Inter-American Economic and Social Council, but it retains automony from that group. The Organization of American States
(OAS), the United Nations Economic Commission for Latin America
(ECLA), the Inter-American Development Bank (IADB), and various United Nations agencies provide technical assistance.

A government desiring financial or technical assistance must present
its request, along with a proposed economic and social development
plan, to an *ad hoc* committee of three members, chosen from the panel
of nine experts. The *ad hoc* committee members study the plan, make
any necessary modifications, and report their recommendations to the
IADB. The Charter cautions the committee members to consider the
principles of self-help in making their recommendations. If the committee approves the plan proposed, the IADB proceeds with negotia-
tions to obtain any external funds necessary to finance the project.

The Implications

Various individuals have observed that the heavy emphasis—in fact,
insistence—on economic planning is a new departure for the foreign
economic policy of the United States. The question immediately arises
as to what implications this has for such factors as the private-market
economy and personal freedom. While this study is not primarily concerned with these implications, it perhaps must be mentioned here that

the author does not view the question as one of black or white. No
economy is completely free and, therefore, the question is really how
much intervention is deemed desirable. The answer apparently suggested by the Alliance for Progress is as much or as little intervention
as is necessary to accomplish specified goals. To the extent that this may
mean limited encroachment on personal freedom and free-market dictates, it is condoned. This is not to suggest either a carte blanche approval of complete government intervention or the end of a free-
enterprise economy. Rather, it suggests a nebulous standard that can be
the only one used in judging many proposals which will be raised in
conjunction with the Alliance. More specifically, it suggests the standard by which the tax proposals, to be made later in this study, will be
tested.

Fiscal and other governmental policy derives meaning and direction
from the aspirations and goals of the society within which it operates.
The goals of the Latin American republics were clearly stated in the
Charter of Punta del Este, and briefly reiterated earlier in this chapter.
The implications of these aspirations for tax-reform measures form the
substance of this monograph. Tax reforms believed necessary for realization of the goals will be recommended; those deemed inconsistent
will be discarded.

A Big Question

The primary emphasis in the Alliance for Progress is apparently "social
development" rather than fundamental "economic development."
What emphasis there is on economic development is oriented toward
increased raw materials production. This fact has caused some economists[9] to question the ability of the Alliance to provide the long-term
effort necessary to assure economic enrichment of a lasting variety.
They have expressed the fear that it might provide only an amelioration
of the present "sore spots."

The final allocation of the internally produced revenues, as well as
the external financial aid, will determine whether a lasting contribution
to real economic development is made. It is with primary concern for
such long-term achievements in economic development that the criterion for tax-revenue measures were selected in this project. For example,
while the short-run social implications of an immediate, highly pro-

[9] See Walter Krause, "El Plan Kennedy," in *Report on Latin America,*
pamphlet, pp. 23–30.

gressive personal-income tax are unquestionable, the implications for long-run development goals are less clear.

A Comparison

The United States aid to Western Europe through the Marshall Plan is often compared to the Alliance for Progress for Latin America. While the comparison may have some relevance, the situations of the two areas—Western Europe and Latin America—are vastly different. The primary distinction is that Western Europe needed only a marginal assistance to *restore* herself following World War II; Latin America needs a complete inner change to *establish* herself, as well as a marginal assistance to accomplish that change. Tax-reform measures are one small part of the necessary inner change; the $20 billion in promised aid constitutes only the marginal assistance.

OBJECTIVES OF THIS MONOGRAPH

This monograph is an attempt to harmonize tax policy with the economic-development-oriented goals stipulated in the Alliance for Progress. While the traditional tax canons of certainty, convenience, and economy of collection still retain some of their validity, in the setting of an underdeveloped country, the aspirations and the institutional factors frequently change priorities and occasionally nullify otherwise important canons.

More precisely, the ultimate objective of this monograph could be stated as the provision of *realistic* guidelines for tax-reform efforts. Alliance-for-Progress external financial aid has been conditioned on the recipient country's attaining minimum progress in tax-reform efforts. Consequently, the provision of realistic guidelines is mandatory for the satisfactory performance of duties assigned to such groups as the Inter-American Development Bank, responsible for an evaluation of loan applications of the Latin American republics.

Tax reform can be narrowly conceived as, for example, measures necessitated to increase government tax revenues. Alternately, tax reform can be broadly conceived as a study to prepare an exhaustive listing, with specific recommendations, of the many aspects of tax reform believed desirable for a particular country. Still a third approach defines tax reform as changes in existing tax programs necessitated to integrate this phase of the economic sphere into the overall development program. This definition permits an *ad hoc* description of tax reform, in each instance relating it to certain social and economic environments and objectives. The third approach is adopted in this study.

In drafting these tax-reform guidelines, and in making recommendations, care was taken to concentrate on those areas most likely to lead to immediate, practical conclusions. In this regard, the words of Professor Alvin Hansen seemed most appropriate:[10] "It follows that the job of the outside critic is not to persuade underdeveloped countries to do something fundamentally different, but to help them to think more realistically about what they are already trying to do, so as to avoid some of the more obvious pitfalls on the developmental path." Failure to follow this good advice is frequently responsible for tax-reform reports resting peacefully in the archives forever.

It must be understood, of course, that where resources, markets, and leadership are wholly lacking, no improvement in any tax system can of itself enable economic development to take place. A good tax system may promote an efficient utilization of scarce resources in a manner consistent with economic development; a bad tax system will simply constitute another impediment to developmental efforts.

The Organizational Plan

Chapter 2 of this study is an attempt to promulge the role assigned tax reform in the overall Alliance-for-Progress program. This is accomplished through a rather exhaustive examination of the basic documents constituting the Alliance: the Charter of Punta del Este; the Declaration to the Peoples of America; and the Act of Bogota. In order better to understand these formal documents, public statements of high-level government personnel from various countries are reviewed. Once the intended objectives for tax reform are clarified, they are intensively examined.

The next four chapters provide a brief sketch of the most important aspects of the existing tax systems of Latin America and suggest, whenever possible, how they might be altered to best accomplish the intended goals of economic development. Chapter 3 begins with a "bird's eye" view of the Latin American fiscal scene. The next three chapters examine, in greater detail, income taxation, wealth taxation, and other taxes, respectively. Primary attention is given to the income tax for reasons developed in Chapter 2.

---

[10] A. H. Hansen, *Public Enterprise and Economic Development,* p. 13.

The Latin American countries as a group have accepted the general notion that economically desirable goals can and should be promoted through special tax-exemption provisions. Therefore, Chapter 7 considers the role of the tax-exemption scheme in an economic development program. Chapter 8 is devoted to problems in tax administration. It may well be that immediate action in tax reform can be restricted to this important aspect of the underdeveloped tax system. Chapter 9 constitutes a summary of the author's findings and recommendations. Chapter 10 concludes the monograph with a review and evaluation of the first post-Alliance tax-reform efforts.

It is hoped that the general reader will find here some comparative material on the different tax systems with which he may be unfamiliar. But more importantly, it is hoped that the administrator-economist-reader will find here some practical considerations of tax reform that could assist in attaining the goals of economic development established for Latin America in the Alliance for Progress.

Two kinds of comparisons are frequently used. One, comparing the tax of a developed and an underdeveloped country, is made whenever it is believed some adaptable experience or relevant idea of the former could be of value to the latter. The second kind of comparison is between underdeveloped countries. In this case the aim is to examine common problems and, where possible, to suggest common solutions to these problems.

The Limitations of This Study

Before we approach this colossal problem, several warnings are in order. First, there is no intention that this effort should constitute a comprehensive study of tax reform for each of the nineteen republics associated in the Alliance for Progress. The study indicates the tremendous need for individual and thorough studies for each country, which will produce the detailed list of recommendations mentioned earlier. Without direct, personal contact in the country involved, such a study would be presumptive indeed. Nevertheless, it is believed that the general direction for real progress in the area of tax reform for Latin America will be developed here.

Second, specific references to particular laws may not be current, although every attempt has been made to keep current. Since the Punta del Este conference, many Latin American countries have initiated tax-reform studies and some have enacted new legislation which was not available to the author. Those noted in embassy dispatches to early

1962 were well summarized in F. R. Fisher's *Tax Reform in Latin America*, and the supplement thereto, and were incorporated in this writing.[11]

Third, a critically important part of government tax policy concerns government expenditure criteria. A letter to the editor of the *Wall Street Journal* suggests that at least one Latin American believes this aspect of tax reform has been too much neglected:[12]

But it is a bit confusing that even though the U.S. Government places so much emphasis on taxes and tax collection, it seems relatively unconcerned on how this new tax revenue is spent. Does it make any difference if it is spent to build hospitals or pay Marxist school teachers? Does it make any difference if it is spent in settling farmers on their own land or in Chinese commune-type agrarian reforms? . . . Does it make any difference if it is spent on nonexistent public services or in maintaining a huge and inefficient bureaucracy for demagogic purposes? Apparently it makes no difference as long as the "wealthy, oppressor, landholder" is squeezed dry.

While the importance of this problem is recognized, it does not constitute any major part of the present project. To investigate criteria for government-expenditure policy, and to determine a proper level of government developmental-investment expenditures, would lead one far afield. The reason for this summary treatment is simply the constraints imposed by time and resources available for a study of this variety.

Finally, the definition of the word "taxes" could be much more broadly construed than it is here. Generally, this monograph restricts the definition to "those government revenues traditionally thought of and reported in government statistics as "tax receipts." In the counties with which this study is concerned, foreign-exchange differentials, profits on government-operated monopolies, commodity-production-board proceeds, and similar revenue producers, could conceptually be included as part of the "tax" receipts. The rejection of the broader interpretation was made, first, to simplify the problem, and second, to permit recommendations that would be both realistic and practical in the majority of the countries. The rejection is not intended to imply that these alternative government revenues are in any way inferior or less real than those discussed.

[11] Frederic R. Fisher, *Tax Reform in Latin America*, Bureau of Latin American Affairs, January 24, 1962. The *Supplement* is dated February 20, 1962.

[12] Carlos A. Ball, "Give Us Our Change," Letter to the Editor, *Wall Street Journal*, July 17, 1962, p. 10.

THE LITERATURE

While there is a substantial body of literature dealing with taxation and tax reform, little of it is specifically directed at the underdeveloped economy. Consequently much of the well-known literature can serve as only a general frame of references for this project. Even thorough, descriptive works on the existing tax-revenue measures of many Latin American countries are not readily available. Accurate statistics on detailed government revenues, particularly at the state and local level, are even more difficult to obtain.

Nevertheless, the body of literature in this vital area is expanding. The writer found the World Tax Series and the Reports of the Conference on Agricultural Taxation and Economic Development, prepared by the Harvard Law School International Program in Taxation, to be particularly thorough and valuable. Numerous studies of individual countries carried out by technical-assistance missions, under United Nations auspices, were also invaluable. The Shoup Commission report entitled *The Fiscal System of Venezuela* is an outstanding example of what can be accomplished in such a country mission.[13] Various branches of, and individuals within, the Pan American Union and the Organization of American States provided interesting and valuable statistics and reports. The annual statistical publications of the United Nations and the International Monetary Fund were equally informative.

Since this topic has so recently become of crucial significance to many Latin American nations seeking aid under the Alliance for Progress, it is safe to predict that within five years many, many more studies, with greatly improved statistical reports, will be available for scholarly investigation. At the same time, many new laws will have been introduced and tested in the laboratory of the political and economic arena. It is only hoped that this work will not be obsolete before the last pages are written.

[13] Commission to Study the Fiscal System of Venezuela, *The Fiscal System of Venezuela*. Carl S. Shoup was director of the Commission. Serving with him were John F. Due, Lyle C. Fitch, Sir Donald McDougall, Oliver S. Oldman, and Stanley S. Surrey.

2. The Objectives of Alliance-Prompted Tax-Reform Efforts

The purpose of this chapter is twofold: first, to promulge the role intended for tax reform in the Alliance-for-Progress program; and second, to make explicit the problems inherent in the major tax-reform objectives. The method used to accomplish the first purpose consists of an intensive culling of the three basic documents of the Alliance, noting all references to tax reform. The documents are the Act of Bogota, the Declaration to the Peoples of America, and the Charter of Punta del Este. In order further to clarify these objectives, explanatory statements by officials of the United States and Latin American governments are reviewed, and the details of the international-agency programs in taxation are considered. The chapter concludes with a discussion of the conceptual problems of the major tax-reform objectives, and their implications for economic development. In short, the chapter attempts to answer this question: Why tax reform?

REVIEW OF THE BASIC DOCUMENTS

The Act of Bogota

The Act of Bogota makes four specific references to tax reform. Two of the references are very general and, therefore, do not reveal much about the intended role of tax reform. They simply suggest that a better tax system, generally, is necessary for the success of the proposed program. However, Title I, Paragraph A, is more specific. It suggests that tax reform should be designed "with a view to assuring equity of taxation and encouraging improved use of land, especially privately owned land which is idle."

Title I, Paragraph E, is also helpful. It suggests that tax revenues be increased to help finance the efforts necessary to accomplish the goals of the program; proposes that this be accomplished simultaneously with increased tax equity and better enforcement of existing tax laws; and advocates a better allocation of the tax revenues collected. The exact wording of Paragraph E is as follows:

E. Measures for the Mobilization of Domestic Resources
  1. This program shall be carried out within the framework of the maximum creation of domestic savings and the improvement of fiscal and financial practices;
  2. The equity and effectiveness of existing tax schedules, assessment practices and collection procedures shall be examined with a view to providing additional revenue for the purpose of this program;
  3. The allocation of tax revenues shall be reviewed, having in mind an adequate social provision of such revenues to the areas of social development mentioned in the foregoing paragraphs.

In addition to these specific references to tax reform, there are at least two additional objectives of the Act of Bogota which could be indirectly assisted through appropriate tax-reform measures. The first of these is land reform. The avowed objectives of land reform include a wider and more equitable distribution of the ownership of land and increased productivity in land use. Chapter 5 will suggest some land-tax revenue measures that could assist in accomplishing these goals. A second objective, that can be vitally assisted through an appropriate tax policy, would be the promotion of international trade and the facilitation of international capital flows. Problems in international taxation are considered at various appropriate points in this monograph.

The Declaration to the Peoples of America

The Declaration constitutes a brief statement by the nineteen signatory countries to the Alliance for Progress proposing common goals for the coming years. In addition, it delineates what they are willing to do to realize their ambitions for economic development. The promises made are extremely demanding ones.

Specified reform measures include the following: making the tax structure more equitable; enforcing tax laws; redistributing the national income in favor of the poorest classes; promoting savings and investment; maintaining reasonable price stability; and contributing more of their domestic resources to economic and social development projects. These are bold objectives that require the highest level of self-discipline for effective implementation.

The words of the Declaration are most precise:

Therefore the countries signing this declaration in the exercise of their sovereignty have agreed to work toward the following goals during the coming years:

. . .

To reform tax laws, demanding more from those who have most, to punish tax evasion severely, and to redistribute the national income in order to benefit those who are most in need, while, at the same time, promoting savings and investment and reinvestment of capital.

To maintain monetary and fiscal policies which, while avoiding the disastrous effects of inflation or deflation, will protect the purchasing power of the many, guarantee the greatest possible price stability, and form an adequate basis for economic development.

. . .

For their part, the countries of Latin America agree to devote a steadily increasing share of their own resources to economic and social development, and to make the reforms necessary to assure that all share fully in the fruits of the Alliance for Progress.

The Declaration to the Peoples of America further stipulates that land-reform measures must be accomplished, and that private enterprise must be encouraged. It advocates the stimulation of private enterprise "in order to encourage the development of Latin American countries at a rate which will help them to provide jobs for their growing populations, to eliminate unemployment, and to take their place among modern industrialized nations of the world." Tax-reform measures, including the provision of tax-exemption schemes, are considered capable of contributing to the creation or expansion of industries deemed desirable in a given economic development plan (typical tax-exemption schemes will be considered in Chapter 7).

The Charter of Punta del Este

The Charter of Punta del Este, the last of three basic documents constituting the framework of the Alliance for Progress, includes numerous references to tax-reform measures. For example, Title I, Chapter II, stipulates the following as "basic requirements" for economic and social development: (a) the maximum use of domestic resources; (b) a more equitable mobilization and use of domestic resources, including appropriate taxation of large incomes and real estate; (c) the improvement of fiscal administration; (d) maintenance of reasonable price stability; (e) stimulation of private saving; (f) elimination of double taxation; and (g) the cultivation of additional foreign private investment. Title II, Chapter IV, promises external assistance in the improvement of tax administrations. Other economic and social goals with tax ramifications mentioned in yet other chapters of the Charter are repetitions of those already considered. They include references to a more equitable distribution of the national income; devotion of a higher percentage of the national product to investment; and diversification and industrialization of the domestic economies.

From this review of the three basic documents of the Alliance for Progress it appears that the framers of these international agreements recognized within Latin America the existence of (1) an "inequitable" tax system; (2) a need for greater capital formation; and (3) a tendency to utilize the land resources in an inefficient manner. Statements by various high-level government officials confirm this interpretation.

FURTHER PRONOUNCEMENTS ON TAX REFORM

Essentially three different groups have expressed an opinion on the tax-reform implications of the Alliance for Progress. They are representatives of the United States government; representatives of foreign governments; and representatives of international agencies, such as the OAS, ECLA, and IADB.

Statements by U.S. Government Officials

Most of the statements by officials of the United States government emphasize one of two objectives for tax-reform efforts in Latin America. Generally, they stress either the need for increased social equity in the tax system or the need for increased capital formation. The following statement by President Kennedy, made to the Inter-American Economic and Social Council meeting at Punta del Este, Uruguay, is typical of those emphasizing the need for greater tax equity:[1]

there is no place in democratic life for institutions which benefit the few while denying the needs of the many even though the elimination of such institutions may require far-reaching and difficult changes such as land reform and tax reform.

The U.S. Ambassador to the United Nations, Adlai Stevenson, echoed President Kennedy's emphasis on the need for greater tax

[1] John F. Kennedy, "Alliance for Progress: A Program for the Peoples of the Americas," *Department of State Bulletin,* XLV (August 28, 1961), 356.

equity when he spoke before the Inter-American Press Association in Manhattan. He said:[2]

> In no area is reform more sorely needed . . . than in taxation—reforming tax systems to relieve the low- and middle-income groups, and ending the tax evasion which costs Latin American governments billions of dollars every year.

The second objective was stressed in the following words by U.S. Secretary of the Treasury Dillon, addressed to the Latin American delegations at Punta del Este:[3]

> First, no developing nation can progress unless it makes heroic efforts to summon its people to the task of development, unless it dedicates a larger portion of domestic resources to the common effort, and unless it calls upon all groups in the society to make fresh and larger contributions to the cause of national progress.

The seriousness with which U.S. officials view the need for tax-reform efforts in Latin America is exemplified in a U.S. Senate document approving President Kennedy's first request for Alliance funds. The Senate Appropriations Committee emphasized[4]

> that these funds are made available because this program is based on self-help, and because it has been assured by the witnesses who testified that land reforms, tax reforms, and social reforms will be among the principal objectives. The committee urges our administrators to withhold the commitment of funds made available in this bill until some of the aforementioned reforms have been accomplished or are in the process of being accomplished.

The idea that tax-reform efforts constitute a precondition to the receipt of U.S. aid has also been expressed by William S. Barnes, director of Latin American Studies at Harvard University and chief U.S.

---

[2] Statement by Adlai E. Stevenson, reported in "The Americas: After the Tax Evaders," *Time*, LXXVIII (October 27, 1961), 41.

[3] Statement by Secretary Douglas Dillon, Press Release #555, August 7, 1961.

[4] Senate Appropriations Committee, *Report on the Inter-American Social and Economic Program and the Chilean Reconstruction and Rehabilitation Program*, Report Number 201, May 3, 1961, p. 2.

officer at an international tax conference,[5] and by Ambassador Teodoro Moscoso, U.S. Latin American area administrator.[6]

Statements by Officials of Other Governments

Statements by officials of other governments are, of course, limited in the English press. Those statements that are available reveal a keen appreciation of the social and political ramifications of the major tax-reform efforts demanded by the Alliance for Progress. In most cases, they also recognize the need for a more equitable distribution of the tax burden and the need for increased tax revenues as the two major objectives of tax-reform efforts.

A clear statement of this attitude is reflected in the following excerpt from an interview between a reporter for the magazine *Américas* and Galo Plaza, the ex-President of Ecuador, currently coordinator of Ecuador's development-planning mission:[7]

Reporter: What seem to be the most urgent reforms?
Galo Plaza: One of the most important tasks is that of reforming our countries' fiscal structures, in order to achieve a more just distribution of the taxpayer's load. This will bring about these two results: that those who are most able to pay, do pay, and a reduction, insofar as possible, in the indirect taxes that unjustly weigh most heavily on those least able to pay. Naturally, that is one of the areas of major legislation that must be passed to reconstruct the tax system so as to put modern methods into effect. When a progressive inheritance tax is proposed, or a new income tax that will not be as easily evaded as the present one is, then we are going to see whether reforms are really desired. If there are no changes in our fiscal systems, we will find that one major obstacle has not been conquered and we will be in a difficult position for executing the rest of the plans for the Alliance for Progress. Let us hope that some of the countries—at least those that have progressive governments—and the privileged classes, and the economic leaders, have a clear vision of the future and realize this is the decisive moment to create the bases for a new future.

[5] As reported in *The New York Times*, "Latins See Gains As Tax Talks End," October 22, 1961, p. 38.

[6] From a speech to the National Conference on International Economics and Social Development, Chicago, July 19, 1962, as reported in "Moscoso on the Alliance," *Américas*, XIV (September 1962), 40.

[7] "Galo Plaza on the Obstacles to the Alliance," *Américas*, XIV (March 1962), 9.

After touring several Latin American countries, a U.S. Senate group reported in early 1962 that government leaders in these countries frequently failed to recognize or accept the "self-help" requirements implicit in the Alliance program. The senators blamed this, in part, on the grandiose manner in which the $20 billion aid program was announced, suggesting that it did not make sufficiently clear the mandatory nature of self-help provisions.[8] Senator Mike Mansfield, a member of this group and a former professor of Latin American and Far Eastern History at the University of Montana, added:[9]

> In some countries visited, it was brought out that little action would be taken on self-help and tax reforms until the next elections, yet these same countries were insisting on external assistance right now. For example, in Brazil, where elections will not be held until October 1962, it was evident that little would be done in the meantime to provide the needed assistance to the country, as stipulated under the Alliance-for-Progress program.

However, members of foreign delegations to the first Alliance-sponsored conference on tax administration[10] generally agreed that "intelligently-designed tax systems, applied with efficacy, may constitute one of the most important instruments *for financing* of Latin America's economic development."[11]

International Agencies and Tax Reform

The actual spadework in the area of tax reform has largely been delegated to the various international agencies concerned with Latin America: the OAS, ECLA, and IADB, working in cooperation with the Harvard University Law School International Program in Taxation. Their resolutions constitute the most concise statement on the intended role of tax reform in the Alliance program available anywhere. Since these are not generally available, they have been reproduced as Appendix 1. Appendix 2 is the text of the joint program on international taxation under the direction of these same agencies.

[8] See Senate Document No. 80, *Special Report on Latin America,* 87th Congress, 2nd Session, p. 3.

[9] *Ibid.,* p. 11.

[10] The reference is to the nine-day tax conference held in Buenos Aires, Argentina, during October 1961. See Appendix 2 for details of the conference.

[11] From page 1 of *Proceedings of the Conference on Tax Administration,* a preliminary draft of the proceedings of the Buenos Aires tax conference (see note 10 *supra*) obtained from Sidney Schmukler, chief, Office of Development Planning, Bureau for Latin America, Department of State.

In summary, these two documents propose essentially the same objectives for tax reform as do the formal Alliance-for-Progress documents; but they do so with greater clarity and precision. In short, their resolutions recognize (1) an urgent and extensive need for capital formation; (2) the desirability of a more equal distribution of income; and (3) the advantages available from the more efficient use of land. They recommend (1) maximum cooperation with tax experts to be appointed to conduct tax-reform studies in individual countries; (2) an intensive effort to improve tax administration; and (3) attendance at two international conferences on taxation.

The joint program on taxation has three basic purposes: strengthening of the Latin American tax systems; improvement of fiscal administration; and technical training of fiscal officers. It attempts to realize these purposes through the organization of tax conferences and the fielding of the tax teams. The program recognizes that eventually each country must draft its own tax system in the light of its own needs and circumstances and consistent with its overall development plan. But it hopes that the overall program will "serve as a ready means of enlisting the cooperation required to facilitate a study of general principals leading to appropriate changes in the tax system."[12]

The OAS sets forth six objectives for its teams of tax experts sent to prepare studies of individual countries. They are[13] (1) to provide practical training in the several phases of tax administration (this is designated the primary objective); (2) to increase the professional and technical level of tax training in the host country; (3) to take inventory of future needs; (4) to select those individuals best qualified for tax training in a foreign country (and thereby to avoid less qualified, political appointees); (5) to cement relations for follow-up technical-assistance missions; and (6) to provide a reasonable target for administrative reforms for IADB use in evaluating loan applications.

In short, the various international agencies also stress the need for tax reform for two primary reasons: (1) to expand government revenues; and (2) to make the distribution of the tax "burden" more equitable. The only major detectible difference between the pronouncements of the international agencies, and those of U.S. and other government officials and of the basic documents of the Alliance for Prog-

[12] See Appendix 2.
[13] From Draft Memorandum, "Suggestions for Fielding Tax Administration Training Missions in Several Latin American Countries," draft memo, OAS: Public Administration Unit, Economic Division, August 11, 1961.

ress, is the increased emphasis in agency statements on the crucial role of improved tax administration. A primary conclusion of this study is that the most *urgent* problem in Latin American taxation—at least for the majority of the countries—is not the need for new tax laws but the improved administration and enforcement of existing statutes. This conclusion is apparently in accord with the thinking of the international agencies.

A Closer Look at the Intended Objectives

To simply state that a tax system should be more equitable or should increase capital formation is not very meaningful. Therefore the remainder of this chapter attempts to explain and evaluate the meaning of these phrases, especially as they relate to economic-development aspirations.

Tax Equity

An inequitable tax system is obviously one in which some individual or some group pays too much (or too little) tax relative to another individual or group. The basis for a tax inequity can stem from either of two conditions. The one, commonly referred to as "horizontal equity," concerns two equally situated taxpayers, whereas the other, called "vertical equity," concerns two unequally situated taxpayers (or groups of taxpayers).

Horizontal Equity

Generally, a tax system is considered "horizontally equitable" so long as equally situated taxpayers make equal tax contributions. Relative to an income tax, the question of what constitutes "equally situated" is interpreted—at least in most English-speaking countries—as meaning "having equivalent amounts of income," after adjustment for such sociological factors as family size, age, and physical infirmities. In Latin America, this notion is not wholly transferable if existing income-tax laws are indicative of accepted notions of horizontal equity. Their schedular income-tax systems frequently distinguish among sources or kinds of income, and they tax the same amount of income differently depending upon the manner in which the income is earned. The advantages and disadvantages of the schedular system for a development-ambitious country will be discussed in Chapter 4.

Vertical Equity

Unfortunately, the concept of vertical equity is even more difficult to state with any degree of precision. The almost universally accepted notion today is that the taxpayer who is "better-off" should make a relatively greater tax payment than should the "less-well-off" individual. But this does not answer the question as to how much more he should contribute. Further, there is no wholly objective way of measuring how "well-off" an individual really is since, ultimately, this involves a state of mind. It is often suggested that consumption spending, property ownership, and/or personal income, provide reasonably reliable indices of this state of "well-being." Income is generally advocated as the most objective of the three alternatives. Most of the statements made in conjunction with the Alliance also suggest income as the appropriate index of tax paying ability. The general contention is that the tax "burden" in Latin America has historically favored the rich at the expense of the poor.

"Tax Burdens"

While this general proposition may have some validity, it must be recognized that it is virtually impossible to determine precisely what the historical real tax "burden" by income group has been. Most individuals who speak of tax "burden" imply that total tax contributions constitute a reliable measure of the tax "burden." Actually, it is the government spending that determines how much of available resources will be diverted from private consumption. Therefore, even if a government collected no taxes but continued to spend, a real "burden" would be involved. Taxes are simply a means of allocating the burden. Even a historical measure of tax allocations by income class is very difficult. To achieve this, it is necessary to know the final incidence of each of the many taxes. Those incidence analyses attempted to date indicate formidable problems. Consequently, the results have not attained any general consensus of expert opinion. Since this is true of incidence studies conducted in the relatively well developed countries, it must be even more true in the underdeveloped areas where reliable statistics on income, spending, and taxation are most frequently lacking. An excellent discussion of the problems involved in incidence studies in less-well-developed areas, and of the unreliability of any results obtained, is provided by the Shoup Commission study attempted in Venezuela.[14]

[14] Commission to Study the Fiscal System of Venezuela, *The Fiscal System*

Equity and Income Taxation

When attempting to extract a greater tax from the wealthier members of society, economists and politicians alike nearly always recommended personal-income taxation. It is generally believed that the incidence of the personal-income tax will rest predominantly with the taxpayer on whom it is imposed, and that this tax can readily be manipulated to require the greatest contribution from those deemed most "able" to pay. For these reasons, increased dependence on personal-income taxation is very often recommended to Latin America and to other less-well-developed areas of the world. The advantages and disadvantages of income taxation in Latin America will be more thoroughly considered in Chapter 4.

Any tax, or tax system may be progressive, proportional, or regressive. A progressive tax system is one that demands a relatively greater percentage of the income (or wealth) of a high income (or wealth) group than it does of a lower income (or wealth) group. A proportional tax system demands the same percentage contribution from every group. The regressive system demands relatively more from the lower income (or wealth) groups. Today, the general consensus of expert and public opinion seems to be that a progressive tax system is the "most equitable" one.

Although an income tax need not be progressive, the vast majority of those enacted in the last half-century do include a progressive tax-rate structure. Incidentally, even the simple granting of a minimum exemption makes an income tax with a proportional rate schedule a progressive tax. This can be simply illustrated as follows: If A has a $6,000 income, and B has a $12,000 income, in a country granting a $3,000 basic exemption and imposing a flat 40 percent tax on the remainder, A must pay $1,200 (40 percent of $3,000) or 20 percent of his income in tax, whereas B must pay $3,600 (40 percent of $9,000) or 30 percent of his income in tax.

Advantages of Progressive Taxation

The advantages often claimed for progressive taxation include the following: (1) it results in the minimum-aggregate sacrifice; (2) it promotes economic stability; (3) it provides a more equal distribution of income; and (4) it approximates the benefits received. The last of the

---

of Venezuela, pp. 455–467. For comparable problems in a U.S. tax incidence study see *Allocation of the Tax Burden by Income Class*, pamphlet, pp. 5–8.

four claimed advantages cannot be substantiated on either empirical or on a priori grounds. That is, it cannot be shown that the inhabitants of a country benefit from their government's expenditures of tax revenues in any direct relation to their personal income. The benefit principle of taxation is applicable to only those government-provided goods and services that can be made subject to a market test and need not be "free-for-the-asking" once provided. Most government expenditures for these items are only a small part of total government spending. The other three claimed advantages of progressive taxation deserve more attention.

The notions of minimum-aggregate sacrifice derive from the economic concept of decreasing marginal utility. This concept suggests that the total utility of greater and greater income is increasing, but at a decreasing rate. From this proposition, many persons jump to the conclusion that imposition of a higher relative tax on higher incomes results in a minimum sacrifice of total utility. The assumptions necessary to substantiate the minimum sacrifice theories were concisely stated by C. Lowell Harriss as follows:[15]

(1) The use of sacrifice as a criterion can apply only to income above a subsistence minimum; (2) the principle of diminishing marginal utility is valid for increasing rates of money income; (3) there is no change in personal sensibilities as income increases; (4) utility curves are reversible, or more simply, to make a man poorer takes away only the utility that was added when he was earlier made richer by the same amount; (5) all persons have the same utility systems; (6) the marginal utility of income is unchanged by expenditures; (7) the real costs necessary to earn a given rate of income, and domestic needs, are the same for all taxpayers.

All of these assumptions are either of restricted applicability or wholly false. Consequently, the "scientific" underpinnings for the notions of minimum-aggregate sacrifice through progressive taxation are indeed shaky. Perhaps in the underdeveloped areas of the world, where the masses live at or near subsistence levels and economic and social development are the primary goals, the more idealistic goal of minimum-aggregate sacrifice would not be of high priority anyway.

The claimed advantage that progressive income taxation promotes

---

[15] C. Lowell Harriss, "Public Finance," in Bernard F. Haley (ed.), *A Survey of Contemporary Economics*, II, 267–268. Harriss gives E. D. Fagan credit for formulating these seven assumptions. See Fagan's "Recent and Contemporary Theories of Progressive Taxation," *Journal of Political Economy*, XLVI (August 1938), 458–485.

economic stability rests on two factors. First, income-tax revenues increase in periods of economic "boom" and fall in periods of "recession." Therefore taxpayers have less after-tax income (relative to other taxes raising equivalent amounts of revenue) for spending in the peak of the economic cycle, but more disposable income in the trough. Most other taxes respond only slowly, or not at all, to economic cycles and thus require the greatest relative contribution at the most inopportune time. The implications for the government are, of course, that it can act contracyclically regardless of revenues, whereas individuals may not have this same ability.

Second, since income taxation leaves the greatest relative share of disposable income in the hands of the lowest-income groups, and since these groups presumably have the highest marginal propensity to consume, the income tax maintains the largest aggregate consumption demand throughout the cycle. (The effect on saving and investment will be separately considered under arguments against progressive taxation.) Once again this claimed advantage of progressive taxation may be of only limited validity in the underdeveloped countries because their cycles are often caused by wholly exogenous factors, such as the world market for a single export commodity. To whatever limited extent economic cycles are attributable to an inadequate domestic-consumption demand in these areas, the claim would have limited validity.

The last argument for progressive taxation—income redistribution—has real appeal for the Latin American countries. It may be, as Henry Simons argues, that this is the only defensible argument for progressive taxation in any country:[16]

The case for progressive taxation must be rested on the case against inequality—on the ethical or aesthetic judgment that the prevailing distribution of wealth and income reveals a degree (and/or kind) of inequality which is distinctly evil or unlovely.

Other writers have been equally forceful:[17]

It may seem a nice job of social engineering to have greater equality achieved as a by-product of raising the necessary revenue, for then the society is not simply and nakedly engaged in redistributing income. On the other hand this may be an advantage; it may make politically feasible a goal which otherwise might prove too divisive and put too great a strain on democratic processes.

[16] Henry Simons, *Personal Income Taxation*, pp. 18–19.
[17] Walter J. Blum and Harry Kalven, Jr., *The Uneasy Case for Progressive Taxation*, p 72.

A real advantage for democratic countries is this fact that progressive taxation can accomplish income redistribution within the market system.

The social discontent in the underdeveloped areas is only in part due to the increased realization of the gap between the standards of living of the developed and the underdeveloped countries. The same accentuated gap among the citizens of a single underdeveloped country also exacerbates the underprivileged masses. Increased reliance on progressive income taxation should help alleviate this irritation and provide greater social justice. Greater social justice means, *ceteris paribus*, improved morale and, therefore, higher productivity—an important element in economic development. A more equal distribution of income should also reduce the demand for luxury imports and free scarce foreign exchange for more advantageous uses.

If income redistribution is to have maximum effectiveness for economic development aspirations, the poorer peoples must often agree to take "their share" of the redistributed income in more education, improved health, and better housing, rather than in immediate and direct supplements to personal, disposable income. Only in this manner can the long-run hopes for continued real improvement in their standard of living be realized.

Once again, a final word of caution seems appropriate. While the ethical and political implications of greater equality of wealth and income in Latin America are undeniably important, the real economic gains available through redistributive finance are limited. The conspicuously large fortunes represent a small aggregate resource considering the tremendous numbers at the other end. The administrative and political problems associated with redistributive finance are equally staggering. These qualifications do not vitiate the arguments favoring progressive taxation and income redistribution, but they do caution against permitting them to carry too much weight in shaping fiscal policy.

Objections to Progressive Taxation

Many objections to progressive taxation have been voiced. Among the more powerful of those frequently heard are the following: (1) it encourages political irresponsibility; (2) it unduly complicates tax laws and tax administration; and (3) it dampens such critical economic incentives as the incentives to work, save, and invest.

The idea that progressive taxation encourages political irresponsibility is in part a corollary to the minimum-sacrifice theories already considered. That is, since progressive taxation results in the minimum loss of aggregate utility for the revenue obtained, it is easier for the government to spend irresponsibly. This would presumably be true since fewer objections would be made than would have been had the same revenue been obtained at greater social cost (*i.e.,* greater utility loss). It is further argued that progressive taxation promotes irresponsibility because the more numerous (and therefore—in a democracy—more politically important) group stands to gain at the expense of the few (the less politically significant group).

An equally convincing case can be made suggesting that progressive taxation promotes political responsibility. Since the wealthy members of society are generally more informed and articulate of the two groups, political irresponsibility in government spending would be more readily detected and restrained if the wealthy were paying a large part of the tax revenue than if the opposite situation were true. And although the wealthy elite may constitute a smaller number of voters than the poorer masses, their votes may (figuratively) count "more than once." This seems especially true in Latin America where many governments have historically been less than democratically constituted.

That progressive taxation complicates tax laws and tax administration cannot be denied. Several economists have suggested various minimum social and economic prerequisites for the successful implementation of an income tax. Nevertheless, in an increasing number of countries, income taxation is being recommended and enacted even when several of the basic prerequisites are not satisfied. Chapter 4 will include a discussion of the prerequisites, and remaining sections of this monograph will propose various techniques that can be useful in making an income tax (and other presumably progressive taxes) successful under less-than-ideal conditions. Acceptance of a few administrative or technical tax reforms, along with increased enforcement efforts, could go a long way in making the existing tax systems of Latin America much more progressive than they have been in the past. To admit administrative complexity need not emasculate the tax-reform efforts.

The effect of progressive taxation on economic incentives is another very complex subject. The objections to progressive taxation, based on these arguments, contend that the incentives to work, save, and invest are all damped by the fact that any incremental income earned will yield smaller and smaller after-tax benefits.

Most of this discussion must proceed in the realm of psychological conjecture for nearly always there are two opposing forces at work. For example, a progressive income tax leaves a man, given an opportunity to increase his income, with less than a full share of "what he has earned." Does this mean he will be discouraged from working harder, or from accepting the greater responsibility—or, in other words, will he prefer more leisure? Or, does it mean he will work still harder to attain the same after-tax income? The answer depends on many noneconomic variables. Empirical studies conducted in the United States indicate that a minimum disincentive exists.[18] Whether the same conclusions would be reached in a similar Latin American study is uncertain; the nature of the Latin culture suggests that a greater value may be placed on leisure.

But even if some disincentive does exist, a progressive taxation that provided more education and better health for the lower-income groups could result in a *net* increase in productivity. The increased morale, labor mobility (through better education), and condition of labor (through better health) should more than offset the disincentive effects attributed to progressive taxation—at least at the rates of taxation and the level of gross national product common to Latin America. Again, it should be noted that this net gain presumes the appropriate investment of the increased tax revenues.

Progressive taxation also has important implications for the incentives to save and invest. These will be considered as part of the discussion of the second major objective for tax reform in the Alliance for Progress: the objective of increased capital formation.

Increased Capital Formation

Most economists concerned with the problems of economic development postulate that one of the fundamental problems in achieving economic growth is the paucity of investment capital in the underdeveloped areas.[19] To prove their point, they suggest that one need but

[18] See Lewis H. Kimmel, *Taxes and Economic Incentives;* Thomas H. Sanders, *Effects of Taxation on Executives;* and John Keith Butters, *Effects of Taxation: Investments by Individuals.*

[19] For example, see Ragnar Nurkse, *Problems of Capital Formation in Underdeveloped Countries,* pp. 1–2; Raul Prebisch, *The Economic Development of Latin America and Its Principal Problems,* U.N., p. 5; Walter Krause, *Economic Development,* pp. 185–187. It is interesting to note that Nurkse and Krause see domestic capital formation, or self-help, as the most important source of capital; Prebisch stresses the essential role of foreign investment.

observe the economic change following the introduction of some minimum capital into an underdeveloped area. Apparently the framers of the Alliance for Progress accept this postulate, since a major objective for tax reform is to increase tax revenues and to utilize the freed resources for appropriate investment projects. Latin Americans are well aware of the necessity of greater capital formation. For example, Antonio Flores, a Mexican economist, says:[20]

In a country like Mexico . . . it seems undeniable that the most pressing need, to which, when necessary, all others must be subordinated, is to achieve greater capital formation at a faster rate. Only in this way will it be reasonable to expect in the long run better and fuller utilization of our natural potentialities and a progressive raising of the standard of living.

A Chilean writer generalized on this same idea:[21]

The main problem being tackled by Chile—and by all the Latin-American countries as well as the other underdeveloped countries—is that of accelerating the rate of accumulating capital, with a view principally to its use in industrial development.

The Meaning of Capital Formation

Capital formation is taking place whenever a country does not engage its entire productive activity in meeting the needs and desires of immediate consumption. Instead, it devotes a part of this activity to the making of "capital goods." This term includes plant equipment, tools, transport facilities, or any other form of real capital that increases the efficacy of productive effort. It can also be construed to include investment in such human capital as technical skills, education, and health. An interesting computation of the "return on investment in education" is attempted in the Shoup Commission report on Venezuela.[22]

The Problem in Perspective

The historical reasons for the shortage of capital and productive investment in the underdeveloped areas are as diverse as the countries involved. Among the reasons frequently cited are the following: high costs, due to low productivity of labor; limited domestic markets; inadequate basic facilities; inadequate external economies; high risk,

[20] Antonio Carrillo Flores, "In Mexico," in United Nations, *Domestic Financing of Economic Development,* p. 160.
[21] Desiderio García, "In Chile," *ibid.,* p. 91.
[22] Commission to Study the Fiscal System of Venezuela, *The Fiscal System of Venezuela,* pp. 406–409.

attributable to both political and monetary instability; limited entrepreneurial ability; and sheer social resistance to change. The most pressing needs in underdeveloped countries are often in the area of social overhead capital (*i.e.,* roads, harbors, education). Since these investments do not yield a profit in a business sense, they must generally be provided by public rather than private investment.

Basically the obstacles to capital formation can be divided between fundamental economic conditions and institutional circumstances. The insufficient inducement to invest, due to the limited domestic market, is a typical economic problem. Another is the low absolute level of real income which, in turn, means a low real ceiling on the capacity to save and invest. Inadequate external economies—due in part to the limited basic facilities—is a third. The implications for developmental fiscal policy are parallel. The wording of a United Nations report emphasizes the difficulty of the fiscal problem as follows:[23] "Fiscal policy is assigned the central task of wresting from the pitifully low output of these countries sufficient savings to finance economic development programmes and to set the stage for more vigorous private investment activity."

Institutional explanations for inadequate capital formation include political instability, lack of education, and inadequate financial organization. Tax-reform measures are generally inadequate and inappropriate for correction of the institutional obstacles. However, other efforts, intended to change the institutional barriers, are equally necessary to insure the long-run, continued success of a development program.

Alternative Sources of Capital

It must also be clearly understood that increased tax revenues by no means represent the only, or even the "best"—in many cases—source of capital funds. There are three basic sources: voluntary savings, compulsory savings, and foreign investment. Compulsory saving encompasses both taxation and inflation; foreign investment can be either of private or public origin. Each of the alternative sources has advantages and disadvantages, as well as real limitations.

Those economists who favor a minimum of government intervention in the market mechanism generally consider stimulation of voluntary saving as the most desirable way of increasing capital formation.

[23] United Nations, *Taxes and Fiscal Policy in Under-developed Countries,* p. 3.

Their recommendations ordinarily include improving or introducing such facilities for private savings as local saving and loan institutions; small denomination government bonds; national lotteries; and, occasionally, social-insurance programs. These methods have been advocated for (and tried in) India, Pakistan, Ceylon, and Mexico. There are two basic limitations to the ideas: (1) the rate of return on these assets cannot be made competitive with alternative avenues of investment, and therefore, unless made compulsory, they are not widely purchased; and (2) they simply do not provide the magnitude of investment funds necessary for real economic development.

Debt financing of economic development may be voluntary or compulsory and it frequently is related to problems of inflation. An interesting example of compulsory debt financing is Brazil's requirement, as part of her revenue laws, that specified businesses invest a given percentage of their profits in government bonds (see Chapter 4). In many underdeveloped countries the only way to float "successfully" a major government debt issue is to have the central bank (really an arm of the central government) purchase the entire issue. To the extent the expenditure of the additional credit adds to the inflationary pressures, it further stimulates involuntary savings through inflation.

On the other hand, voluntary debt financing of economic development may provide for economically and socially productive investment without imposing restrictions on consumption expenditures, as taxation ordinarily must. Deficit financing will not be inflationary if it simply offsets hoarding or if the increased purchasing power is just enough to engage previously unemployed resources in productive activity. Therefore debt financing should be considered and utilized in those countries with excess productive capacity and unemployed resources. In this setting, so long as the expenditure is productive, there is a strong case for borrowing. In many Latin American republics debt financing has been eschewed because of the inherent inflationary bias of these economies, short on marketable goods and services, suddenly swelled with a substantial increase in the monetary resources.

It is also conceivable that foreign capital could provide the funds for real economic development. The major limitation is, once again, that an adequate supply of such capital does not appear likely. Foreign *private* capital presents some additional problems: it must be channeled into the "right" enterprises; it must be maintained in a proper flow; and it must be accompanied by the necessary technical and financial skills. A complicating factor is the spirit of nationalism that tends to deprecate any possible good deriving from foreign private investment in an underdeveloped area. There is historical evidence to prove the likelihood of such investment being concentrated in export industries, particularly those of an extractive nature. The depletion of "wasting-assets" has not helped quell the nationalist cries opposing foreign private investment.

On the other hand, there is historical evidence to prove (a) that technical experience and managerial ability tend to follow foreign private investment; (b) that the income-generating effects of foreign private investments, both in new service industries and in domestic demands, have been substantial; and (c) that foreign investments are frequently accompanied by increased investment in basic "social overhead" facilities. All of these factors substantially speed up the process of economic development and do so in a less arduous and socially disruptive manner than would be possible were foreign capital not present.

Foreign *public* aid, as promised in the Alliance for Progress, presents fewer problems. It can readily be channeled into the most advantageous facility; it evokes less emotional feelings of nationalism; it can be provided on a grant basis, or on terms most favorable to the borrowing country; but it cannot be provided in the necessary quantities. Even the $20 billion in Alliance aid is admitted to be but the marginal effort necessary for development in Latin America. Furthermore, as Professor Ragnar Nurkse points out in the following quotation, once a country is truly capable of using outside aid to its best advantage, it should also be capable of substantial domestic capital formation.[24]

But once the receiving countries are capable of devising the necessary controls for the productive use of outside aid, they should be equally capable of using such policies for the mobilization of potential *domestic* sources of capital (*e.g.,* skimming off resources now absorbed by luxury consumption, making use of labour set free from the land through better farm methods or recruiting any surplus labour already existing on the land). It is far from my intention to suggest that in these circumstances foreign aid becomes unnecessary. Yet this consideration does shift the emphasis upon the need for domestic policies to ensure that in the overall use of resources, domestic as well as external, investment is given top priority.

Still another source of investment capital is "compulsory saving." As

[24] Ragnar Nurkse, "International Investment To-day in the Light of Nineteenth-Century Experience," *The Economic Journal*, LXIV (December 1954), 744–758.

already noted, this is a primary objective for tax reform in the Alliance program. The problems and advantages of the alternative methods of raising revenue and forcing saving through taxation, and the implications of the revenue methods selected for economic development, constitute the essence of this study .

Taxation and Capital Formation

In one sense, increased taxation and increased capital formation are conflicting goals. That is, increased taxation—especially progressive taxation—may mean a decrease in private domestic saving, and therefore, private domestic investment. The argument made to substantiate this claim is based on two factors: first, the incontrovertible fact that individuals with the larger incomes are the only ones who save any substantial portion of their income.[25] Progressive taxation demands most from these individuals. Therefore, if the tax obligations are paid from that portion of income that would otherwise have been saved, there may be a net decrease in investment. The arguments against progressive taxation, on the grounds that it decreases saving and investment, proceed on the additional assumption that the government "spends" all of the revenue collected on consumption, or simply reallocates it in direct redistribution schemes. Henry Simons states the argument thus:[26]

> Increasing progression means augmenting incomes where saving is impossible and diminishing incomes too large to be used entirely for consumption. Thus, it means diversion of resources from capital-creation to consumption uses. The classes subject to the highest rates will not greatly curtail consumption; and persons at the bottom of the income scale, paying smaller taxes will use their additional income largely to improve their standard of life. . . . That the net effect will be increased consumption, however, hardly admits of doubt.

A second argument made against any increased income taxation emphasizes the fact that increased taxation means a decrease in the

---

[25] James S. Duesenberry found that even in the "affluent" U.S., 75% of the families save nothing (*Income, Saving and the Theory of Consumer Behavior*, p. 39). Ragnar Nurkse contends that this is not because the other 75% are too poor to save, but because the consumption pattern of the 25% so whets their appetite that nothing is left for saving. If Professor Nurkse's contention is correct, a significant level of forced saving will be necessary in the underdeveloped countries for a long time.

[26] Simons, *Personal Income Taxation*, pp. 22–23.

return of any profitable investment. This, presumably, makes consumption spending a more desirable alternative to additional investment. In reality there are conflicting forces at work. The decreased return on investments could cause taxpayers to save and invest even more if their objective is to attain a specified after-tax earnings stream.

Ultimately the *net* increase or decrease in capital formation resulting from an increase in taxation is primarily dependent upon what the government does with the revenues obtained. Assuming no change in the basic propensities, if the government invests all the proceeds the net effect would at worst be no change in investment. Even this would be the result only in the unlikely case that the entire tax was collected at the expense of an equal amount of private domestic saving. The objectives of increased tax revenues and increased capital formation are consistent so long as the public investment is greater than any decrease in private investment, and the additional public investment is at least as productive as the curtailed private investment would have been.

One of the problems with private domestic investment in Latin America has been the tendency to "invest" in such nonproductive assets as gold, jewelry, foreign and domestic currency, and commodity hoards. With as much emphasis on economic development planning as there is in the Alliance for Progress, there is no valid reason to believe that public investment would be any less productive than even the best private domestic investment. (Results may not be directly comparable since public investment returns can frequently be meaningfully calculated only in a social sense.) In short, "the appeal to spare the goose that lays the golden eggs is not very strong when the goose is not laying many eggs of any kind."[27]

The only conceivable situation that would result in a net decrease in aggregate investment would be where the combined decrease in private domestic saving and private dissaving (associated with "flight capital") would be greater than the incremental government investment. If foreign exchange controls are utilized, there should be effective ways of preventing this development. In all fairness, however, the phenomenon of "flight capital" is not an unusual Latin American reaction to tax reform.[28]

[27] Nurkse, *Problems of Capital Formation*, p. 145.

[28] The report of the First Annual Meeting of the Inter-American Economic and Social Council cited the need of terminating "the existing substantial flow of private capital out of Latin America." The report is summarized in the *International Financial News Survey*, November 23, 1962, pp. 373–374. Gun-

Saving Through Inflation

An alternative form of compulsory saving is available through inflation. Rampant inflation is, of course, wholly inconsistent with economic
development objectives. It creates expectations and behavior patterns
that wholly negate the desired results. A slow, controlled inflation may
be an effective way of forcing saving for development objectives. The
problem is controlling the inflation within the desired constraints. Historically, inflation has constituted a serious problem for several Latin
American republics. Professor Hansen suggests that part of the explanation for the historical problem of inflation is political. He states it
this way:[29]

> But to the politician, with his eye on the immediate electoral impact of his
> policies, the inflationary way of mobilizing capital resources is usually easier
> than the imposition of new taxes. It can be made to appear the result of
> "nature causes," or even better, of "external circumstances over which we
> have no control," such as the unreasonable tight-fistedness of the Americans,
> and not the consequence of any deliberate governmental action.

The opinion of a group of experts assembled by the United Nations
was that economic development should be achieved with a minimum
of inflation. They suggested the following order of preference for the
alternative sources of capital funds: (1) voluntary saving, (2) taxation, (3) direct controls plus external financing. They then add:[30]

> If even these latter are not sufficient and the development programme is es-
> sential, inflationary borrowing or printing of money may be considered as a
> last resort; however, this method is a dangerous one. Nevertheless, develop-
> ment should not be suspended in order to avoid inflationary methods.

The reluctance to accept inflationary financing as a generally desirable alternative is partially due to the difficulty in predicting and controlling the inflationary profits. They will be beneficial only if the
recipients do *not* spend them on additional consumption, hoard them,
or use them to speculate in existing commodities. Unfortunately each

---

nar Myrdal once estimated that such "clandestine movements of capital" were
greater than the annual lending of the International Bank (see Myrdal's *An
International Economy*, p. 106). Stephen Raushenbush estimates between $8
and $10 billion has been withdrawn from Latin America since World War II
in this manner (see Raushenbush's *The Challenge to the Alliance for Progress*,
pamphlet, p. 51).

[29] A. H. Hansen, *Public Enterprise and Economic Development*, p. 84.
[30] United Nations, *Domestic Financing of Economic Development*, p. 34.

of these is a likely alternative. Inflationary financing is also eschewed because investment taking place under inflationary conditions is apt to flow into "luxury industries" rather than into industries producing essentials. Further, if labor is well organized, there is a danger that a demand-pull inflation will precipitate a cost-push inflation. Finally, inflation can be devastating in terms of the foreign-exchange position of the inflationary country. In most underdeveloped countries the so-called "hard" currencies are already in short supply and domestic inflation merely adds to the difficulties by increasing the demand and decreasing the supply of foreign exchange. Any subsequent currency devaluation is equally disruptive.

Inflation also tends to increase, rather than decrease, the existing inequalities in income and wealth. It may also prompt dissaving as consumers try to maintain former real levels of consumption. As previously noted, the exact opposite prescriptions have been assigned top priority as objectives for tax reform in the Alliance-for-Progress program. In short, there are a multitude of good reasons for the hesitancy in recommending inflation as a major method of increasing capital formation.

Price Stability

The severity of the inflationary problem since World War II has varied widely in the Latin American republics. Several countries, including Costa Rica, the Dominican Republic, Ecuador, El Salvador, Guatemala, Honduras, Panama, and Venezuela, have experienced only mildly inflationary conditions. Colombia, Mexico, and Peru have experienced a somewhat more pronounced, but not an uncontrolled, period of inflation. Rapid inflation has been characteristic of Argentina, Bolivia, Brazil, Chile, Paraguay, and Uruguay. For the decade 1946–1956, Bolivia's average *annual* inflation exceeded 60 percent! A comparison of the general price index for the years 1953–1964 for five of these countries is given in Table 2.

The mere existence of significant inflation presents numerous complicating factors for successful taxation. Capital-gains taxation and property taxation are tremendously complicated by significant price-level changes. Income measurement—an obvious essential for income taxation—becomes very difficult as inflation becomes more and more pronounced. The determination of "taxable income" is essentially a problem of matching costs and revenues. If the time period elapsed

TABLE 2

Comparison of Consumer Price Index (all items)
for 1953, 1955, 1958, 1961, and 1964

Country	1953	1955	1958	1961	1964
Argentina	100	117	217	670	1,302
Brazil	100	142	237	607	3,000
Chile	100	302	752	1,253	3,000
Colombia	100	109	153	185	294
Mexico	100	122	150	164	171

Source: United Nations, *Monthly Bulletin of Statistics,* Vol. 16, No. 1 (April 1962), pp. 140–147, Table 48; Vol. 19, No. 5 (May 1965), pp. 156–160, Table 60.

between the incurrence of the cost and the realization of the revenue is very long, net profit, or taxable income, is largely illusory in an inflationary setting. This is particularly true as applied to cost deductions for depreciation, depletion, and year-end inventories.[31]

Inflation further complicates income taxation by making necessary frequent redeterminations of basic cost-of-living exemptions and progressive tax rates. Tax assessments not paid immediately become less real as the value of the monetary unit declines. In fact, given quite rapid inflation, it may be advantageous to delay tax payments even if this means paying a fine and interest. In this extreme situation, tax evasion is wholly rational.

The increased taxation, recommended in the Alliance, will serve to decrease the effective demand of the private sector, but it is not likely to decrease the inflationary pressures. The mere fact that the governments intend to expend the revenues collected means that there will be no net decrease in effective demand. It will simply change the nature of the demand. If the tax programs are successful, the shifts in demand should be substantial and the necessary reallocation of resources will not be accomplished without a significant amount of inflation, at least

[31] In an attempt to deal with these problems Brazil passed a bill in July 1964 allowing depreciation deductions based upon cost figures increased by price-level factors set by the National Economic Council. The same bill gives the taxpayer a choice of (1) paying an additional tax equal to 5% of the increased asset valuations or (2) purchasing treasury bonds equal to 10% of the same quantity. In any event the revaluation is mandatory and failure to elect an option creates an overdue tax payment which is also revalued upward.

in restricted markets. In other words, "bottleneck inflation" is apt to constitute a real problem for the developing economies in years to come.

In addition to possible bottleneck inflation, it is likely that several of the Latin American republics will continue to experience significant cyclical price movements. This will remain a problem until their economies are sufficiently diversified, and thereby freed from the present heavy dependence on the world market for a single commodity or two. Further insulation from exogenous forces will be possible whenever industrialization and economic-integration ambitions are realized.

Occasionally tax measures are suggested as an appropriate tool in the maintenance of reasonable price stability. Unfortunately, tax systems are simply not very efficacious for controlling price movements in underdeveloped countries. This is true because of the unsatisfactory state of economic forecasting; the slowness of the legislative process; the period of lag between a tax law and any economic results; and the effect of escalator arrangements in labor contracts. In a developmental setting, a heavy tax program may decrease consumption spending but it may not decrease it to the extent, or in the markets, considered most desirable. Frequent and well-timed changes in tax systems, necessary if taxation is to act contracyclically, are politically difficult to attain. They may also be economically disruptive if they engender adverse expectations on the part of buyers. It is not unlikely that frequent and substantial tax changes would encourage still more commodity hoarding, speculation, and other unproductive "investments." Direct controls, such as price and wage ceilings and commodity rationing, are much more effective, especially in controlling bottleneck inflations, than are general tax controls.

In conclusion, it must be re-emphasized that the maintenance of reasonable price stability—as a goal of the Alliance for Progress—is most desirable. Confidence in the stability of the currency unit facilitates planning and encourages private saving and investment in truly productive enterprise. Price stability also contributes significantly to the feasibility of desirable taxation. The only objection raised here is against assigning tax reform the objective of achieving and maintaining reasonable price stability. It does not appear that tax *revenue* policy, at least, is efficacious for this purpose. Constraints on government spending in periods of serious inflation can be defended. However, these constraints should not generally apply to spending on basic economic development projects, since only through their successful completion can lasting price stability be achieved.

SUMMARY

A review of the basic documents of the Alliance for Progress suggests several objectives for tax reform. The two primary objectives are making the average Latin American tax system more equitable and freeing more resources for increased capital formation. Statements by high-level government officials, and the provisions of tax programs instituted by international agencies, both confirm this analysis. Other basic objectives of the Alliance have significant ramifications for tax policy, either directly or indirectly. Those dealing with land reform and international trade and capital flows are particularly important to tax-reform efforts.

On closer investigation, it becomes apparent that "greater tax equity" is generally intended to mean "more progressive taxation." Perhaps the greatest advantage in progressive taxation for the Latin American republics is the assistance it lends to income redistribution ambitions. Administrative complexities constitute a formidable disadvantage; the real significance of other claimed disadvantages are not always clear-cut.

Increased capital formation is considered essential to the attainment of economic development aspirations. Fundamental economic conditions and institutional arrangements explain the historical shortage of capital in these countries. An exclusive reliance on compulsory saving through taxation, as a source of needed capital, should be avoided. In most underdeveloped countries the fiscal machinery is underdeveloped too.

In conclusion, tax reform measures should avoid subsistence level taxation and the adjunct depletion of human capital to the maximum extent possible. A reasonably progressive tax system—one that would minimize shifting and adjust somewhat to changes in income—is desired. Increased revenues and income redistribution are accepted goals. Tax laws must not be overly complex, even at the expense of limited interpersonal equity, since ease of administration and compliance will remain a significant factor in any successful Latin American tax system for several years. The time-honored tax canons of certainty and economy of collection do not ordinarily rank as high for the underdeveloped countries as they do for the more economically developed nations. Even the avoidance of economic distortion of existing economic patterns can be omitted as a criterion for tax policy in a developing country.

3. A Summary of the Current Latin American Fiscal Scene

The purpose of this chapter is to provide a "bird's-eye view" of some important aspects of the present-day fiscal practices in Latin America. The chapter includes statistical data on the level of taxation (*i.e.*, the ratio of taxes to national income); the relative importance of direct and indirect taxes in the total tax yield; and additional detail on the composition of the overall tax structure in several Latin American countries. The chapter also contains comments on the policy of restricting various taxes to specified levels of government, or the alternative practice of allocating a portion of the revenue from exclusively central-government taxes to lower levels of government; and on the dangers of earmarking tax revenues for development projects. Before the presentation of any statistical data, the reader is alerted to the multifarious inadequacies inherent in international comparisons of public finance statistics.

PROBLEMS IN INTERNATIONAL COMPARISONS OF PUBLIC FINANCE STATISTICS

There are three kinds of difficulties in making intercountry comparisons of public finance statistics. First, in most underdeveloped countries adequate and reliable statistics are simply not available. Second, the statistics that are available are frequently not comparable. Third, many important factors in public finance cannot be measured in quantitative terms.

The dearth of reliable statistics is widely recognized and limited corrective action is already underway. The United Nations and the International Monetary Fund are devoting substantial resources to this task.[1] The two Alliance-sponsored conferences on tax reform included supplemental efforts to encourage Latin American countries to make available complete and accurate statistics about government revenues and expenditures (see Appendix 2). The statistics presented in this chapter are adapted in large measure from an Agency for International Development (AID) culling of year-end embassy economic reports, IMF consultation papers, and IBRD economic surveys, because they were the most recent data available.[2]

The incomparability of available statistics results from a host of problems. A few of the more critical ones include the following: (1) the descriptive nomenclature is not universally interpreted; (2) the reporting period varies from country to country (*i.e.,* calendar years are used in some countries, fiscal years in others); (3) the accounting in some countries, and for certain taxes, is on a cash basis, whereas in other countries, or for other taxes, an accrual basis is followed; (4) the currentness of the reported data varies widely, and frequent and material revisions of earlier reports are common; (5) the definition of "taxes" varies by country (a particularly troublesome variation exists as to the handling of "payroll taxes," or "social insurance contributions," which tend to be quite high in the underdeveloped countries); and (6) the relative significance of various taxes by levels of government differs widely, and often the available statistics are for the central government only. The unreliability of exchange rates makes conversion of tax-revenue data, to a common monetary base, statistically hazardous. Even comparisons of the ratio of tax revenues to national income in different countries are of limited validity because of the dubious accuracy of the income estimates.

The irregular distribution of natural resources, and wide variations in nontax revenues, account for further large differences in the tax revenues of many countries. For example, the existence of great quantities of petroleum in Venezuela completely dominates her tax-revenue statistics. Nontax revenues may or may not be significant in amount. They run the gamut from profits on government-operated enterprises (communication and transportation facilities are the most common) to fees for services that only a government unit could logically provide (such as lighthouse fees and various inspection and

[1] For example, see the United Nation's annual *Statistical Yearbook*, and its *Monthly Bulletin of Statistics*; see also the International Monetary Fund's monthly *International Financial Statistics*.

[2] Frederic R. Fisher, *Tax Reform in Latin America*, Part II.

regulatory fees). Generally, the more productive the nontax revenues, the less the reliance on purely tax revenues. The source of significant nontax revenues may alter the tax structure too.

International comparisons of budget estimates are even more precarious than comparisons of historical data. Budget estimates are generally optimistic and not infrequently colored by political considerations. Estimates of revenues and expenditures are always difficult to make with accuracy—and especially so when domestic political stability, world prices, natural calamities, and inflation loom as significantly as they do in the underdeveloped countries. The only advantage of using budget estimates is their availability and timeliness.

The degree of enforcement of existing tax statutes, the real incidence of many taxes, and the effect of recession and/or inflations on the tax revenues of any particular year, are examples of factors that are important to public-finance statistics but are not readily measurable in quantitative terms. Statistical attempts to measure these and other factors are admittedly abstract and heavily dependent upon numerous questionable hypotheses.

In spite of these serious limitations, the next section of this chapter consists of some statistical data on Latin American taxes. Table 3 attempts to measure the "level of taxation." Because of the many statistical infirmities mentioned above, the results must be considered only as general propositions without too much weight being assigned to the precise numbers. Only in this sense can they be more helpful than misleading.

THE LEVEL OF TAXATION

The ratio of tax revenues to some aggregate national income measure (gross national product, net national product, or national income) is frequently cited as an appropriate measure of the "level of taxation." Exactly which of the three bases is most appropriate for measuring the level of taxation is a matter of conjecture. A National Bureau of Economic Research study concluded that net national product was the best alternative.[3] The authors of that study reject gross national product because it implies that taxes could be met from capital consumption allowances. They reject national income because it excludes from the denominator indirect business taxes that are included in the numerator.

[3] National Bureau of Economic Research, *The Tax Burden in Relation to National Income and Product*, pamphlet.

Whatever base is used, the literature suggests that the higher this ratio, the closer a country is to its "tax capacity."

In the early 1950's, Colin Clark popularized the notion that once 25 percent of the national income of a country is collected in taxes, any additional taxation is conducive to inflation.[4] The ensuing debate culminated in a symposium conducted by the Tax Institute in late 1952. The general consensus of expert opinion was that there is no doctrinaire answer as to the optimum level of taxation applicable to all countries, or even to a single country at different times. The experts suggested that the limits of tax capacity are a function of such diverse factors as tax rates, administration, voluntary-compliance habits, accounting and assessment procedures, the level of income, the distribution of income, the overall tax structure, and human attitudes and motivations. Monteath Douglas, executive director of the Canadian Tax Foundation, concluded:[5] "the elements of taxable capacity prove on closer investigation to be so contingent, subjective, and variable—to be so much a matter of circumstances of time and place, of institutional arrangements, and public attitudes—that they defy generalization, and any conclusion expressed in absolute or final terms is bound to misrepresent the very nature of the problem itself." He goes on to suggest that the problem is really a political (rather than an economic) one. The *practical* limit of tax capacity is reached, according to Mr. Douglas, when the nonfinancial and social costs associated with taxation seriously dampen economic vitality and taxpayer morale, after all structural improvements to the tax system have been made. These limits depend "on the voters' appreciation of economic consequences on the one hand and their political value judgments on the other."[6]

Mission reports of the technical-assistance experts in public finance generally conclude that most underdeveloped countries could increase the tax-to-national-income ratio without economic detriment.[7] As discussed in Chapter 2, this is one of the primary objectives for tax reform in the Alliance-for-Progress program. The second major objective, increasing tax equity, involves deciding the mode of the tax change believed to be most appropriate.

[4] Colin Clark, "The Danger Point in Taxes," *Harper's Magazine*, CCI (December 1950), 67–69.

[5] Monteath Douglas, "Taxable Capacity and British and Canadian Experience," in Tax Institute, *The Limits of Taxable Capacity*, p. 31.

[6] *Ibid.*, p. 35.

[7] United Nations, *Taxes and Fiscal Policy in Under-Developed Countries*, pp. 6–7.

The ratio of taxes to gross domestic product is estimated at 11.1 percent for Latin America as a whole.[8] Table 3 indicates the level of taxation in eight Latin American countries based both on national income and on gross national product. The ratio based on net national product is not shown because of the unavailability of net-national-product data. The two different ratios in Table 3 are not wholly comparable for reasons explained in the footnotes. Obviously, if they were comparable, the same ratio based on net-national-product statistics should be somewhere between these two estimates.

Even granting the many statistical limitations of Table 3, the figures

TABLE 3

The Level of Taxation in Eight Latin American Countries in 1960

Country	Taxes as a Percent of National Income[1]	Taxes as a Percent of Gross Private Domestic Product[2]
Chile	17%	14%
Colombia	10	10
Costa Rica	14	11[3]
El Salvador	14	11
Guatemala	14[4]	11[3]
Honduras	10	9[3]
Mexico	8[5]	9
Peru	14[5]	11

[1] These figures were compiled by the author from data in the United Nations, *Statistical Yearbook, 1961*, pp. 545–557, Table 175, and the United Nations, *Monthly Bulletin of Statistics*, Vol. 16, No. 2 (November 1962), pp. 150–151, Table 13. The figures involve taxes at central-government level only, excluding extra-budgetary receipts, for the calendar year 1960, unless otherwise noted. All figures have been rounded to the nearest whole percent.

[2] These figures were adapted from Inter-American Development Bank, Social Progress Trust Fund, *First Annual Report, 1961,* Part Three. The percentages were calculated by the fund administrator from data supplied to him by the individual countries. Taxes are for all levels of government for the calendar year 1960 unless otherwise noted. All figures have been rounded to the nearest whole percent.

[3] Includes only central-government receipts.

[4] Tax revenues are for the fiscal year 1959–1960.

[5] Both tax revenues and national income are for 1959, the last data available.

[8] Social Progress Trust Fund, *First Annual Report, 1961,* p. 28.

do support the contention of the technical-assistance experts concerning the real possibility of increased taxation in most underdeveloped countries. The relatively low level of taxation in these eight countries is not particularly surprising. The following considerations are particularly important: (a) economic production occurring outside the market can be imputed in the computation of gross national product, but remains extremely difficult to tax; (b) the masses of people live at or near subsistence levels of living and, therefore, the collection of taxes becomes exceedingly difficult, if not improper; (c) the profligate members of the society are unwilling to make large tax contributions, and the governments are unwilling or unable to collect even those taxes imposed. Under these circumstances, a suggestion that the level of taxation be immediately increased to, say, 25–35 percent of national income, as is common in some of the more economically advanced countries, makes little sense.

However, it is sensible to expect this ratio to increase as economic development takes place. Real development necessitates increased government expenditures and, therefore (in most countries), higher taxes. In the early stages of development, it is especially probable that government expenditures will increase more rapidly than national income.

Relative Importance of Direct and Indirect Taxes

Individuals concerned with tax reform in underdeveloped countries often support statements about tax regressivity and demands for greater equity with statistics revealing that these countries rely heavily on indirect taxation over direct taxation. The discussion proceeds on the explicit or implicit assumption that indirect taxation is generally regressive because low-income individuals spend a greater percentage of their incomes on taxed services and commodities than do individuals higher on the income scale.

The accuracy of this contention depends upon many facts. For example, indirect taxes, such as sales taxes, that exempt "necessities" are not particularly regressive. Indirect taxes, such as excise taxes on "luxuries," have no real significance to the vast majority of low-income individuals since these commodities (or services) are not generally represented in their purchase. Furthermore, indirect (as well as direct) taxes can be wholly or partially shifted to persons other than those initially paying the tax and no adequate method of determining the final incidence has been devised. Export duties, a common indirect tax in many underdeveloped nations, have many similarities to a gross income tax. In short, it cannot be assumed without qualification that heavy indirect taxation necessarily means a highly regressive tax structure.

In at least two separate attempts to measure statistically the progressivity of indirect taxation in the Latin American countries, the conclusion was that some progressivity exists up to fairly high income levels. Although both studies admit serious statistical limitations and, therefore, the possibility of substantial error, it is believed that these conclusions are sufficient to raise serious doubt as to the validity of the common belief that indirect taxation is always regressive. In the higher income brackets, the progressivity was found to be highly irregular.[9]

Table 4 indicates the relative percentage of direct and indirect taxes in total ordinary revenue for ten Latin American countries in 1960. The relatively heavy dependence on indirect taxes can be justified on two grounds: first, most indirect taxes are easier to administer than are

TABLE 4

Percentage of Direct and Indirect Taxes in Total Ordinary Revenue for Ten Latin American Countries in 1960

Country	Percent Direct	Percent Indirect
Chile	32.8	67.2
Costa Rica	16.6	77.7
Ecuador	16.9	67.2
El Salvador	10.0	85.2
Guatemala	9.1	90.9
Honduras	15.1	84.9
Mexico	31.5	68.5
Nicaragua	13.2	86.8
Paraguay	17.3	71.3
Uruguay	20.6	79.4

Note: Percentages may not add to 100% because of "other taxes."
Source: Adapted from Frederic R. Fisher, *Tax Reform in Latin America,* Appendix B.

[9] See Commission to Study the Fiscal System of Venezuela, *The Fiscal System of Venezuela,* Table 1–8, p. 40, and Henry C. Wallich and John H. Adler, *Public Finance in a Developing Country,* pp. 132–134. The Wallich and Adler study dealt with El Salvador.

direct taxes; and second, indirect taxes are capable of producing substantial amounts of revenue.

The tendency to eschew indirect taxation is particularly common to fiscal scholars educated in the United States. Dr. A. K. Eaton, Assistant Deputy Minister of Finance of Canada in 1952, emphasized the contrast between U.S. and Canadian thinking as follows:[10]

There seems to be among your [U.S] leaders and writers in the field of public finance a far greater reverence for income tax as a fiscal instrument than there is in Canada. It could be that your professors have over-sold you on this idea, and perhaps you learned too well the rather lofty classroom doctrines of a few decades ago. In Canada we tolerate the income tax but certainly we do not go into raptures over it. As for indirect taxes, many of your writers seem to regard them as somehow inherently evil things and have an abhorrence of them that verges on the unnatural and, if I may say so, seems slightly old maidish. We, who have lived for three decades under a general sales tax at the manufacturers' level coupled with a generous sprinkling of miscellaneous excise taxes, can, perhaps, not be expected to cringe or come out all over goose pimpled on hearing repeated academic criticisms of these taxes south of our border—and I do not mean down Mexico way.

U.S. tax reformers must also remember that our own heavy dependence on direct taxation via income taxation—at least on the federal level—is a rather recent phenomenon. The following facts are illustrative: In 1915 a family of four with a net income of $10,000 paid $60 in federal income tax; in 1930 they paid $82.25; in 1940, $440; and in 1952, $1,773.60.[11]

DETAILS OF THE TAX STRUCTURE

Intercountry comparison of detailed tax sources—beyond a general division such as the direct-indirect comparison of Table 4—becomes virtually impossible. William Sprague Barnes, head of the Harvard Law School International Program in Taxation and one of the best informed U.S. tax scholars, estimates that for Latin America as a whole, 20–25 percent of the tax revenues come from income taxes, 70–75

---

[10] A. Kenneth Eaton, "Taxing Income in Canada," in National Tax Association, *Proceedings of the Forty-Fifth Annual Conference of the National Tax Association, 1952*, p. 21.

[11] In these computations "net income" means income after allowing all possible deductions but before personal exemptions.

percent from sales, excise, import, and export taxes, and 0–10 percent from property and other capital taxes.[12] The comparable figures for the U.S. emphasize the difference in the two areas. In 1960, the combined U.S. federal-state-local percentages were approximately 66, 17, and 17 percent, respectively.

The series of tables presented here suggest the wide variety in the tax structure of the individual Latin American countries. Although the nomenclature is not entirely comparable, the detail is highly varied, and the statistics are questionable, the figures are revealing and some generalization is possible. For example, several Latin American countries rely heavily on customs duties for significant portions of their tax revenues. Costa Rica, El Salvador, Guatemala, Haiti, and Nicaragua can be included in this group as indicated by Tables 5a to 5e. Older actual data, and more recent budget estimates, suggest that Bolivia and Honduras could also be included with this group of countries.

TABLE 5

Detailed Tax Structure of Five Latin American Countries Relying Heavily on Customs Duties for Ordinary Government Revenues

a. Costa Rica: Tax Structure in 1960

Type of tax	Receipts in millions of colones	Percentage of total
Income tax	37.1	12.0
Tax on banana-company profits	*	*
Land tax	14.3	4.6
Customs duties (largely on coffee)	192.7	62.5
Coffee tax	12.2	4.0
Other indirect taxes	34.7	11.2
Other revenues	17.6	5.7

* This tax was temporarily suspended in 1960 to compensate the banana companies for an overpayment of wages per an earlier government instruction. The 1961 budget estimate included the tax at an estimated .9 million colones.

Source: IMF—SM/61/39, August 31, 1961.

[12] Joint Economic Committee, *Hearings Before the Subcommittee on Inter-American Economic Relationships of the Joint Economic Committee,* 87th Congress, 2nd Session, May 10 and 11, 1962, p. 10.

TABLE 5 Continued

Detailed Tax Structure of Five Latin American Countries Relying Heavily
on Customs Duties for Ordinary Government Revenues

b. El Salvador: Tax Structure in 1960

Type of tax	Receipts in millions of colones	Percentage of total
Import duties	69.8	40.7
Export taxes	26.3	15.3
Income-of-property taxes	17.1	10.0
Excise and consumption taxes	30.1	17.9
Gov't. service fees and sale of goods	8.3	4.8
Other receipts	19.3	11.3

Source: IMF—EBS/61/82, July 5, 1961.

c. Guatemala: Tax Structure in Fiscal Year 1959–1960

Type of tax	Receipts in millions of quetzales	Percentage of total
Import duties	28.0	36.7
Export duties	9.7	12.6
Excises on alcohol and tobacco	16.0	20.9
Business-profit taxes	7.0	9.1
Other taxes	10.8	14.1
Other current revenue	5.1	6.6

Source: IMF—EBS/61/104, August 2, 1961.

TABLE 5 Continued

Detailed Tax Structure of Five Latin American Countries Relying Heavily
on Customs Duties for Ordinary Government Revenues[1]

d. Haiti: Tax Structure in Fiscal Year 1960

Type of tax	Receipts in millions of gourdes	Percentage of total
Import duties	55.6	33.3
Export taxes	25.4	15.1
Other customs duties	1.4	.8
Internal taxes	45.5	27.1
Other revenues	4.4	2.6
"Non-fiscal" revenues	22.6	13.5
Special coffee-export tax	9.5	5.7
Other special revenues	3.1	1.9

Source: IMF—EBS/61/131, September 18, 1961; IBRD—R 61–99, September 21, 1961.

e. Nicaragua: Tax Structure in Fiscal Year 1959–1960

Type of tax	Receipts in millions of cordobas	Percentage of total
Import duties	108.7	46.2
Export duties	5.2	2.2
Consular fees	19.8	8.4
Income tax	23.4	9.9
Capital tax	7.6	3.3
Consumption tax	38.4	16.3
Other current receipts	32.2	13.7

Source: IMF—SM/61/55, June 21, 1961.

[1] The information contained in Table 5 has been adapted by the author from Frederic R. Fisher, *Tax Reform in Latin America,* a mimeographed paper, and the source references above are those given by Mr. Fisher.

A great deal of work needs to be done in analyzing the impact of these taxes through studies of individual countries. Detailed comments on customs duties will be included in Chapter 6. Suffice it to note here that a heavy dependence on customs duties makes budgeting extremely difficult. As prices and quantities fluctuate, so do tax receipts. Although specific duties lag seriously behind an inflationary impact, they are widely used. Ad valorem duties are more responsive to economic changes. The ultimate incidence of customs duties is virtually impossible to determine accurately. Most of them are undoubtedly shifted to various sectors of the domestic economy.

Brazil, Chile, Colombia, Mexico, and Uruguay have a more balanced tax structure. This can in large part be attributed to the larger size and greater diversity of the economies involved. In this group, all but Uruguay collect significant portions of their tax revenues from income taxation. Consumption, sales, and property taxes are also used in varying degrees. The detailed composition of the tax structure in each of these five countries, for a recent period is provided in Tables 6a through 6e. Recent budget estimates suggest that Argentina, Paraguay, and Peru could be roughly classified with the group of countries included in Table 6.

TABLE 6

Detailed Tax Structure of Five Latin American Countries with "Reasonably Balanced" Tax Structures

a. Brazil: Tax Structure in 1960

Type of tax	Receipts in billions of cruzeiros	Percentage of total
Customs duties	22.0	10.6
Consumption tax	83.5	40.2
Income tax	62.2	30.0
Stamp tax	25.5	12.2
Electrification tax	1.7	.8
Other taxes and fees	1.9	.9
Patrimonial, industrial and other income	11.1	5.3

Source: IMF—Brazil—Request for Stand-by Agreement, May 12, 1961.

TABLE 6 Continued

Detailed Tax Structure of Five Latin American Countries with "Reansonably Balanced" Tax Structures

b. Chile: Tax Structure in 1959

Type of tax	Receipts in millions of escudos	Percentage of total
Income taxes	88.0	14.3
Mining-income taxes	94.4	15.2
Property taxes	20.7	3.3
Sales and purchase taxes	126.0	20.3
Production taxes	54.9	8.9
Service tax	62.0	10.1
Taxes on juridical acts	33.0	5.3
Import taxes	137.3	22.3
Miscellaneous taxes	2.4	.3

Source: IBRD—Current Economic Position and Prospects, June 1, 1961; IMF—SM/61/30, April 11, 1961.

c. Colombia: Tax Structure in 1959

Type of tax	Receipts in millions of pesos	Percentage of total
Direct taxes (income and property)	868.0	46.9
Indirect taxes (customs, excise, *etc.*)	662.4	35.8
Fees and fines	92.5	4.9
Royalties and property income	89.8	4.8
Other revenue*	142.1	7.6

* Includes amounts released by Banco de la Republica to the Treasury from special export tax.

Source: IMF—SM/61/54, June 19, 1961.

TABLE 6 Continued

Detailed Tax Structure of Five Latin American Countries with
"Reasonably Balanced" Tax Structures[1]

d. Mexico: Tax Structure in 1960

Type of tax	Receipts in millions of pesos	Percentage of total
Income tax	3,638	31.5
Sales and excise taxes	2,734	23.6
Import duties	1,670	14.4
Export taxes	805	6.8
Other tax revenues	713	6.2
Fees and other receipts	2,031	17.5

Source: IMF—EBS/61/79, July 5, 1961.

e. Uruguay: Tax Structure in 1959

Type of tax	Receipts in millions of pesos	Percentage of total
Import duties and consular fees	132.8	12.7
Excises (consumption taxes)	193.5	18.5
Sales and transactions taxes	153.6	14.7
Income taxes	58.5	5.6
Property taxes	157.0	15.0
Stamp taxes	147.1	14.1
All other (including business taxes)	202.8	19.4

Source: IMF—SM/61/63, July 17, 1961 (p. 18).

[1] The information contained in Table 6 has been adapted by the author from
Frederic R. Fisher, *Tax Reform in Latin America,* a mimeographed paper, and
the source references above are those given by Mr. Fisher.

The fiscal system of Venezuela is so dominated by the existence of the petroleum industry, it must be considered separately. The taxes on petroleum companies provide nearly two-thirds of the total Venezuelan tax revenues. Excluding the oil taxes, nearly 45 percent of the remaining revenue is from customs duties; another 30 percent is from income taxation.[13] The detailed breakdown for fiscal year 1959–1960 is given in Table 7.

TABLE 7

Venezuela: Tax Structure in Fiscal Year 1959–1960

Type of tax	Receipts in millions of bolivares	Percentage of total
Oil royalties	1,520	29.9
Oil-income tax	1,267	24.9
Exchange profit	419	8.2
Import duties	721	14.3
Income tax on iron-ore companies	61	1.2
Direct taxes	492	9.7
Indirect taxes	426	8.4
Other	175	3.4

Source: IBRD—R 61–62, June 21, 1961 (Adapted by the author from Frederic R. Fisher, *Tax Reform in Latin America,* Part II.)

In all of the above tables, revenue is limited to "ordinary revenue" actually collected during the period indicated unless noted to the contrary. That is, the tables exclude such extrabudgetary items as grants received, bond proceeds, government-operated-entity profits, and monopoly receipts. The revenue figures given are for the central government only. In most cases, this is equivalent to saying it represents the large majority of the total tax receipts. Data for lower levels of governments are generally difficult to obtain and are of dubious accuracy.

In other countries, such as Ecuador, the fiscal system is so complex it is difficult to classify the country in any of the above groups. Ecuador's central government budget accounts for less than one-half the

[13] Commission to Study the Fiscal System of Venezuela, *The Fiscal System of Venezuela,* pp. 2–4.

"public sector" operations but it is divided into three separate, yet overlapping, budgets. Tax revenues are allocated to the various budgets. The *operations* budget (only) for 1960 indicates that just over 50 percent of the receipts come from customs duties. Income taxation adds another 17 percent. Details on other budgets are not available.[14]

Any more detailed investigation of the Latin American tax structure would have to proceed on a country-by-country, or tax-by-tax, basis. For example, some import and export duties are imposed strictly for revenue reasons, others for protection only, and most for a combination of these (and other) reasons. Excise taxes vary on each item, level of imposition, and tax base. Any of these details considered important for economic development aspirations will be considered in subsequent chapters.

TAX SHARING IN LATIN AMERICA

In the problematic area of intergovernmental fiscal relations, the "underdeveloped" countries are in one sense more advanced than some of the "well-developed" nations. The problem derives from the fact that if each tax is collected by the most efficient level of government, the resultant revenue allocation may not be consistent with the expenditure requirements for the most advantageous functional distribution of governmental activity. The failure to delineate the jurisdiction of each level of government, relative to each of the various taxes, frequently results in an undesirable duplication of taxes in economically developed countries. This duplication compounds any economic disadvantages associated with a tax.

Many taxes can be most efficiently administered at the central (or federal) government level. Therefore, in the absence of tax sharing, the lower levels of government are left with insufficient revenues to provide those government goods and services they are best equipped to provide. Even taxes that can be effectively administered at lower levels of government are most desirable (or least undesirable) when they are uniformly imposed. And uniformity in taxation is often obtainable only through compulsory measures.

Tax-sharing is common among the different levels of government in Latin America. Common practices can be illustrated from the laws of Mexico, Brazil, and Venezuela. Article 127 of the Constitution of

---

[14] For a detailed discussion of the Ecuador system see Fisher, *Tax Reform in Latin America*, Part II, "Ecuador."

Venezuela provides that not less than 12½ percent, nor more than 25 percent, of the annual federal governmental receipts are to be redistributed in state grants. Of this amount, 30 percent is divided equally among the states; the remaining 70 per cent is allocated according to population. The constitution leaves the Venezuelan state with little independent revenue-producing power. Consequently, for the period 1956–1959, in excess of 90 percent of the Venezuelan state and territory revenues came from federal grants.

Since 1934, the Constitution of Brazil has provided each level of government with exclusive jurisdiction over specified taxes. Import duties, specified excise taxes, the *"imposto único"* (a tax on fuels, lubricants, and electricity), income and excess-profits taxes, taxes on foreign-exchange transactions, and stamp taxes on legal documents regulated by federal law, are examples of exclusively federal taxes. Brazilian state governments hold sole rights to the rural-land tax, the real-property-transfer tax, sales taxes (by far the most important), and stamp taxes on legal documents regulated by state law. The municipal governments receive all revenues from the urban-real property tax, license taxes on activities subject to municipal regulation, the amusement tax, and a "business tax" imposed on anyone engaged in industry, commerce, or a profession, regardless of profitability.

In addition to the exclusive tax rights, the Brazilian Constitution further provides that the federal government must remit 10 percent of the income-tax collections to the municipalities (exclusive of state capitals), and 60 percent of the *imposto único* to its "source of origin." Any "nonexclusive taxes" collected by the state governments must be shared on a 20–40–40 (federal-state-local) basis. The obvious effect of this provision is a strong deterrent to state imposition of any nonexclusive tax. A final tax-sharing provision requires the Brazilian state to remit 30 percent of any *excess* of state tax collections over municipal tax collections in the same city to the city concerned.[15]

The Constitution of Mexico provides a similar system of exclusive tax jurisdiction. For example, the federal government retains complete tax jurisdiction on all matters of exclusively federal domain—such as export taxes, import duties, taxes on foreign commerce and on water power. In addition, the numerous unspecified taxes are in practice relegated to the federal level by the practice of required allocation to

[15] A thorough discussion of the details is available in the Harvard Law School International Program in Taxation, *World Tax Series: Taxation in Brazil*, pp. 41–42.

"coordinating" states. States voluntarily electing coordination release their rights to tax the same transaction. In exchange, Article 73, Section XXIX, of the Federal Constitution guarantees the coordinating state the right to share in any revenues collected. The distribution system is determined by various federal laws. In this system, *"municipos"* are further guaranteed a share of the state's allocation.[16]

In addition, 40 percent of the federal excise tax on electric energy produced in Mexico is remitted to the state governments. One-fourth of the 40 percent (or 10 percent of the total) goes to the state in which the energy is produced; the remaining three-fourths (or 30 percent of the total) goes to the state in which the energy is used. Once again the *municipos* share in the state's share, as specified by the state legislature.

Federal grants-in-aid and federal-state-city tax-participation agreements are common in many other Latin American countries. Except in Brazil, Mexico, and Colombia, state and local taxation is relatively insignificant. Because of the increased uniformity in taxation and the reduced administrative requirements, it would seem that this practice could be highly recommended throughout Latin America and other less-developed areas. However, two noted authorities recently suggested that this same practice has been an important factor in the antitax attitude so prevalent in Latin America.[17] They contend that as long as tax revenues are remitted to a distant government, there will be no grass-roots acceptance of the tax reforms deemed essential to the Alliance for Progress. They further contend that the absence of local government financial autonomy has been an important contributing factor in the slow development of community initiative and governmental administrative ability.

THE EARMARKING OF TAX REVENUES

At present, the practice of earmarking tax revenues varies widely in Latin America. In one extreme case (Bolivia), nearly 90 percent of the

[16] The interested reader should consult the Harvard Law School International Program in Taxation, *World Tax Series: Taxation in Mexico,* pp. 84–85, for additional details.

[17] The two experts are William Sprague Barnes, Director of the Harvard Law School International Program in Taxation, and Dr. Elba Gómez del Rey de Kybal, a Pan American Union economist from Argentina. See their testimony before a Joint Economic Committee, *Hearings Before the Subcommittee on Inter-American Economic Relationships of the Joint Economic Committee,* 87th Congress, 2nd Session, May 10 and 11, 1962, pp. 9–12, 21–25.

taxes are earmarked. More limited activity in this area is common. For example, Mexico imposes a tax on the consumption of electric energy and telephone service that is earmarked for specified public-utility organizations. Although Venezuela has no earmarked revenues, revolving funds, or trust funds per se, she does utilize several autonomous "institutes" that perform similar functions.

Colombia has recently imposed several special taxes and earmarked the proceeds for development projects. One of these, Law No. 81 of December 22, 1960, imposes a 6 percent tax on the after-income-tax income (in excess of 20,000 pesos) of corporations and silent partnerships. The revenue collected is destined for the construction of dwellings for middle and working classes. Various payment options (including stock and bond subscriptions in nonprofit dwelling corporations) are provided. Another special Colombian tax is imposed and earmarked to aid in the development of electricity, iron, and steel production.

In conjunction with Alliance-for-Progress tax-reform discussions, it is not unusual to discover a sentiment favoring the earmarking of new and/or revised tax revenues for economic and social development projects. Knowledgeable individuals have suggested that the wealthy of Latin American society would not be so averse to payment of taxes if they could but be convinced that the resources thus released would not be foolishly squandered by the recipient government's officials.[18] Unfortunately, history records enough cases of irresponsible government to make the contention serious. The suggested solution is the earmarking practice.

While it is true that earmarking might restore confidence and decrease opposition to tax changes, the dangers inherent in this practice more than outweigh the possible benefits since other less costly methods of attaining the same benefit are available. Neither development plans nor other governmental functions should be restricted by the yield of any particular tax or taxes. Generally, there is no logical relation between the developmental (or other) expenditure and the tax imposed; therefore, the "benefit principle" cannot justify the practice either. Earmarking seriously complicates the budgeting and planning processes. Special taxes, such as those illustrated by the Colombian example, further complicate the tax system, increase the difficulty in gaining

---

[18] For example, see Elba Gómez del Rey de Kybal, "Why More Taxes? Mobilizing for the Alliance," *Américas*, XIV (April 1962), 12.

voluntary compliance, and make accurate economic analysis extremely hazardous.

The much preferred alternative to earmarking tax revenues is to simplify the tax system under a reasonable number of laws; work diligently for an improved administration of the simplified laws; allocate the revenues judiciously; and then engage in an extensive public-relations campaign to explain the why and wherefore, and the results of the tax system. In an unusually clever metaphor, a Canadian, Monteath Douglas, speaking to a group of U.S. fiscal experts, dissects this problem of the reluctant taxpayer. His prescription is equally applicable to the underdeveloped nation struggling with the problem of tax reform:[19]

> Preparation of the budget each year in our country [Canada] has to cope with the ravages of a disease known to us as *fiscal schizophrenia*. The symptoms, which are widespread, are a persistent disposition during ten months of the year to regard oneself (or one's constituents) as the worthy beneficiary of generous projects of government expenditure, followed during the other two months, before and after the budget, by a species of amnesia which causes the patient to be conscious only of his role of taxpayer. The infection originates in undetermined organs of the body politic and becomes active and communicable when people meet their elected representatives. Among the latter, resistance has sometimes been so low that the cynics who first detected this condition were inclined to suppose that it was an occupational malady attributable to the strain of public life. But it is now believed that politicians are simply the victims of unavoidable exposure, and life appointment to the Senate has been observed to establish complete immunity, often marked by vigorous indications of allergic reaction.
>
> If this contagion should ever penetrate the United States, I can tell you that there is only one known remedy. *Susceptibility has been traced to an insufficient diet of nutritional information and to lack of the tonic benefit of informed discussion.*

SUMMARY

Whereas intercountry comparisons of public-finance statistics are of only limited validity, some generalization from the available statistics for the Latin American countries as a group is possible. First, the ratio of tax receipts to national income is low enough in most of these countries to suggest a real possibility for increased taxation—especially

[19] Monteath Douglas, in Tax Institute, *The Limits of Taxable Capacity*, pp. 39–40, (emphasis mine).

when accompanied by economic growth. Second, indirect taxes are greater revenue producers than are direct taxes. Third, the smaller Latin nations tend to rely quite heavily on customs duties for their tax revenues. Fourth, several of the larger and more diversified economies have reasonably well-balanced tax systems. Fifth, a few Latin American countries are so dominated by a particular industry that their tax systems cannot readily be included in other groups.

The practice of sharing tax revenues among the different levels of government is well established in several Latin American countries. On the one hand, this is advantageous because it permits the collection of tax revenues by the most efficient level of government, increases the uniformity in taxation, and minimizes administrative costs and requirements. On the other hand, the practice may be disadvantageous since it increases resistance to tax reform, stifles grass-roots development programs, and suppresses local government autonomy and the development of administrative abilities.

Lastly, the procedure of earmarking tax revenues is often advocated as a method of "selling" Alliance-prompted tax-reform measures. In most cases this is an undesirable alternative even if the revenues are earmarked for economic development projects. The pressure for earmarking should be directed instead into general tax-education campaigns.

4. Income Taxation

The last two chapters indicate the desire and the tendency for the developing nations of Latin America to look to direct taxation—particularly to income taxation—for an ever increasing portion of their tax revenues. While there are hazards and limitations in income taxation for a developing country, they are not sufficient to discourage many of these countries from enacting income-tax laws. This chapter includes a brief discussion of some of the more important problems, and reports on the existing state of the income-tax art in several of the Latin American republics.

It is obviously impossible within the confines of a chapter or two, to discuss, even in a general way, the numerous important provisions of each of the income-tax codes of the nineteen signatory members of the Alliance for Progress. A thorough examination of even a single country's code is equally impossible. This chapter does include a discussion of a few of the more common and significant aspects of the income-tax laws selected from these many codes. Distinctive features, having a particular advantage or limitation for economic development aspirations, are given primary consideration. The chapter ends with four illustrative calculations of income taxes in two Latin American countries.

PROBLEMS OF INCOME TAXATION

The problems of income taxation are administrative and political as well as economic. A truly productive income tax must tap the middle-income classes as well as the high-income group. This, in turn, is both expensive and difficult. Success demands an honest and efficient tax-collection machine, including a capable civil service. Unfortunately, success further depends upon a rather complex law and a substantial degree of voluntary compliance. Many underdeveloped nations are lacking in each of these areas. A brief consideration of some of the administrative problems is made in appropriate subsections of the present chapter. A more detailed analysis of the administrative aspects, and recommendations for administrative improvements, will be considered separately in Chapter 8.

The core of the income-tax problem is frequently political. In several of the Latin American republics, and in many other underdeveloped countries, the governments either cannot or will not impose and collect a truly progressive income tax. Although the following portions of this chapter identify several apparent weaknesses in the various Latin American income-tax laws, the overwhelming impression left with the present writer, after this study of their laws, is not how poorly the laws are written, but how surprisingly sophisticated they are! Therefore it seems that, except in limited areas, the *major* task facing these countries is political and administrative, not legislative.

Before tax administration can be effective, the power-dominant groups must be willing to give more than lip service to the income-tax laws. Nicholas Kaldor, an internationally known economist, makes the same point this way:[1]

To the detached observer, fiscal reform undoubtedly appears as the most appropriate instrument for transforming the feudal or quasi-feudal regimes which inhibit the healthy evolution of so many of the underdeveloped countries and prevent them from following the path toward the kind of mass-prosperity civilization which has evolved in Western Europe and North America. But the advocacy of fiscal reform is not some magic potion that is capable of altering the balance of political power by stealth. No doubt, expert advice on tax reform can be very useful in making men of good will— ministers or officials—conscious of the precise nature of the legislative and administrative changes that are required. But what can actually be accomplished does not depend merely on the individual good will of ministers or on the correct intellectual appreciation of the technical problems involved. It is predominantly a matter of political power.

The big question that remains in much of Latin America is whether the acceptance of tax, economic, and social reforms can ever be accomplished without a major shift in the balance of power through revolution. Making Alliance-for-Progress financial aid the *quid pro quo* for long-overdue reforms is an obvious attempt to do so. It is to be hoped that political leaders of Latin America will also realize that the voluntary relinquishing of some historical privileges is necessary

[1] Nicholas Kaldor, "Will Underdeveloped Countries Learn to Tax?" *Foreign Affairs*, XLI (January 1963), 418.

for social stability and, therefore, in their own best long-run interest. It must also be emphasized that the formal political structure is not a factor of major significance as far as successful income taxation is concerned. Professor Hansen suggests that authoritarian governments may be in an even better position than democratic ones when it comes to attaining success in progressive taxation in a developing nation:[2]

> . . . it may be of very little significance that the formal sources of governmental authority are democratic. Indeed, many of the formally democratic political systems of the underdeveloped countries fully justify the opprobrious adjectives that Lenin applied to "bourgeois democracy" in general—"inevitably narrow, subtly rejecting the poor, and therefore, hypocritical and false to the core." Conversely, an openly dictatorial regime, such as Colonel Nasser's Egypt, may be far more genuinely popular in character than the so-called democratic regimes that have preceded it.
>
> In an underdeveloped country a broadly-based, popular, authoritarian government will have much greater freedom to tax the higher incomes than a wealth-dominated "democratic" one.

The economic problems inherent in income taxation were considered in Chapter 2. To recapitulate briefly, these include the possibility that increased taxation could hamper business activity, decrease the incentive to work, and discourage private investment. On the other hand, the counterbalancing economic forces, induced by the concomitant public investment, could more than compensate for any detrimental effects. Very little useful generalization about the economic effects of progressive taxation is possible short of an intensive investigation of each specific situation. Such an investigation is outside the scope of this project.

Suffice it to say that in the Alliance-for-Progress program (1) higher taxes are believed imperative to help finance the investments necessary for real economic development; (2) a more progressive tax system is considered the most desirable way of raising a good portion of the necessary tax revenue; and (3) the task is finding a solution that can offset any detrimental disincentive effects through the positive effects of the development-oriented public-expenditures program.

PRECONDITIONS FOR SUCCESSFUL INCOME TAXATION

Technical-assistance-mission reports written just before and after World War II frequently urged the adoption of income taxation. They

[2] A. H. Hansen, *Public Enterprise and Economic Development*, p. 78.

were followed in the early 1950's by a series of articles stressing the fact that the institutional setting of the developing countries was such as to preclude the successful implementation of the earlier income-tax recommendations. Prior reports were criticized for including too many of the ideological precepts of the tax advisors, and too little appreciation of the institutional setting of the host country.

The prevailing opinion of the time was well summarized in the report of the U.N.-sponsored Technical Assistance Conference on Comparative Fiscal Administration, held in Geneva, July 16 to 25, 1951.[3] A basic conclusion of this conference was that, for most underdeveloped countries, income taxation could only be a long-range objective. During the same year, Richard Goode's now famous paper was read before the Forty-Fourth National Tax Association Conference.[4] In this paper, Mr. Goode proposed six prerequisites to a successful income tax. Essentially, his list included (1) a money economy; (2) general literacy; (3) minimum accounting records; (4) acceptance of the idea of voluntary compliance with tax laws; (5) political acceptance of an income tax; and (6) an efficient administrative machine.

By the mid-1950's, Goode's list of prerequisites was still cited with approval. However, it was then seen as a delineation of the lines along which corrective action had to be taken. Income taxation, at least on the upper-income groups, was again being recommended for the here and now. The following statement, from a U.N. study, reflects this change in attitude:[5]

A recitation of such limitations is, of course, a counsel of caution, not of despair. It suggests the lines along which action must be taken to remove the barriers listed and underscores again the necessity of improving administration and compliance to the limits possible within the framework of existing social institutions. At the same time, it calls for ingenuity in adapting and modifying advanced fiscal instruments to the conditions existing in economically underdeveloped countries. In the case of the income tax, for example, the difficulties encountered in many countries do not rule out the income tax entirely but strongly suggest that it not be used as a mass tax. . . . A personal income tax with a narrow base but high rates on large income,

[3] An excellent statement of the agenda, and a summary of the discussion of this conference, is contained in the United Nations, *Taxes and Fiscal Policy in Under-Developed Countries*, pp. 28–42.

[4] Richard Goode, "Reconstruction of Foreign Tax Systems," in National Tax Association, *Proceedings of the Forty-Fourth Annual Conference of the National Tax Association, 1951*, pp. 212–222.

[5] United Nations, *Taxes and Fiscal Policy*, p. 20.

buttressed by administrative efforts concentrated on this area, may be a suitable instrument for achieving some of the ends of economic policy and distributive justice.

The position stated in this quotation represents the essence of the position of the author. This position appears consistent with the overt expressions of a majority of the Latin American governments: witness the fact that, effective July 1, 1961, each of the signatory nations to the Alliance had an operative income-tax statute on the books. Uruguay was the last country to join this list. Others, such as Mexico and Brazil, enacted income-tax laws as early as 1921 and 1922, respectively. Guatemala's income-tax law is the only one that does not include a tax on purely personal income; it is restricted to a tax on commercial profits. Most of these tax codes were extracted from French settings and, therefore, they contrast notably with the typical English-oriented tax law.

DISTINGUISHING FEATURES OF SOME OF THE LATIN AMERICAN INCOME-TAX CODES

The distinguishing features of each Latin American income-tax code vary from the obvious, apparent on even a first reading of the law, to the very subtle technical distinctions that can remain hidden until a new case suddenly exposes them to light. A complete appreciation of the distinctions is beclouded by the constantly evolving nature of the economies and the tax laws. The object of this portion of the present monograph is to note some of the more obvious distinctions, and to comment on some possible ramifications for economic development aspirations.

Tax Proliferation

Even a cursory examination of the tax systems of Latin America reveals a tendency toward tax proliferation. In considering income taxes, it is often necessary to consider not one or two major laws, but a whole host of apparently separate tax laws, all based upon some sort of income measurement. The basic income tax usually consists of from four to ten "schedular taxes." If separate schedules are not provided for business income, an additional "business tax" is typical (schedular taxation and taxes on business income are considered in greater detail below). Finally, a progressive "complementary tax" on total taxable income from all sources is common to those countries having proportional schedular tax rates. A combination of the basic schedular taxes, business-income taxes, and the complementary tax, can provide an effective tax based on income. However, many of the Latin American countries have enacted still other income-based taxes.

The following examples, drawn from the Brazilian tax system, serve to illustrate the sort of income-tax proliferation that is common to many of the Latin American countries. In 1941 the "law for the Protection of the Family" was enacted. This law imposes an additional income tax equal to 15 percent of the total schedular and complementary tax liability for any taxpayer over twenty-five and either unmarried or widowed without children. The rate decreases to 10 percent if the taxpayer is married but remains childless. At age forty-five and over, the tax rate is 5 percent if the taxpayer still has only one child.[6]

The Brazilian tax scene is further complicated by a tax that is in some ways more closely akin to a forced loan. Since 1951, any taxpayer having a total schedular and complementary tax liability of between 20,000 and 250,000 cruzeiros is required to "invest" a sum equal to 15 percent of his income-tax liability in the Brazilian Economic Development Program. For those taxpayers with an income-tax liability in excess of 250,000 but less than 1,000,000 cruzeiros, the rate increases to 20 percent; if the tax liability exceeds 1,000,000 cruzeiros, the rate is 25 percent (261.52 Brazilian cruzeiros equal one U.S. dollar). Revenue raised in this manner constitutes a special fund from which expenditures are limited to port and railroad rehabilitation, warehouse-capacity expansions, cold storage and slaughterhouse facility construction, the generation of electric energy, and "basic" industrial and agricultural development projects. All funds "invested" are "repaid" with a 25 percent premium in four years. Payment is in the form of 5 percent federal bonds, maturing in twenty annual installments of 5 percent each, beginning one year after issue. Considering the fact that the consumer price index in Brazil increased from 142 in 1955 to 607 in 1961, it becomes difficult to distinguish precisely between such a forced loan and more ordinary taxation.

A complete picture of the Brazilian income-tax structure would further include details on a 4 percent "business-reserves" tax (again,

---

[6] For a country with an annual population growth rate already in excess of 2.4%, the necessity of such a law is not immediately evident to the North American observer.

this is formally worded as a compulsory loan rather than an outright tax) and a 30 percent "excess-reserves" tax. Parallel illustrations of tax proliferation in Colombia were briefly mentioned in Chapter 3. Similar situations are typical of many of the Latin American republics.

Any income-based tax beyond the schedular taxes, the business-income tax, and a complementary-income tax, are wholly unnecessary. If these three basic taxes are not considered sufficiently progressive, or if increased revenues are considered mandatory, the proper solution lies in the adjustment of the existing rate structures, exclusions, deductions, or exemptions. All too frequently, the solution accepted in Latin America is the imposition of another "new" tax. This solution demands new definitions, exclusions, and administrations, for each law. The result is—at best—haphazard income taxation.

Concepts of Taxable Income

Another fundamental difference between many tax codes concerns the basic concept of "taxable income." The three different concepts in the United States, Mexico, and Brazil, serve to illustrate the possible breadth of this distinction. The U.S. Code provides that any income not expressly exempt by law is taxable income. The Mexican Code takes just the opposite position: any income not specifically mentioned in the detailed revenue laws is not taxable income (incidentally, the Mexican provisions are reasonably comprehensive, and therefore, little income escapes taxation). The intent of the Brazilian Code is to restrict the concept of taxable income to recurring receipts only.

The evolution of a "commercial code" is reflected in the concept of taxable income utilized in some Latin American countries. For example, in Mexico the commercial law (*actos de comercio*) regulates (1) transactions performed by persons characteristically engaged in the business sphere; (2) transactions entered into with a "speculative intent" (*i.e.,* the intention to make a profit); and/or (3) transactions primarily involving property of a commercial nature (*i.e.,* negotiable instruments, ships, and so forth). Other transactions are regulated by civil law (*actos civiles*). The significance of the distinction for tax purposes is that any profit or income resulting from a transaction regulated by commercial law is subject to income taxation, whereas profits from transactions regulated by civil law are held not to constitute taxable income. Even though the formal distinction was amended in Mexico in late 1959, "the tax on profits from non-commercial contracts has not been enforced."[7] The laws of Guatemala and Ecuador utilize still more restricted concepts of taxable income.

Generally, the legislative definition of taxable income is weak in the less developed countries of Latin America. Because many of the tax laws are transitional, the precise definitions and concepts conducive to the better tax system are not developed rapidly enough through administrative experience. Therefore, it can generally be recommended that the legislative definitions of taxable income be made quite explicit. As an improved administrative machine becomes a reality, and the laws become more stable, less reliance on legislative definitions is necessary. In order to avoid undesirable economic distortion, and to raise the maximum revenues, it is also recommended that the definitions of taxable income be made as inclusive as possible.

Source Rules

Prior to World War II few, if any, of the Latin American republics taxed transactions effected beyond their national boundary. In postwar revisions, and in new revenue laws, a change in this attitude is apparent. There is a growing assertion of the right to tax foreign-source income. Joseph Crockett, a tax consultant to the Pan American Union, General Secretariat of the Organization of American States, contends that this assertion is not "based on any deep rooted convictions or . . . productive of any substantial amount of revenue. It would appear to be more in the nature of a retaliatory measure adopted in the response to the long reach of the United States, or as one Latin American official put it, 'necessary for prestige'."[8]

The change is not yet complete. For example, Argentina and Venezuela still tax only income from domestic sources. Brazil taxes a resident individual's income from any source, but a resident entity's income only if from a domestic source. Nonresidents (individuals and entities) are subject to the Brazilian income tax on only that portion of the income from a Brazilian source. The revised laws of Mexico impose a tax on the income of residents and/or citizens (individual or entity) from any source in the world. Nonresident aliens and/or entities are taxed only on income from a Mexican source.

The problem of source rules is that the "source of income" is not

[7] Harvard Law School International Program in Taxation, *World Tax Series: Taxation in Mexico*, 1961 Supplement, p. 19.

[8] Joseph P. Crockett, "Tax Pattern in Latin America," *National Tax Journal*, XV (March 1962), 95.

readily determined. Does the interest income accruing on a loan have its "source" in the country (a) in which the loan arrangement is completed? (b) in which the creditor (or debtor) resides? (c) in which the capital is actually utilized? or (d) in still some other country? Similar questions can be raised about income deriving from property, from the rendering of a personal (or professional) service, from the sale of merchandise, or from any other activity. Mr. Crockett found that "despite the importance of determining source . . . only three Latin American republics have legislative definitions of source, and tax administrations of other countries seem unaware of the problems involved in a determination of source, seeming to regard source as simply obvious."[9]

From even this brief consideration of source rules, it is apparent that many precise definitions are necessary—but they frequently are not available. Definitions of numerous other tax terms, such as "gross income," "resident," "domicile," and "entity," are essential to a complete understanding of the source rules. Unfortunately, none of these terms are universally understood or accepted either. The foreign tax adviser must be particularly careful to determine the exact meaning intended for all of them before making recommendations. Any efforts the various international agencies might undertake to achieve a more uniform tax terminology would be beneficial. In the meantime, the individual legislatures and tax administrators should be encouraged to make explicit the meaning intended for any of these controversial, though fundamental, tax terms.

A second economic development ramification proceeding from source rules pertains to the growing assertion of the right to tax incomes earned outside territorial boundaries. This practice could result in multiple taxation of a single transaction and thereby rapidly bring to an end the many economic advantages being sought through the "common market movement," as prompted in the Latin American Free Trade Association (LAFTA). A world-wide tax concept for "residents" and, perhaps, citizens, is not harmful so long as a single income stream is not subject to multiple income taxes without provision for tax credits for the tax paid in another jurisdiction. In short, the problem for tax reform is not to repeal the progress that has been made in defining taxable income, even when it includes income from foreign source, but rather to encourage the enactment of foreign-tax credits that will permit individuals and companies operating interna-

[9] *Ibid.*, p. 100.

tionally to offset taxes paid in one country from those taxes imposed on the same income by another country. Generally the capital-exporting country should be the one to forego the revenue.

In wording any international tax agreement, care needs to be taken to provide for tax credits on "excused taxes" as well as on taxes actually paid. If one country enacts a provision to excuse new industries from part or all of the internal taxes for some limited time period, the net result for a foreign investment company might simply be increased taxation in the home country (see Chapter 7 for the details of some of these tax-exemption schemes and their place in development aspirations).

Schedular Income Taxation

The most obvious distinction between the "typical" Latin American income-tax code and the U.S. Code is the fact that the former provides a series of separate classifications, or "schedules," for different "kinds" of income, whereas the latter presumedly imposes a single tax on all "kinds" of income. Each of the so-called tax schedules is part of the general income-tax law of the country, but each is generally described in a separate chapter and each has its own regulations and provisions. The schedular system is of French origin (although the French have subsequently abandoned it themselves); the "global (or unitary) system" is of U.S. and British extraction. In reality, neither system is found in pure form; most income-tax systems contain features of each. In comparing the two here, it must be remembered that the primary issue at stake is how can a developing country best assess income accurately and still maintain the widest coverage of all income earners. The form or administrative device chosen is dependent upon the specific circumstances of the country in which the income tax is to operate. The accepted social institutions are an important consideration.

The disparity between the two systems is largely a matter of emphasis. The schedular system overtly recognizes social distinction in "kinds of income," and it frequently provides different tax rates for the different incomes. The unitary system—by caprice of administration if not by law—usually makes similar distinctions. Think, for example, of the U.S. treatment of (a) imputed income and certain bond interest (wholly tax exempt); (b) capital gains, dividends, and income from mineral exploitation (partially tax exempt); and (c) earned income from wages and salaries (wholly taxed). Walter Heller, professor of Economics at the University of Minnesota and formerly chairman of the President's Council of Economic Advisors, states that: "Available figures suggest that the [U.S.] income tax applies with 95 percent effectiveness to wage and salary income, about 75 percent to dividends, and possibly only 50 percent or even less to interest, rentals, and farm incomes."[10]

The number of schedules—and, therefore, the number of different "kinds" of income recognized—the definitions, exclusions, deductions, exemptions, tax rates, and so forth, vary widely among the twenty Latin American republics. For example, Venezuela has nine schedules; Brazil, eight; Mexico, seven; Chile, six; and the Dominican Republic, five. Most of these codes provide a "catch-all" schedule for the reporting of income not properly reported elsewhere. However, even this cannot be interpreted literally since, as was mentioned in the earlier discussion of taxable-income concepts, some countries intentionally impose the income tax only on those gains arising from "commercial" transactions, or gains from recurring receipts.

The major single disadvantage of the schedular system is the necessity for numerous fine distinctions in classifying income. The descriptive titles of the various schedules listed in Table 8 are suggestive of the problems encountered. For example, income from the rendering of a service may be reportable under one schedule if rendered as an employee; under another schedule if rendered independently, as a professional; or under still a third schedule if rendered as a commercial service that is held to constitute a business activity. This opens the door to political discrimination and unduly complicates the tax administrator's task. These distinctions become increasingly critical as the variations in the tax rates of the different schedules increase. The schedular rates (only) for Brazil, Mexico, and Venezuela, are shown in Table 8. (The reader is cautioned not to jump to the unwarranted conclusion that these are the "effective" income-tax rates in these three countries.) Taxpayer preferences for the alternative schedules are further intensified by the complexity of the returns, and by the varied deductions allowed, exclusions permitted, records required and additional information requested under each of the schedules.

The greatest advantage of the schedular system is the providing of standard tax forms and tax laws specialized and complicated only to the degree necessary for the kind of income being reported on each schedule. In other words, the descriptive materials and the tax forms

---

[10] Walter Heller, "Limits of Taxable Capacity with Respect to Income Taxation," in Tax Institute, *The Limits of Taxable Capacity*, p. 76.

TABLE 8

A Comparison of the Schedular Income-Tax Rates in
Three Latin American Republics

a. Brazil: Schedular Tax Rates

Schedule and Income Included	Tax Rate
Schedule A: Interest from nominative government securities	3%
Schedule B: Interest from other sources and certain other income from capital	10%
Schedule C: Compensation for personal services as an employee	1%
Schedule D: Compensation for independent personal services	2%
Schedule E: Income from real property	3%
Schedule F: Income from distributions by entities, business income of individuals, and foreign income	0%
Schedule G: Income from agriculture	0%
Schedule H: Income from gainful occupations not includible under another schedule	5%

Source: Harvard Law School International Program in Taxation, *Taxation in Brazil,* p. 49.

b. Venezuela: Schedular Tax Rates

Schedule and Income Included	Tax Rate
Schedule 1: Rents from real property	2½%
Schedule 2: Interest, royalties	3 %
Schedule 3: Business profits	2½%
Schedule 4: Oil and mining profits	2½%
Schedule 5: Agricultural profits	2 %
Schedule 6: Profits from noncommercial professions	2 %
Schedule 7: Salaries and wages	1 %
Schedule 8: Gains from sales of real property	3 %
Schedule 9: Lottery prizes and other chance winnings	10 %

Source: Commission to Study the Fiscal System of Venezuela, *The Fiscal System of Venezuela,* p. 88.

TABLE 8 Continued

A Comparison of the Schedular Income-Tax Rates in
Three Latin American Republics

c. Mexico: Schedular Tax Rates Schedule and Income Included	Tax Rate*
Schedule I: Income from commercial activities	From 5% on income over 2,000 to 39% on income over 2,000,000
Schedule II: Income from industrial activities	Same as for Schedule I
Schedule III: Income from agricultural, livestock raising, and fishing activities	From 3.2% on income over 2,000 to 25.9% on income over 1,500,000
Schedule IV: Wages, salaries, and other personal compensation	From 1.7% on income over 500 to 50% on income over 7,000
Schedule V: Income from professional services, arts, and crafts	From 3.0% on first 2,000 to 33.0% on income over 1,000,000
Schedule VI: Returns from capital investment (interest, royalties, rental, *etc.*)	From 10.0% on first 2,000 to 50% on income over 840,000
Schedule VII: Income arising from government concessions	From 20.0% on first 2,000 to 55.0% on income over 2,000,000

* All figures are in Mexican pesos.

Source: Arthur Andersen & Co., *Highlights of Taxation in Mexico for United States Businessmen,* pamphlet, pp. 17–22.

appropriate to report income received as an employee can be made exceedingly simple and remain essentially separate from the relatively detailed forms and laws applicable to, say, a manufacturing firm. Even within manufacturing, separate regulations and tax forms can be provided for different types of industries, if deemed appropriate.

Considering the fact that the schedular system is well ingrained in most of the Latin American republics, it does not appear advisable to recommend its sudden abandonment in favor of a unitary system, at least at the present time. Since Alliance-induced tax-reform efforts are, at best, tolerated, those reforms that can accomplish the essential objective with a minimum of antagonism can be most highly recommended. The major advantage of the schedular system can be retained, and the major disadvantage minimized, if these countries can be persuaded to work toward a narrowing of the tax-rate differentials applicable to the different schedules. An income tax is, after all, a tax on people, and income is simply the measuring stick of relative prosperity. Therefore, the "kind" of income should not be a major consideration in tax rates. The ultimate goal should be equal rates for all schedules. The present income-tax systems of Brazil and Venezuela represent reasonable proximities to this objective. When combined with their complementary taxes on total schedular incomes, they also can provide an effective means of progressive taxation. Incidentally, any preferred tax treatment deemed socially desirable can easily be provided by the enactment of tax credits, basic exemptions or exclusions, subsidies, rebates, or other special provisions.

Concomitant efforts to standardize deduction allowances, exemptions, and required records—at least within major reporting groups—should also be commended to the developing nations of Latin America. Acceptance of these alternatives would bring the preferred taxpayer's position clearly into focus and would permit a more accurate economic analysis of the overall tax system than is currently possible in many Latin American republics.

Business-Income Taxation

Another major distinguishing feature of some of the Latin American tax codes concerns the taxation of business income. The problems of business-income taxation are neither new nor peculiar to the developing nations. The essence of the problem derives from the fact that certain legal entities can generally earn income and withhold the distribution of the income, partially or wholly, from the ultimate owners. The income-tax dilemma follows. If the legal-entity concept is pierced, and the entire income attributable to the entity's operations is imputed to the owner(s), even though an actual distribution of profits is not forthcoming, the individual taxpayer may be in no position to pay the tax demanded of him. On the other hand, if the entity concept is not pierced, and the income tax is imposed on the entity only (as a separate legal "person"), the moneyed taxpayer can completely avoid the intended progressiveness of income taxation by a "proper" fracturing of his business interests.

Because of the relative simplicity of most sole proprietorships, partnerships, joint ventures, and certain limited liability forms of business organization, the laws of the more economically advanced nations typically provide that the earnings of these entities are potentially available to the ultimate owner(s), even if an actual distribution is not accomplished. In these cases, the owner's income tax is based upon a figure including his share of any such business income, and the entity is not subject to any separate income tax. However, because of the relative size and complexity of the ownership of many incorporated entities, a contrary position is deemed appropriate for the corporate form of business organization. The corporate-income tax is imposed on the corporate income, separate and distinct from the income of the stockholders. Any distribution of the corporate income to the stockholders is taxable to the recipient, in varying degrees, in the different countries.

In the United States, cash dividends paid to a corporate stockholder are generally included in the recipient's tax base, along with any other income he may have received in the same year. The result is, of course, that income earned by the corporation is in reality taxed twice: once via the corporate-income tax and again, following distribution, via the personal-income tax. In order to allay some of the many objections voiced against this double taxation, the U.S. has recently permitted each taxpayer to receive $100 per year in dividends tax free, and granted him a tax credit equal to 2 percent of the remainder. Other economically advanced countries have solved the same dilemma through a "dividends-received-tax-credit" approach or a "dividends-paid-deduction" approach.[11]

The Latin American tax practices present an interesting contrast to the accepted practice in the more developed countries. There are two essentially different approaches followed there: the Brazilian system is illustrative of the one; the Mexican system, of the other.

The legal fictions of Brazil extend the notion of a "juridical person" to include even the sole proprietorship, so long as it is engaged continuously in a business activity. The tax laws provide a separate business tax, similar to the U.S. corporate-income tax, on the earnings of such juridical persons if gross income is 180,000 cruzeiros or more in a year. The basic rate of this tax for most legal entities is 28 percent. An excess-profits tax is further imposed at rates from 10 to 50 percent of the earnings in excess of a "basic profit." Any distributions of business income are reported by the individual taxpayer in Schedule F.

[11] The advantages and limitations of each of these solutions are well developed in John F. Due, *Government Finance*, pp. 241–246.

Although this schedule imposes no schedular income tax, it must be included in the computations for the complementary tax. The latter tax is a progressive tax based on total schedular income (in Brazil, the top marginal rate of 50 percent is imposed on net taxable incomes in excess of 3,000,000 cruzeiros). Under this Brazilian system, the term "distribution" is not restricted to the payment of a dividend. A sole proprietor's income is deemed distributed as soon as it is determined; a partner's income is deemed distributed whenever it is actually disbursed, *or* whenever it is credited to the partner's capital account. So long as the partnership income is held in a suspense account no distribution is implied.

The income-tax system of Mexico includes three schedules devoted exclusively to the taxation of business income (see schedules I, II, and III, Table 8c, *supra*). Any taxpayer, real or juridical, divides his income among the various schedules as appropriate. Until 1962 there was no complementary tax on the total earnings reported by an individual in the various schedules. In this situation, it is obviously advantageous to the taxpayer to diversify his income so that it will be reported in several different schedules. Since the law recognizes as a separate taxpaying entity any firm optionally or obligatorily registered with the Commercial Registry, it is to further advantage of the wealthy taxpayer to divide his investments among several firms.[12]

In addition to the progressive schedular taxes, the Mexican law imposes a distributable-profits tax on the profits of commercial entities whether distributed or not. The tax rate is a flat 15 percent. There is no further tax on entity-profit distributions, either to the entity or to the ultimate owner.

The problems involved in attaining a proper taxation of business income are numerous, particularly as applied to widely owned firms. The present system of business-income taxation in some of the Latin American countries does not provide an adequate solution to these

---

[12] Even the sole proprietorship can be registered at the owner's option. The effect of the 1962 revision on the second of the two weaknesses cited is not yet clear. The most important provision in the 1962 law is the initiation of an additional progressive tax on the aggregate income earned by an individual. It is to apply to individuals earning in excess of Ps. 180,000 ($14,412). The new complementary-tax rates begin at 3% on aggregate income between Ps. 180,000–275,000, and rise to 15% on aggregate income in excess of Ps. 1,450,000. However, combined income taxes cannot exceed 30% of the individual's income. See "New Tax Laws in Mexico," *International Financial News Survey*, 14 (January 12, 1962), 7–8.

problems because it leaves open a great number of unnecessary possibilities for widespread tax avoidance. Generally, the income of entities with relatively restricted ownership should be imputed to the owners and taxed to them whether the earnings are formally distributed or not. When this is done, any separate tax on the entity income is wholly inappropriate. The refusal to pierce the entity veil seriously hampers any attempt to attain a truly progressive tax system.

Income earned by widely owned entities cannot be handled in the same manner. Therefore, to avoid a major loophole, these firms are best taxed under a separate law, generally with only a single tax rate, or with very limited progression.[13] Earnings distributed by widely owned entities should be deductible for purposes of computing the entity tax, but should be wholly taxable to the recipient individuals. Among the major advantages of this procedure are the facts that (a) it minimizes the possibilities of evading the intended progressiveness of personal-income taxation; (b) it eliminates double taxation of *distributed* profits; and (c) it is administratively easy to handle.

The development-oriented economist might object that this procedure also encourages the distribution of entity income whereas a re-investment of income is the more desirable alternative. This objection can be answered by the further recommendation that income reinvested in an authorized manner also be deductible for purposes of computing the entity-income tax. While this does mean a loss in government revenues, it can accomplish the same ultimate goal if the administrative control over the deduction provision is well handled. Deductions for "reinvested earnings" are already common to most of the Latin American republics (see Illustrations 1 and 2).

Exclusions

Virtually every country's tax law excludes some income from the general income-tax base. Two of these, nonrecurring receipts and profits on "civil transactions," were mentioned earlier. This section deals with still other items frequently excluded either by special provisions in the tax laws or by conceptual limitations. While a discussion of the taxation

[13] Limited progression may be justified as a special consideration for small business. Continued progression, as in a personal-income tax, would result in corporate split ups and would hinder any exploitation of economies of scale. It would also reward the inefficient (low-profit) firms by taxing them at low rates. None of these results are consistent with economic development aspirations.

of capital gains would be appropriate under this heading in many of the Latin American countries, it is deferred until later.

The exclusion of various items of income from the tax base is commonly justified on one of three grounds. One, the exclusion is believed consistent with the best interests of "social equity." Two, the exclusion is considered an effective incentive for the attainment of a socially desirable goal. Three, the exclusion is deemed necessary to make the tax law administratively feasible.

In the third group, the nearly universal exclusion of most items of income-in-kind is illustrative. Even the most economically advanced nations fail to include these items in the income-tax base because they are not valued in the market place and, therefore, are difficult to value accurately. Since tax administrations, independent appraisers, and communications systems are generally less developed in the relatively underdeveloped nations, it would *not* be advisable to recommend that these countries generally try to include such items in their income-tax base either. However, it is interesting to note that at least one Latin American republic is already taxing the imputed income derived from residential housing.

Colombian law provides that any taxpayer owning a house, an apartment, or a country home, in which he resides, must estimate and declare an imputed income from the enjoyment of these properties so long as the value of the land and buildings is greater than 100,000 pesos ($1 U.S. equals 6.70 Colombian pesos). The valuation basis to be used is the official cadastral valuation if available; if not, the historical cost is used. The income is imputed to be 6 percent of the valuation base if that is between 100,000 and 300,000 pesos; 10 percent if between 300,001 and 500,000 pesos; and 12 percent if over 500,000 pesos. Provision is also made in this law to impute the same income should the taxpayer try to avoid the tax by renting from another individual, at some low rental (in a less than "arm's length transaction"), or by having a firm provide his housing.[14]

Perhaps the "advanced" nations should investigate the Colombian experience in this attempt to tax a major item of imputed income. Certainly such income represents a significant and integral part of the real income of the well-to-do taxpayer. If the provision can be made administratively expedient, it provides a preferred method of taxing property ownership. Since the Latin American countries are already

[14] Donald O. Wallace, (ed.), *Colombian Income Tax Service*, pp. 388–389.

accustomed to the widespread use of tax sharing, this change would not have to be made at the expense of a major revenue producer for lower levels of government (in the U.S. many local governments are almost wholly dependent upon property taxation for their revenues).

Exclusions commonly justified on the grounds of social equity include the income of educational, charitable, religious, scientific, artistic, and fraternal associations; retirement income payments; gifts and inheritance; insurance proceeds; and indemnification payments. With the possible exception of gift and inheritance receipts, these exclusions from income taxation can be justified in most instances. If the government were to impose any significant tax on these income streams, it would often have to supplant the curtailed service, or the decreased income, with an equivalent public service. In these cases, little net gain from the increased taxation could be anticipated. Although the inclusion of inheritances and gifts in taxable income can be recommended on theoretical grounds,[15] a contrary tax treatment is so infused in most existing social institutions that it would be inadvisable to make such a change a precondition to Alliance-for-Progress financial assistance. Inheritance and gift taxation will be considered in greater detail in Chapter V.

The other group of exclusions—those justified as an incentive for attaining specified social goals—provide the greatest contrast between the "typical" Latin American tax system and the U.S. system. Generally, the Latin American countries are more prone to accept this justification. The one exclusion common to each system is that granted to interest on certain government debt obligations. In the U.S., the exclusion is limited to income from debt instruments of lower-than-federal levels of government, and it is purportedly granted only to guarantee these governments a relatively broad and "inexpensive" (re interest rates) market in which to operate. In the underdeveloped countries, the exclusion commonly extends to interest on any and all government securities. It is provided in the hope that it may stimulate private saving and thus expand the market for these securities. Even with the added tax incentive, the money markets are so limited in most of these countries that the only method for "successfully" floating a government security issue is through central bank operations.

Interest paid on bank savings accounts in Latin America is often excluded from income taxation on the grounds that this also contributes

[15] See Henry Simons, *Personal Income Taxation*, Chapter 6.

significantly to the stimulation of private savings. In some countries, this exclusion is limited to the interest earned on a specified amount of savings. For example, in Colombia the interest on a maximum savings of 5,000 pesos is exempt; in Uruguay, the figure is 10,000 pesos; and in Venezuela, it is 10,000 bolivars (converting these figures at the July 1, 1962, official rates of exchange yields approximately $746, $911, and $2,985 respectively). On the other hand, Mexico places no limit on this exclusion.

A next step, already accepted in several of these countries, is the exclusion of interest paid by approved mortgage banks, agricultural institutions, and industrial firms. The advisability of the exclusion of interest, partially or wholly, from income taxation is questionable. It can be argued that since the primary purpose of the increased taxation in Latin America is the release of resources for developmental investment, and since this is accomplished by any saving, regardless of the form it takes, tax-induced private saving should constitute an acceptable (if not a preferred) alternative to forced saving through taxation. Even though these arguments have real appeal, they tell only half the story.

Other exclusions granted in some countries of Latin America, and justified as necessary for the attaining of a socially desirable goal, include the following diverse items: rents on properties constructed after specified dates; dividends on "new" industries; salaries and emoluments paid to certain ecclesiastic leaders (in some cases this is restricted to those practicing a given cult); all remunerations paid to professors and teachers (in Brazil!); and the income of journalists, including royalties to authors. The above list is not intended to be comprehensive; it simply suggests the latitude of the items not infrequently excluded from income taxation on "social grounds" in Latin America.

The objections to all of these exclusions are both numerous and material. First, once the precedence is set, it is extremely difficult to combat effectively the granting of many more requests. Special-interest groups seize upon the opportunities presented and thereby make effective income taxation tremendously difficult. In this sense, exclusions compose a veritable Pandora's box. Second, the advantage gained from the exclusion provision is, in most instances, directly related to the wealth of the taxpayer. In the Latin American setting, just the opposite sort of relationship is desired. The question thus reduces to this: which social goal—a more progressive tax system or (say) increased *private* saving—is paramount? Third, the exclusions generally provide no benefit whatsoever to those individuals in the lowest-income group. In fact, they may be indirectly detrimental to their interests if the decreased revenue from income taxation is recouped elsewhere. Fourth, the exclusions constitute such a serious erosion of the tax base that the income tax becomes much less than its name implies. As the list of exclusions grows, the tax often degenerates into a tax on "earned income," particularly as applied to wage and salary payments. Finally, widespread exclusion provisions make effective tax reform exceedingly difficult.

Deductions

It is hazardous to make many general statements concerning what deductions are permitted in the computation of taxable income since these deductions vary widely among (1) the different countries of Latin America; (2) the different income-based taxes within a single country; and (3) the different schedules provided for the reporting of different kinds of income. What is attempted here is a very brief discussion of some elementary distinctions between the deduction provisions of the U.S. Internal Revenue Code and those deduction provisions frequently found in the Latin American codes. In no sense is the discussion comprehensive; emphasis is again deliberately placed upon those deduction provisions with the greatest ramifications for economic development. For purposes of this discussion only, deductions are categorically, though artifically, divided between those appropriate for the computation of what might be labeled "investment" and "earned" income.

Investment-Income Deductions

The two most significant, distinguishing features of the Latin American income-tax laws, relative to allowable deductions for the computation of investment income generally, are at opposite ends of a continuum. At the one end, many tax laws are written with only a general reference stating that *any* expenses necessary to the creation, maintenance, or preservation of the income are deductable.[16] Typically, this general proposition is followed by a condensed list of examples that is wholly unsatisfactory for the adjudication of administrative decisions that indubitably accompany a provision of this nature. In addition, equally conjectural limitations are sometimes imposed. For example,

---

[16] Illustrations could be cited from even such "developed" tax laws as those of Mexico, Uruguay, and Venezuela.

expenses may be deductible only if they are "reasonable" in proportion to the volume of the taxpayer's operations; or if they are "common to the industry."

At the opposite end of the continuum, it is not unusual to find, in selected income-tax laws of the various Latin American republics, unrealistic restrictions on the deductibility of valid expenses. For specified taxes, deductions are often exclusively restricted to from two to six specified expenses. Other expenses—even if actually incurred and wholly necessary to the production of the revenue—are disallowed. The Brazilian Schedule E (rental income) is a classic example; the seven specified deductions do not even include depreciation or mortgage interest! Whenever the approved list of deductions excludes fundamental expenses, the tax can rapidly become onerous.

Certain restrictions on expense deductions can be economically sound and administratively useful, especially when they can be quantitatively expressed. A particularly prevalent limitation of this sort concerns salary payments to entity owners. If these payments are not restricted, profit distributions frequently masquerade as salaries. However, finding a good base for an appropriate restriction can be an extremely difficult task. For example, if owners' salary deductions are limited to a percentage of profits, as several Latin American codes prescribe, no owner-salary payments are allowed in years reporting a net operating loss. If they are tied to paid-in capital, another common provision, reasonable salaries may be disallowed after even mildly inflationary periods.

What is needed in the countries at both ends of this continuum is a much more extensive cataloguing of deductible and nondeductible expenses. Any limits that must be imposed should be reconsidered frequently to determine if the intended objective is still being attained. The detailed cataloguing of expenses, and the imposition of limitations, may have to be accomplished legislatively in those countries with a relatively weak tax administration. Countries more fortunately situated could promptly provide equivalent "guidelines" through published administrative rulings when not prohibited by law.

The provisions for loss deductions are in most cases far too stringent in Latin America. This stringency can most easily be explained by the relatively heavy emphasis placed upon taxation as a revenue tool, rather than upon its role as a crucial economic force operating in the economy. This same attitude is responsible for the fact that what loss-deduction provisions there are nearly always are restricted to loss carry-forwards, excluding loss-carrybacks. Still further revenue consciousness is deducible in the restriction of loss offsets to the liability for the schedular income taxes, even when the complementary tax produces the higher liability. Other countries restrict loss offsets to firms with negative "surplus." That is, in some countries, all losses must be offset against any accumulated earned and/or capital "surplus" before they are deductible from even future earnings!

The limitations on loss deductions are wholly inconsistent with economic development aspirations. The inability to deduct operating losses strongly discourages new ventures, and it makes older firms unnecessarily cautious. Even though revisions permitting generous loss deductions and carryback provisions could contribute to serious government budget problems in any one year, the energizing force such provisions would inject into a rapidly changing and growing economy should not be underestimated. It seems likely that a much larger continuing government expenditure would be required to generate another force of equal impact. This becomes increasingly true as income taxation assumes a major role in the overall tax system.

A final undesirable deduction provision, common to those countries of Latin America imposing only a territorial-source income tax, concerns the treatment accorded expenses incurred outside the territorial boundaries. The corollary rule is that generally any expense incurred outside the country imposing the income tax is not deductible in the computation of net taxable income (limited statutory exceptions to this general rule are not uncommon). The problems inherent in the determination of a proper deduction for an expense incurred in another country are substantial because it may be virtually impossible for the taxing government to verify the accuracy of the deduction claimed. The proper valuation of internationally operated, parent-subsidiary transactions are an integral segment of this problem.

Although the difficulties are obvious, the governments of Latin America should be encouraged to establish reciprocal rights and privileges in international expense verification requests. The failure to attain the necessary degree of accord on this issue will constitute another serious stumbling block on the road to effective economic-area integration. Cooperative efforts of international agencies are essential and they need to be encouraged.

Other deductions, with exceptions, are similar to those permitted in the United States. These include a deduction for the cost of goods sold (on different inventory costing methods), bad debts, maintenance expenses, wages and salaries, specified taxes, advertising, entertainment, travel, depreciation (with a few notable exceptions), utilities, insurance premiums, and interest. In one area—holding the line on depletion allowances—the Latin American countries have been more successful than their northern neighbor. They have no provision for statutory-depletion-deduction allowances in excess of cost. A contributing factor, of course, is the fact that the extractive industries of Latin America are typically owned and operated either by foreign firms or by the national governments.

Earned-Income Deductions

Relative to the deductibility of expenses in the computation of taxable earned income, nearly polar positions are again typical. One group of the Latin countries permits virtually no deductions whereas another group permits great latitude in the deduction of personal expenses. The rationale for the former position is based upon a fundamental distinction between the schedular and the global tax systems in "pure" form. The Harvard tax experts explain the difference this way:[17]

the schedular system of the law does not recognize any personal or family allowances or the deduction of expenses which are not strictly related to the particular schedular income. It is felt that only a global or "personal" income tax may properly give consideration to the circumstances of the taxpayer.

The other group of Latin American countries, even though utilizing the schedular tax approach formally, have for some reason or another taken an opposite position. The following items are frequently deductable in these countries: interest on personal debts; contributions to charitable, scientific, educational, and literary organizations; certain taxes; life-insurance premiums (usually limited); burial expenses; and education costs. The suggested rationale for the acceptance of these "personal" expenses as tax deductions is either a social judgment concerning the desirability of the end-product of the deductible expenditures, or an attempt to provide greater interpersonal tax equity for hardship situations. The parallel with the "other itemized deductions" accepted in the U.S. personal-income-tax law is striking. Except for

[17] Harvard Law School International Program in Taxation, *Taxation in Mexico*, p. 120.

education costs, burial expenses, and insurance premiums, the two lists are highly comparable, though the limitations on each item vary somewhat.

In a developed country, excluding the hardship cases, a strong argument can be made supporting the position that the only appropriate deduction is a personal exemption allowance that reasonably approximates the cost of living. Beyond this, free-market forces should guarantee the "most desirable" allocation of expenditures. Underdeveloped countries, striving for difficult and far-reaching changes in behavior patterns, naturally look for possible tax incentives to assist in attaining the desired changes. For example, accepting expenditures on education as a tax-deductible item could provide a desirable incentive in attaining a better educated populace, an important goal of the Alliance for Progress. Accepting expenditures on medical and dental services as tax deductions could provide a desirable incentive in attaining increased general health standards, another primary goal stipulated in the Charter of Punta del Este. In this sense, these deduction provisions are consistent with economic development aspirations.

On the other hand, the mere acceptance of such deduction provisions does decrease the apparent progressivity of the income tax. The same deduction granted to two taxpayers, one in a 50 percent marginal tax bracket and the other in a 20 percent marginal bracket, obviously generates a larger absolute tax saving for the taxpayer with the higher income. In this sense, the "tax benefit" is directly related to income. Since the group in which the greatest change is desired is, generally, the lowest-income group, an inverse relation would be more appropriate. Attempts to restrict the tax benefit of generous deduction provisions to the lower-income groups are not unknown. Some tax laws provide that particular deductions will be granted to only those taxpayers with a total income of less than a specified amount; others grant only some fractional share of the deduction to the taxpayer with an income in excess of a specified amount. For example, Colombia restricts the deduction of medical and dental expenditures to taxpayers with a total-annual-schedular income of 36,000 pesos (approximately $5,373) or less. The taxpayer with five or more dependent children gets 50 percent of the deduction after his income exceeds the Ps. 36,000 limitation.

Even though these deduction provisions complicate the tax law and introduce an erosion of the tax base, the benefit obtained may be enough to justify their retention, especially if the benefits are withheld from the higher-income taxpayers. The greatest danger lies in the fact that

once a privileged deduction is granted, it becomes politically difficult—
if not impossible—to retrieve.

Minimum Exemptions

The tax laws of many countries include a minimum-exemption provision. This exemption can be handled in any one of three ways. First,
the exemption may be granted only to those individuals (or firms)
earning less than a stipulated amount of income during a given time
period, generally one year. The major fault of this exemption treatment
is that it makes the marginal tax rate on incomes just over the minimal
fantastically high. Consequently, this treatment is not widely used. Exceptions to this general rule can be found in the laws of Venezuela. For
example, Venezuela grants a monthly exemption of 1,000 bolivars to
any taxpayer earning wages and salaries of Bs. 1,600 ($478) or less
per month. No exemption is permitted if the monthly wage and salary
income exceeds Bs. 1,600. Therefore the marginal rate of taxation on
the 1601st bolivar earned is over 1600 percent! (The schedular tax is
imposed on wages and salaries at the rate of 1 percent.) This injustice
rapidly disappears at higher income levels.

Second, the exemption may be made to vary inversely with total income. The very low-income taxpayer gets the full exemption; they very
high-income taxpayer gets no exemption; and middle-income taxpayers' exemptions are graduated. The English system includes exemptions of this general variety. None of the Latin American systems
seem to have adopted this treatment for minimum exemption; however an equivalent procedure is utilized in some of these countries as far
as "itemized deductions" are concerned. The Colombian treatment of
medical and dental expenses (see preceding section) is illustrative.

The third possible method allows the same exemption to all taxpayers regardless of their total income. The U.S. $600 personal ex-
emption is typical. Obviously this sort of exemption again provides a
greater absolute tax saving to the taxpayer in the higher marginal tax
bracket than it does to a lower-income taxpayer. An alternative *tax
credit*, calculated at the lowest marginal tax bracket rate, would over-
come this difficulty. In most of the countries of Latin America having a
minimum personal or family exemption provision, some derivation of
this third method is followed. For purposes of computing the complementary tax, Brazilian law excludes from the definition of a taxpayer
any individual with an aggregate schedular income of 60,000 cruzeiros

or less. Additional "abatements" are allowed as follows: 50,000 cruzeiros for a spouse; 25,000 cruzeiros per dependent child; 10,000 cruzeiros for certain other dependents within a family relationship; and 6,000 cruzeiros for any destitute child raised, but not adopted, by the taxpayer. Variations in the amount of the personal exemption, based upon the family relation between the taxpayer and the dependent, are common in Latin America. To the extent these exemptions are supposed to reflect a minimum cost of living allowance, the distinctions are not at all clear.

In the early stages of income-taxation experience, it is generally wise to establish a minimum exemption high enough to exclude a significant fraction of the lower-income earners from the tax base.[18] This is advisable on administrative as well as humanitarian grounds. It is especially recommended for countries where the preconditions for successful income taxation are not satisfied. In most countries with low average per capita incomes, this will be the case. Strong early efforts for strict compliance with a law of limited coverage can pave the way for subsequent extensions largely dependent upon voluntary compliance and self-assessment.

Capital-Gains Taxation

The ubiquitous problems involved in taxing capital gains are responsible for some of the least satisfactory tax laws in the most well-developed countries. Consequently, it is not surprising to discover that the majority of the Latin American countries simply exclude, partially or completely, capital gains from income-tax provisions. A brief statement of the diverse capital-gains provisions of a few Latin American countries follows.

Uruguay is one of the few countries to construe "income from industry or commerce" to include both occasional and accidental income

[18] Most countries will do this automatically. A rough computation by the author indicated that aggregate personal exemptions for a family of four (father, mother, and two dependent children) are approximately 85% of four times the average per capita income in Colombia. Using this sort of rough test, it would appear that nearly one-half the Colombians are automatically excluded from income taxation. Given the setting, the high percentage does not appear unreasonable. Equivalent computations for Argentina and for the U.S.A. yield figures of approximately 35% and 20% respectively. For purposes of the complementary tax only, the figure was 220% in Venezuela. Venezuela, like Brazil and Mexico, provides no minimum exemption in the calculation of the *schedular* income-tax liability.

as well as routine business income. In fact, in Uruguay, gross income is *explicitly* defined to include capital gains. The exclusions and deductions are sufficiently generous, and the tax rates are sufficiently low, that no "special" provisions were deemed necessary for capital gains. In Brazil, capital gains accruing to individuals are excluded (except for gains on the sale of real property), whereas those accruing to corporations and other business entities are included with business income, and subject to the business-income tax. Venezuelan law excludes a pro rata portion of each capital gain (the exact amount depending on the date the capital asset was acquired) and permits increasing the cost basis of capital assets by an imputed (6 percent) interest each year the asset was held. The imputed interest is not taxed.

In Mexico, the exclusion of all gains on "civil transactions" automatically excludes most capital gains from income taxation. That is, most transactions involving a capital gain are deemed to arise from a civil, rather than a commercial, origin. In specified circumstances, even if a transaction is deemed of commercial origin, a Mexican taxpayer may be entitled to the tax-preferred "occasional act of commerce" treatment. The Dominican Republic explicitly excludes the gain on sale of securities from any income taxation. In other countries, security profits attain preferred tax treatment through the widespread use of bearer shares.

For the development-oriented economist, the most disturbing aspect of excluding capital gains from income taxation is not the revenue loss, but the economic incentive provided for the purely speculative, nonproductive investment. The tendency to "invest" in foreign exchange, diamonds, real estate, and other "riskless" assets is already so prevalent it intensifies the shortage of capital for essential development projects. A capital-gains tax, at least as high as the income tax on productive investments, would serve both to increase needed tax revenues (at minimum social cost) and to decrease the unwarranted tax benefit currently provided the least productive forms of investment.

The strongest arguments opposing capital-gains taxation are couched in terms suggesting that the imposition of such a tax actually constitutes an encroachment on the capital base rather than a levy on income. These arguments are especially powerful when it can be demonstrated that any increase in monetary value is wholly attributable to inflationary forces, as it might well be in several of the underdeveloped countries of Latin America. In these cases, retention of a given real earnings stream demands reinvestment of the entire proceeds obtained from the sale of a capital asset, not those proceeds less some tax. Therefore, the mere existence of the tax is said to be detrimental to economic growth because it unduly discourages the free exchange of capital assets. A final argument that has merit, and opposes capital-gains taxation, points out that the capital gain often accrues over several years time, but since the gain is not generally recognized for tax purposes until the year it is realized, the progressive income-tax rates impose an unreasonably high tax in the year of realization.

In short, there are sound arguments on both sides of the capital-gains question. However, many of the cogent arguments that oppose the inclusion of capital gains in the income tax base are equally applicable to other sources of income. For example, the income from wages and salaries also reflects the impact of inflation. Yet no one seems too worried about the maintenance of the laborers' real income stream. It is sometimes even argued that the progressive tax rate serves, in this instance, as a desirable anti-inflationary force in the economy. This reply would be equally applicable to other profits. The objections based on the multiple-year accrual, single-year-tax, factor could be solved by abandoning the realization criterion or by instituting some averaging device.

Abandoning the realization criterion cannot be widely recommended until an impartial, realistic, and inexpensive method of appraising assets is discovered. Contrary to the general practice, the tax laws of Brazil and Argentina suggest that both of these countries accept the idea of asset revaluations and income recognition prior to realization. They also exhibit a willingness to tax—to a limited degree—the imputed income arising from the asset revaluation. The Argentinian "patrimony tax" includes an appropriate coefficient to determine the amount of the annual increase in asset values. Since the coefficient is solely dependent on the date the asset was acquired, the possibility that particular asset values would not move with the general price level is not recognized. Any possible harm resulting from this assumption is mitigated (if not swamped!) by a combination of low tax rates and an exclusion of 50 percent of the imputed gain. In a country experiencing relatively rapid inflation, such a general provision is undoubtedly less oppressive than the complete inclusion of capital gains with ordinary income in the year of realization. Nevertheless, it fails to provide a really satisfactory solution to the capital-gains problems.

Various averaging methods are frequently proposed, but they are seldom accepted. The tax experts studying the Venezuelan tax system recommended averaging capital gains over the shorter of the actual holding period or four years.[19] Similar recommendations have often been rejected by more economically advanced countries on the grounds of administrative difficulty. In short, recommended procedures must depend largely on the circumstances existing in each country. But in all developing countries, some form of capital-gains taxation can be highly recommended.

A COMPARATIVE ANALYSIS OF INCOME TAXATION IN MEXICO AND VENEZUELA

In concluding this chapter on the Latin American income-tax systems in general, it should prove instructive to pause briefly for a more detailed examination of particular income-tax laws in specific factual situations. This section includes four examples illustrating how two different income streams are taxed in Mexico and Venezuela. Illustrations 1 and 2 suggest the income-tax computation as applied to income earned by a corporation. Illustrations 3 and 4 suggest the income-tax computation as applied to income earned by an employee. Taken together, the four examples illustrate several of the distinctive features of the Latin American income-tax systems mentioned earlier in the chapter. For example, a study of these four illustrations would demonstrate, among other things, (a) the technique of a schedular approach to income taxation; (b) the role of the complementary tax in a system having proportional schedular tax rates; (c) the tendency to tax proliferation; (d) the different treatment accorded minimum exemptions; and (e) the diversity in provisions intended to encourage the reinvestment of entity profits.

It must be emphasized that a comparison of income taxes between two or more nations can never be entirely equitable because of a number of factors. The three following are considered particularly important.

1. The diverse definitions, exclusions, deductions, and exemptions peculiar to each tax system cannot be presented concisely. The four illustrations have been based on extremely restrictive assumptions in order to maximize the comparability of the results. This advantage can be attained, of course, only at a significant loss in the realism of the illustration. The assumption of a more elaborate factual situation would

[19] Commission to Study the Fiscal System of Venezuela, *The Fiscal System of Venezuela*, p. 165.

be informative of many important distinctions that do exist between the income-tax systems of Mexico and Venezuela, but it would contribute little to a general appreciation of the role of tax reform in the over-all Alliance-for-Progress program.

2. The income-tax rates reflect the relative significance of the income tax in the entire tax structure of each country. If the tax system tends to give relatively greater emphasis to other than income-based taxes, or perhaps only to income-based taxes in a particular industry, then it is virtually impossible to determine much about the impact of income taxation from the examination of only the one tax. Venezuela is a case in point: the income tax on the petroleum industry contributes approximately two-thirds of the total national tax revenues and, therefore, the effective income-tax rate on other industries is significantly lower than in other countries with a less-dominant industry.

3. It is virtually impossible to evaluate the degree of enforcement of the tax law in each of the countries. Furthermore, the laws may be written so "loosely" that even minimum efforts at tax-planning can serve to emasculate the apparent intention of the law. For purposes of these four illustrations, it was assumed that a "letter-of-the-law" enforcement existed, and that no tax loopholes were available to the taxpayer concerned.

Although there are many limitations to the conclusions that can be derived from a restricted, comparative analysis of income taxation as attempted here, it is possible to draw a few significant conclusions. First, it is evident that in some countries the present income tax law does (or could) provide a significant degree of income taxation on the income earned by a corporate entity, without any major legislative changes. The effective tax rate of nearly 45 percent on the Mexican corporation of Illustration 1 is highly comparable to the effective tax rate on similar entities in the most economically advanced nations of Europe and North America. A United Nations' study reports nearly equally high rates of effective corporate-income taxation in Argentina, Brazil, and Chile.[20] Therefore, the possibilities for increasing income taxes on industrial income, without the likelihood of incurring serious economic disincentives in these countries, appears limited. Considering the role of industrialization in the developmental process, a temporary reduction of these taxes could even be considered a desirable alternative.

[20] United Nations, *Foreign Private Investment in the Latin American Free-Trade Area*, p. 22.

Second, in other Latin American countries, typified by Venezuela, there does appear to be some real possibility for increased income taxation on at least selected industrial activities. Countries that are well endowed with a particular natural resource are frequently dilatory in taxing other sectors of the economy. Developmental aspirations, as well as equity considerations and sound financial planning, may dictate the need for additional sources of revenue in these countries.

Third, the effective (or average) rate of taxation on earned incomes is not generally very high in Latin America. This is true even at income levels well in excess of the national per capita average. While the lack of administrative refinements, necessitated in many countries by the existing social institutions, may well dictate tax rates below the level found in the more economically developed nations, it is evident that a real potential exists for increased income taxation on at least the higher personal incomes. Furthermore, the tax rates are sufficiently low now that the danger of any economic disincentives from increased personal-income taxation seems quite remote. The greater apparant danger is that loopholes and exclusions will provide more rewarding opportunities for the erudite individual, and thereby dissuade him from accepting otherwise acceptable employment subject to even mildly progressive taxation. In other words, the detrimental effect of the income-tax system on the labor force could be better attributed to the "negative" than to the "positive" *disincentive* effects.

Finally, the need for consolidating several income-based taxes into a single tax is especially apparent in Illustration 1. In most countries utilizing a progressive schedular tax, adequate income taxation could be obtained through a single tax. The tendency to impose additional taxes on even the same "kind" of income, rapidly increases the administrative complexity of the tax law. Each law must provide its own "special rules," definitions, exclusions, deductions, tax base, and rate structure. This makes the law extremely lengthy and difficult to understand; it also increases the difficulties encountered in trying to investigate the impact of the income tax on the country's industrial and economic development.

The four illustrations follow.

ILLUSTRATION 1

Illustrative Calculation of Income Taxes on Industrial Income in Mexico[1]

		In Mexican Pesos		In U.S. Dollars[2]
Assumed Owners' Equity		24,980,000		2,000,000
Assumed Net Income before Income Taxes		6,245,000		500,000
Calculation of Income Taxes:				
A. Schedular Tax (Schedule I or II)[3]				
Income Subject to Schedular Tax		6,245,000		500,000
Tax Computed as Follows:				
On 1st Ps. 2,000,000	623,858		49,949	
On Next 4,245,000 @ 39%	1,655,550		132,550	
Total Schedular Tax		2,279,408		182,499
Net Income after Schedular Tax		3,965,592		317,501
B. Excess-Profits Tax[4]				
Tax Computed as Follows:				
On income equal to 1st 15% of owners' equity	Exempt		Exempt	
On next Ps. 218,592 @ 5% (5% since amount does not exceed another 5% of owners' equity)	10,930		875	
Total Excess-Profits Tax		10,930		875
Net Income after Schedular and Excess-Profits Taxes		3,954,662		316,626
C. Distributable-Profits Tax[5]				
Exemptions:[6]				
Legal Reserve	197,733		15,831	
Reinvestment Reserve	395,466		31,663	
Total Exemptions		593,199		47,494
"Distributable Income" (or amount subject to tax)		3,361,463		269,132

ILLUSTRATION 1 Continued

	In Mexican Pesos	In U.S. Dollars[2]
Distributable-Profits Tax (15%)	504,219	40,370
Recap:		
Schedular Income Tax	2,279,408	182,499
Excess-Profits Tax	10,930	875
Distributable-Profits Tax	504,219	40,370
Total Income Taxes	2,794,557	223,744
Effective Tax Rate 44.7%		

Notes:

[1] Illustration 1 is based on a hypothetical Mexican corporation engaged in a "commercial" or "industrial" activity (excluding agriculture, livestock raising, and fishing), that realizes a net taxable income of $500,000 (6,245,000 pesos). Total owners' equity is assumed to be $2 million (24,980,000 pesos).

[2] The conversion from Mexican pesos to United States dollars is based on the January 1, 1963, "official rate" of exchange: 12.49 pesos equal 1.00 dollar.

[3] The Mexican Income Tax Act of 30 December 1953, published in the *Diario Oficial* of 31 December 1953, as amended by a Decree of 28 December 1960, provides that income reportable under Schedule I or II be taxed on a progressive rate scale. The published scale stipulates that net taxable income in excess of 2,000,000 pesos is subject to a base tax of 623,858 pesos plus 39% on all taxable income in excess of 2,000,000 pesos. (This is the highest marginal tax bracket in Schedule I or II.)

[4] Income Tax Acts, Articles 170–180, define "excess profits" as those exceeding 15% of "invested capital." "Invested capital" is defined to include paid-in capital, capital reserves, and surplus—here assumed to be 24,980,000 pesos. Thus, in this illustration, profits in excess of 3,747,000 (15% of 24,980,000) are deemed "excess." The tax base for the excess-profits tax is the same as for Schedule II purposes less the schedular-income tax. The excess-profits-tax rates begin at 5% on profits in excess of 15% but not more than 20% of invested capital and continue at progressive rates until reaching a maximum rate of 25% on profits in excess of 50% of invested capital. A qualifying limitation states that the total excess-profits tax cannot exceed 10% of the excess-profits-tax base. The limit is reached when taxable income exceeds 51.67% of invested capital.

[5] The gross base for the distributable-profits tax is taxable income as defined for Schedule I and II less the schedular and excess-profits taxes. Income Tax Acts, Articles 138–140 and 145, provide a flat distributable-profits-tax rate of 15%.

[6] Special exemptions are granted in the calculation of the distributable-profits tax base. The limit is reached when taxable income exceeds 51.67% of invested distributable profits is mandatory until the total reserve is equal to 20% of

owners' equity. An additional "reinvestment reserve" equal to 10% of distributable profits is available at the taxpayer's option so long as the profits are set aside and not distributed to the owners. In addition, firms engaged in "manufacturing" may exempt additional reserves of up to 30% without specific permission and up to 95% with advance permission from the Treasury Department. Only the "legal" and "optional" reserves are assumed to apply in this illustration.

ILLUSTRATION 2

Illustrative Calculation of Income Taxes on Industrial Income in Venezuela[1]

	In Venezuelan Bolivars		In U.S. Dollars[2]
Assumed Net Income before Income Taxes		1,675,000	500,000
Calculation of Income Taxes: A. Schedular Income Tax (Schedule 3)[3] 2.5% of Assumed Income		41,875	12,500
B. Complementary Tax[4] Tax Computed as Follows: On 1st Bs. 1,400,000	202,320		60,394
On next Bs. 275,000 @ 20%	55,000		16,418
Gross Complementary Tax	257,320		76,812
Less Reinvestment-Reserve Tax Credit[5]	25,732		7,681
Net Complementary Tax		231,588	69,131
Total Income Tax		273,463	81,631
Effective Tax Rate 16.3%			

Notes:

    [1] Illustration 2 is based on a hypothetical Venezuelan corporation, engaged in a business (excluding the oil, mining, and agricultural industries) that realizes a net taxable income of $500,000 (1,675,000 bolivars).

    [2] The conversion from Venezuelan bolivars to United States dollars is based on the January 1, 1963, "official rate" of exchange: 3.35 bolivars equal 1.00 dollar.

    [3] The current income-tax law of Venezuela is based on the 1956 law, published August 8, 1955, effective January 1, 1956, as amended by Decree No. 476 of December 19, 1958. This law provides that business income reported in Schedule 3 is subject to a proportional tax of 2.5%.

[4] The complementary tax, described in the same basic law, is imposed on the aggregate schedular incomes of both corporations and individuals. The corporation is not granted any exemptions but can deduct charitable contributions if the total of such contributions is in excess of Bs. 5,000. The schedular tax is not deductible in the computation of the complementary-tax base. Complementary-tax rates begin at 2% on the first Bs. 8,000 and increases progressively until reaching a maximum rate of 45% on all income in excess of Bs. 28,000,000 ($8,358,209). The marginal rate appropriate for the taxpayer in the Bs. 1,400,000–2,000,000 bracket—as in Illustration 2—is 20% for all income in excess of Bs. 1,400,000. The complementary tax aggregated from all lower brackets is Bs. 202,320.

[5] The 1958 law provides two complementary-tax reductions for "reinvested income." The one, available to taxpayers in the last three tax brackets only (*i.e.,* those with taxable incomes in excess of Bs. 14 million) is not applicable to this illustration. The other is available to any taxpayer engaged in the manufacture of industrial products so long as (a) at least 80% of the income reported in Schedule 3 is from the sale of the manufactured articles, and (b) the profits are reinvested in the fixed assets of the business. In order to make this illustration as comparable as possible to Illustration 1, it was assumed that the Venezuelan corporation met these criterion and reinvested between 10% and 20% of its net income. This assumption entitled the corporation to a 10% tax credit against the complementary tax. (The amount of the tax credit is dependent upon the percentage of income reinvested: a 10% tax reduction is granted for reinvestment of between 10% and 20% of the profits; a 25% tax reduction is granted for reinvestment of between 90% and 100% of the profits.)

ILLUSTRATION 3

Illustrative Calculation of Income Taxes on Personal Income in Mexico[1]

	In Mexican Pesos	In U.S. Dollars[2]
Assumed Income afterAll Exclusions and Deductions Other Than Personal or Family Exemptions	149,880	12,000
Schedular Income Tax (Schedule IV)[3]		
Tax on 1st 12,000 pesos[4] 977		78
Tax on next 490 pesos @ 18% 88		7
Total *Monthly* Income Tax 1,065		85
Total Income Tax (Monthly Tax times 12)	12,780	1,020
Effective Tax Rate 8.5%		

Notes:

[1] Illustration 3 is based on a hypothetical Mexican-resident citizen who receives a $1,000 (12,490 peso) *monthly* salary as an "employee." It is further assumed that this taxpayer has no other wage or salary income. Although it is of no significance for Mexican income-tax purposes, in order to make the comparison with Illustration 4 as comparable as possible, it is further assumed that the taxpayer is married and has two dependent children.

[2] The conversion from Mexican pesos to United States dollars is based on the January 1, 1963, "official rate" of exchange: 12.49 pesos equal 1.00 dollar.

[3] The Mexican Income Tax Act of 30 December 1953, as amended by the Decree of 28 December 1960, provides that the tax on wage, salary, and other personal income reported in Schedule IV, will be withheld on a monthly basis and based solely on gross earnings. The employer must remit the tax withheld by the fifteenth of the month following payment of the salary. No exemptions or deductions are allowed and no return is required from the individual.

[4] The tax rate is determined by reference to a table that exempts the first Ps. 500 and taxes monthly income in excess of Ps. 70,000 at 50%. The 18% marginal tax rate is applicable to taxpayers earning between Ps. 12,000 and Ps. 14,000 per month.

ILLUSTRATION 4

Illustrative Calculation of Income Taxes on Personal
Income in Venezuela[1]

	In Venezuelan Bolivars	In U.S. Dollars[2]
Assumed Income after All Exclusions and Deductions Other Than Personal or Family Exemptions	40,200	12,000
Schedular Income Tax (Schedule 7)[3]		
1% of Taxable Income	402	120
Complementary Tax[4]		
Gross Tax Base	40,200	12,000
Less Family Exemption	22,000	6,567
Difference—Subject to Tax	18,200	5,433
Tax Computed as Follows:		
On 1st Bs. 14,000[5]	330	99
On next Bs. 4,200 @ 3.5%	147	44
Total Complementary Tax	477	143
Total Personal Income Tax	879	263
Effective Tax Rate 2.2%		

Notes:

¹ Illustration 4 is based on a hypothetical Venezuelan-resident citizen who receives a $1,000 (Bs. 3,350) *monthly* salary as an "employee." It is further assumed that this taxpayer has no other personal income, of any kind, and that he is married and has two dependent children.

² The conversion from Venezuelan bolivars to United States dollars is based on the January 1, 1963, "official rate" of exchange: 3.35 bolivars equal 1.00 dollar.

³ The 1956 Income Tax Law, as amended by Decree No. 476 of December 19, 1958, provides a 1% schedular income tax on all wages and salaries earned by residents and reported in Schedule 7. Taxpayers earning less than Bs. 1,600 monthly are exempt from Schedule 7 tax; those earning more than Bs. 1,600 get no exemption. The tax is withheld on a monthly basis and generally no further adjustment or payment is necessary. In other words, if a taxpayer earns less than Bs. 1,600 in two months and more than that in the other ten months, these is no further tax payment required even though the monthly average exceeds Bs. 1,600. In the event a taxpayer receives compensation in kind—housing, for example—an additional payment must accompany an annual declaration form. No deductions are permitted.

⁴ A complementary tax, applied at progressive rates, is imposed on the total net income reported in the nine schedules. Certain exemptions permitted in the computation of the schedular-tax base are disallowed in computation of the complementary-tax base. In this illustration, where it is assumed that the taxpayer has no income other than his salary, the only possible difference between the two tax bases would be in those cases where the taxpayer has made charitable contributions in excess of Bs. 5,000 or has incurred medical and dental expenses. If charitable contributions exceed Bs. 5,000, they are deductible in full; medical and dental expenses, regardless of amount, are also deductible in full so long as the taxpayer supplies receipts for the payments. For purposes of this illustration, it was assumed that neither of these provisions were applicable. However, all individual taxpayers get a special exemption of Bs. 12,000 as respects the complementary tax. The married taxpayer receives additional allowances of Bs. 4,000 for a spouse; Bs. 3,000 for each child, parent, or grandparent, dependent on him (except that males of legal age cannot be claimed as dependents unless incapacitated); and Bs. 900 for other individuals supported. The exemption shown in Illustration 4 is based upon the assumptions stated in note 1.

⁵ The computation is made as follows:

First	Bs. 8,000	@ 2.0%	or	Bs. 160
Next	Bs. 2,000	@ 2.5%	or	Bs. 50
Next	Bs. 4,000	@ 3.0%	or	Bs. 120

The marginal complementary-tax rate for the Bs. 14,000–20,000 bracket is 3.5%.

SUMMARY

Although there are obstacles to effective income taxation in any underdeveloped country, most of these countries have already enacted income-tax laws. This is also true for each of the nineteen signatory nations to the Alliance for Progress. Unfortunately, enforcing an income-tax law often proves more difficult than enacting it. Whenever this is true, the efficacy of sound legislative and administrative reforms is minimized until a shift in either the existing balance of political power or in political thinking is accomplished. The withholding of external, Alliance-prompted, financial aid, pending action on long overdue economic and social reforms—including tax reforms—is an apparent attempt to effect just such a change, sans revolution.

The income-tax laws of the Latin American republics as a group contrast notably with the United States' Internal Revenue Code. The most obvious difference is the Latin American adoption of the French schedular approach, as opposed to the U.S. global approach, to income taxation. On closer investigation this disparity becomes a matter of degree. Another distinctive feature, at least until very recently, concerns the reluctance of the Latin countries to tax income earned outside their territorial boundaries. The United States taxes the income of citizens and residents from both foreign and domestic sources.

In general, the income-tax laws of the Latin American republics are quite sophisticated. However, some aspects of these laws frequently need the tax reformers' attention. (1) The need to consolidate unrelated, income-based taxes is evident in several countries. (2) The need for numerous legislative definitions of varied tax terms is equally apparent. (3) The liberal granting of exclusions, and the accepted practices in business-income taxation, facilitate the wealthy taxpayer's attempt to evade truly progressive income taxation, even when the letter of the law is enforced. These loopholes should be closed. (4) Provisions for tax deductions vary from onerous restrictions to a predatory erosion of the income-tax base. An extensive cataloging of deductible and nondeductible expenses is desperately needed; provisions for loss deductions should be extended. (5) The widespread omission of capital gains from income taxation provides an undesirable incentive for nonproductive forms of investment. Capital gains should be taxed.

These five problem areas in income taxation are neither weak in *each* of the nineteen Latin American republics nor the most significant in any particular country. However, this list does suggest five of the more profitable areas for investigation by tax experts assigned to evaluate Alliance-for-Progress aid applications. The need for studies of individual countries is obvious.

5. Wealth Taxation

Although income flows are widely accepted as an appropriate index of human well-being and, therefore, of the ability to pay taxes, income is not the only accepted base for progressive taxation. Alternative progressive taxes are based on stock concepts of existing wealth. Net wealth, estate, inheritance, gift, and real-property taxation are all important variants of the latter group. The tax systems of the Latin American countries commonly include one or more of these taxes. However, none of them are currently productive of large amounts of revenue.

This chapter considers the role of wealth taxation in the overall tax structure of the Latin American republics. It attempts to answer such questions as these. (1) Since wealth taxes are not prolific revenue producers, would it not be advisable to abandon them? (2) What are the implications of wealth-based taxes for economic development aspirations? (3) What wealth-tax reforms, if any, are consistent with non-tax objectives of the Alliance for Progress?

Once again, due to time and space limitations, it is necessary to make a rather cursory examination of complex subjects. Primary attention in this chapter is focused on land taxation because it has a crucial role to play in the Alliance-for-Progress program. Generally, information on wealth taxation in Latin America is difficult to obtain. This can probably be attributed to the relatively unimportant role these taxes have played in the recent Latin fiscal systems.

NET-WEALTH TAXATION

A tax levied on the net wealth of individuals could theoretically make an excellent adjunct to a progressive income tax. It would be especially helpful in accomplishing a redistribution of the existing wealth, a common goal of many developing nations. A net-wealth tax would also increase the equity of the overall tax systems as between the recipients of labor and property income, and the owners of valuable assets.

From an economic development standpoint, a net-wealth tax would have both desirable and undesirable incentive effects. The net-wealth tax could be preferred to the income tax since it would have no disincentive effect on the desire to work. That is, a worker's marginal income would not be reduced by a tax imposed at progressive rates. On the other hand, the incentives to save and invest could be significantly damped by a net-wealth tax. Consumption spending would be preferred to noncredit investment because the net-wealth tax would impinge only on the individual who accumulated assets. The net effect on development aspirations of these two incentive considerations is wholly conjectural.

Another economic disadvantage of a net-wealth tax, vis-à-vis an income tax, derives from the fact that the base of the former tax is as of some arbitrary moment in time, whereas the latter tax reflects important changes taking place during a given time period. Therefore, the net-wealth tax results in a continuing preference for low-value assets, as well as a differential movement in assets values as the tax-base inventory date reoccurs.

Regardless of the purely economic considerations, a comprehensive net-wealth tax does not appear to be a likely candidate for inclusion in the tax system of most developing countries in the near future. Serious administrative problems and strong political opposition would undoubtedly destine any contrary suggestions to certain rejection. Reasons for the political opposition are obvious.

One of the most serious administrative complexities is the necessity of placing a market value on nonmarketed assets. A truly comprehensive net-wealth tax would even have to include an estimate of the value of an individual—*i.e.,* of the personal services the individual might perform—based, perhaps, on the discounted value of an estimated-earnings stream. The difficulty in estimating market values, selecting the appropriate discount rate, and estimating an income stream are apparent. Even a wealth tax restricted to more conventional assets is made administratively difficult because of the ease of concealing numerous assets. This is especially true of jewels and antiques, stocks, bonds, foreign and domestic currencies, and other instruments of indebtedness that typically constitute a substantial percentage of the wealth existing in the developing country. Because of these and other administrative difficulties, what wealth taxation exists, is either based on selected (usually real) assets only, or is imposed at infrequent intervals.

In spite of the many difficulties associated with a net-wealth tax, the participants at the second Alliance-sponsored tax conference, meeting at Santiago, Chile, December 5–14, 1962, reached the following general consensus of opinion:[1]

that in addition to a progressive income tax there should also be a tax on net wealth of individuals or families. For this purpose "wealth" should include property in the form of real estate and financial assets—as well as valuable personal possessions—and "net wealth" should be the excess of the value of such property over liabilities. Such a net wealth tax should be levied at relatively low rates on the wealth in excess of some reasonable multiple of the *per capita* national income. It was recognized that the net wealth tax required a high degree of efficiency of tax administration, and therefore its introduction in the near future may only be advisable for countries possessing these administrative prerequisites.

Although a general net-wealth tax may have to remain a long-run goal for most Latin American republics, more limited forms of wealth taxation should be considered in the shorter run.

Death and Gift Taxation

Death and gift taxes, like the net-wealth tax, can be of assistance in the redistribution of existing wealth. The economic effects of death taxes have been argued for years. In general, it is agreed that they have a minimum effect on the incentives to work, save, and invest. Some U.S. studies suggest, however, that the mere existence of death taxes encourages people to keep their estates in a relatively liquid form.[2].

In the Latin American countries, death and gift taxes have been imposed at only very moderate rates and with only limited success. Consequently, it is doubtful that they have had much—if any—influ-

---

[1] *Provisional Report of the Conference on Fiscal Policy*, OAS, Santiago, Chile, December 5–14, 1962, pp. 6–7.

[2] See John F. Due, *Government Finance*, pp. 367–371; C. Lowell Harriss, "Liquidity of Estates and Death Tax Liability," *Political Science Quarterly*, LXIV (December 1949), 533–559.

ence on human economic behavior. Because of administrative difficulties and the insignificant amount of revenue produced, Mexico abolished the inheritance tax in the December 1961 tax revisions.[3]

The abolition of death taxes in Latin America generally would have undesirable consequences. In countries imposing no capital-gains tax, or in those countries imposing it at relatively low tax rates (compared to the income tax), a significant amount of wealth accumulation can take place without being taxed. The inequity of taxing only earned income that has been realized can be partially ameliorated through the imposition of a tax on the market value of an estate left by a deceased taxpayer. In other words, accumulated capital gains should be considered "realized," and taxed at progressive rates, at the time of the taxpayer's death. Such a tax is usually called an estate tax.

The estate tax alone does not satisfy the equity criterion because it fails to take into consideration the recipient's ability to pay. To correct this deficiency partially, an inheritance tax—based on the aggregate value of the property transferred to each legatee—is generally imposed on the recipient. Most Latin American inheritance taxes provide tax rates that vary with the relation of the recipient to the decedent, and with the amount received. That is, the more distant the relationship, and the greater the value received, the higher the tax rate. In most countries, the established rates are outdated and unnecessarily low. For example, the Venezuelan law dates to 1936, with minor adjustment in 1939, and imposes rates from 0.5 to 30 percent. The top marginal rate applies only to amounts in excess of 4 million bolivars left to strangers.

In order to prohibit a taxpayer from wholly evading death taxes by giving away his estate prior to death, it is also necessary to tax *inter vivos* gifts. Ideally, this would be done on a cumulative basis with progressive rates. Historically, it is on an annual basis with rates similar—if not identical—to those provided in the inheritance-tax laws. Even the combined estate, inheritance, and gift taxes do not wholly satisfy equity considerations unless gratuitous transfers of wealth are regarded as a distinct indicator of the ability to pay. That is, unless, as a tax base, they are regarded as separate and distinct from the income and wealth of the recipient. To resolve otherwise would necessitate

---

[3] In 1960 the Mexican inheritance tax yielded approximately 27 million pesos ($2.2 million). This was only 0.3% of the central government tax collections that year.

a complete integration of income, death, and gift taxes. This, in turn, demands a level of administrative competence not found in most countries.

Even the conventional methods of taxing gratuitous transfers of wealth present serious administrative problems. Probably the most difficult of these involve valuation and discovery. Assets that are not frequently exchanged in a free market introduce formidable valuation problems; small-business ownership is a typically troublesome asset to evaluate. Gifts and intangible assets are easily concealed; consequently, minimum exemptions from the tax base are administratively compulsory.

In one form or another, however, the developing countries of Latin America should be encouraged to utilize a progressive tax on gratuitous transfers of wealth, even if this is administratively difficult and productive of little revenue. It is necessary because it is the only satisfactory method of taxing certain forms of wealth accumulation that should not be permitted to escape taxation entirely. These taxes also serve to redistribute the existing wealth, to increase revenues (albeit to a limited extent), and to demand more from those who have most. All three of these results are in accord with Alliance-prompted tax-reform objectives.

REAL-PROPERTY TAXATION

Conceptually, the taxing of real property is a poor substitute for a general-net-wealth tax. It selects a single form of wealth as an appropriate tax base and arbitrarily permits all other forms of property ownership to remain untaxed. Furthermore, with limited exceptions, it is cast in an impersonal (or "in rem") form, completely ignoring the status of the liable taxpayer. In spite of the obvious inequities of real-property taxation, it is one of the oldest forms of taxation known to mankind. Its popularity can largely be attributed to two facts. First, until relatively recent times, land ownership constituted one of the best indices of an individual's wealth. This tends still to be true in developing nations. Second, tax administration problems are reduced since land ownership is difficult to conceal. Introduced in Asia and the Near East, land taxes originally consisted of 10 percent of the value of the produce. New-World adaptations generally based land taxes on capital values, rather than on an actual or estimated, gross or net produce basis.

Land Taxation in Latin America

Land taxes provided an important share of the total tax revenues in many Latin American countries prior to the twentieth century. Since then, their relative importance has declined. According to the last available data, only in Paraguay and Panama are land taxes still producing more than 5 percent of the total tax receipts.[4] The explanation for the decline in their relative importance can be attributed to both the increased tax receipts from other sources, and to the fact that land taxes based on capital values do not automatically adapt to economic growth or inflation. Most of the Latin American countries' land taxes, like those in the U.S., are based on capital values.[5]

Considering the fact that the agricultural sector typically accounts for a large percentage of the national output in many of these countries, it seems reasonable to expect that a major portion of the tax revenue would derive from the same source. Except for export levies on agricultural products produced for world markets, and restricted situations involving unfavorable exchange rates or production-board prices, this has not been the case. Instead, the agricultural sector has been able to escape, partially or wholly, many of the taxes currently used to raise most of the tax revenue.

Income taxation seldom reaches the degree of effectiveness in the agricultural sector that it does in the industrial sector because (a) farmers are notoriously poor record keepers; (b) many agricultural expenses are not readily verified; and (c) taxes cannot be withheld at the source. Even if taxable-agricultural income were easily calculated, it frequently is given advantageous treatment in the schedular income-tax rates imposed in Latin America (see Table 8 *supra*). Furthermore, by engaging in barter transactions, and by remaining largely outside the monetary sector of the economy, agriculturalists can avoid even the indirect taxes that individuals living in urban areas must pay. For all of these reasons it is believed that the agricultural sector represents a significant source of untapped tax capacity in some of the developing countries of Latin America.

Some form of land taxation may be the only practicable method of obtaining significant revenues from the rural sector at the present stage

[4] Haskell P. Wald, *Taxation of Agricultural Land in Underdeveloped Economies*, p. 62.

[5] Argentina, Paraguay, Panama, Costa Rica, Mexico, Chile, Nicaragua, El Salvador, Guatemala, Bolivia, and Brazil all impose land taxes on capital value.

of economic development. The Japanese experience, under the Meiji regime in the last three decades of the nineteenth century, proves what can be accomplished when economic development aspirations are underwritten (in large measure) by a high rate of rural taxation. Professor Hansen reports that in spite of the oppressive land taxes in Japan, productivity per acre increased 100 percent between 1884 and 1935.[6] Land taxation may even be particularly appropriate for development-oriented countries "because the land tax yields not just revenue but the right kind of revenue; it enlarges the supply of foodstuffs to urban areas, and thus the amount of employment that can be offered outside agriculture without creating inflation."[7]

The belief that greater amounts of revenue should be raised through increased property taxation is increasingly accepted in Latin America. Proof of this fact is included in the report of the 1962 tax conference. The report states, as a general consensus of opinion, that "among the most important causes for the insufficiency of such revenue is the failure of the tax system to impose effective levies on the propertied classes and to collect existing ones."[8] Then, in recommending corrective action, it advocates "the collection of more revenue from taxes on urban and rural property, which are additional to personal income taxes on the income derived from such property and which should also be coordinated with other forms of special taxation of income from property . . ."[9]

Administrative Considerations in Land Taxation

Successful land taxation, based on capital values, depends upon the existence of a complete and accurate register of property ownership

[6] Alvin H. Hansen, *Public Enterprise and Economic Development*, p. 89. Professor Hansen goes on to admit that "the peasant had to shoulder a burden in the interests of capital-formation, which has rarely been equalled elsewhere." The only other possibly comparable situation concerns the collectivization of Russian agriculture. The implication for Latin America may be displeasing to many. Mr. Hansen stated it this way: "The moral, possibly, is that the degree of parliamentary democracy and of civil liberties that an economically developing country can afford to allow is dependent on the pace of the development that it chooses to pursue" (p. 89).

[7] Nicholas Kaldor, "Will Underdeveloped Countries Learn to Tax?" *Foreign Affairs*, XLI (January 1963), 413–414.

[8] *Provisional Report of the Conference on Fiscal Policy*, OAS, Santiago, Chile, December 5–14, 1962, p. 2.

[9] *Ibid.*, p. 3.

and on a reasonably accurate assessment of property values. The explanation for the relatively poor showing of land taxation in Latin America in recent years is attributable to the combined factors of incomplete registers, outdated assessments, and low tax rates. Harvard's Professor Barnes estimates that the average Latin American real-estate tax is approximately 1 percent "of a greatly understated and under assessed valuation."[10] A recent survey in Maracaibo, Venezuela, undertaken with the assistance of a professional management firm, revealed that only 10 percent of the potential urban real-estate tax was being collected.[11]

The appropriate corrective action must begin at widely varying points in the Latin American countries. The First Annual Report of the Social Progress Trust Fund states that six countries (Chile, El Salvador, Guatemala, Honduras, Peru, and Venezuela) have very recently organized steps to carry out some form of land survey or reassessment procedure. Since this work constitutes an integral first step in successful land taxation, any financial or technical assistance requested should be promptly provided to assure rapid completion of the work begun. Other countries should also be encouraged to undertake similar projects.

It may be possible to obtain adequate assessments of both rural and urban properties through self-assessment procedures. Such a procedure could at least supplement direct valuation by fiscal officers. One possible method of self-assessment would require every owner to declare the value of his property in a public record. Other persons, and/or fiscal officers, would be free to submit bona fide bids to purchase the property. If a bid was significantly greater (say 20–25 percent) than the owner's valuation, the owner would be given the option of accepting the bid and selling the property, or of revaluing his property to the amount of the rejected bid. In order to stimulate the solicitation of bona fide bids, a frustrated bidder could be awarded some percentage of the incremental property tax collected in the following year. Using this system, in countries where inflation tends to be serious, automatic readjustment of assessed values may be mandatory between successive self-assessment declaration dates.

[10] Joint Economic Committee, *Hearings Before the Subcommittee on Inter-American Economic Relationships of the Joint Economic Committee*, 87th Congress, 2nd Session, May 10 and 11, 1962, p. 11.

[11] Commission to Study the Fiscal System of Venezuela, *The Fiscal System of Venezuela*, p. 334.

Whether such administrative techniques should become a permanent feature of real-property taxation, or whether they should be used only during a transitional period, cannot be stated with any certainty. If the experience proves favorable on a trial basis, some countries may prefer to retain the procedure permanently. It would indubitably be superior to the existing situation in many countries where a small staff, with few professional appraisers, are assigned the nearly impossible task of appraising all real properties.[12]

Land Reform and Land Taxation

Among the numerous nontax objectives of the Alliance for Progress, land reform best illustrates the inextricable entwine of tax policies and other social institutions. Land reform is an inherently complex subject. It includes such factors as pioneering, homesteading, irrigation, reclamation, transportation, electrification, communication, and education. However, the essence of the problem can be divided into two separate elements. The one element concerns the existing pattern of land tenure; the other concerns the low level of agricultural productivity. Low productivity can be attributed to such diverse factors as under use, farms of inefficient size, poor technology and education, unavailability of credit and capital, and the inaccessibility of great expanses of land. Some of these problems of land reform are amenable to *partial* correction through improved systems of land taxation.

Land-Tenure Aspects

Land ownership is highly skewed in nearly all of the Latin American republics. There are concurrently a very small number of very large farms, and a very large number of very small farms. Table 9 indicates

[12] For example, as of 1954, only four of nine "departments" in Bolivia (political subdivisions corresponding roughly to U.S. states) had ever been assessed professionally. A staff of sixteen was responsible for assessing all urban property; only eight of the sixteen were appraisers (see the United Nations, *Taxes and Fiscal Policy in Under-Developed Countries*, pp. 47–48). Other administrative problems will be discussed in Chapter VIII. However, it might be noted here that a related problem concerns the pay of assessors and tax collectors. In Guatemala, a revision of assessments started in 1945 was only 20% completed four years later. A possible explanation may be that some tax collectors were paid 20% of their collections up to a maximum of 100 quetzales ($100) per month. Since few collections were ever made after this maximum had been earned, there was little incentive to finish the reassessment project intended to increase tax revenue (see *Ibid.*, p. 74).

the extent of the land tenure problem. Illustrative statistics supporting this table could be drawn from almost any country:[13] In both Mexico and El Salvador, approximately 1 percent of the farms account for 50 percent of the farm land, while approximately 80 percent of the farms are less than five hectares each. In Honduras 1.8 percent of the farms occupy 46 percent of the area, while 65 percent of the farms are between one and nine hectares each. In Venezuela, 2.5 percent of the farms account for 82 percent of the area. In Guatemala 158 farms (less than 1 percent of the total) occupy 40 percent of the farm land, while 266,000 farms (76 percent of the total)occupy 9 percent of the land.

The popular reaction against this concentration of ownership has from time to time erupted in violent actions of expropriation and confiscation. As a partial solution to this problem, underdeveloped countries might consider the imposition of a land tax with rates graduated on the basis of the value of the owner's aggregate holdings. That is, the greater the aggregate value of land owned, the higher the tax rate. Such a tax could assist in the breaking-up of large estates, with a minimum of social disruption. Land taxes very similar to this have very recently been enacted by some of the Latin American nations. For ex-

TABLE 9

Estimated Percentage Distribution of Land Holdings in
Latin America, Around 1950

Size of Farms (in hectares)*	Per Cent of Farms	Per Cent of Land Area
0–20	72.6	3.7
20–100	18.0	8.4
100–1,000	7.9	23.0
Over 1,000	1.5	64.9
Total	100.0	100.0

* One hectare equals 2.471 acres.

Source: Based on a regional summary by Oscar Delgado, *Estructura y reforma agraria en Latinoamerica,* prepared for the Sociedad Economica de Amigos del Pais, Bogota, 1960 (mimeographed), as reported in Albert O. Hirschman (ed.), *Latin American Issues: Essays and Comments,* p. 165.

[13] These statistics were selected from Social Progress Trust Fund, *First Annual Report, 1961,* Part Three.

ample, Law No. 2825, of October 1961, provided Costa Rica with a land tax with rates varying from 0.25 percent of capital value on properties of one hundred to five hundred hectares to 2.5 percent for properties greater than five thousand hectares. Many other countries have graduated their land-tax rates partially on the value of aggregate holdings and partially on productivity considerations.

It must be emphasized that the breaking-up of large estates may not increase agricultural productivity. Indeed, if the large estate is already "well-managed," it may actually decrease productivity. From the viewpoint of solely economic considerations, only the poorly utilized land should be redistributed. This could, of course, include efforts to consolidate privately owned plots that are too small for efficient cultivation. A tax intended to accomplish this objective would generally be discarded on social grounds.

Productivity Aspects

The social ramifications of a highly concentrated land ownership are, of course, very important. However, to the economist, an even more disturbing fact is that many of the large landowners permit much of their land to remain idle, or to be utilized in a very inefficient manner. If an economic development program is to be effective, it is absolutely essential that agricultural productivity be increased to something approaching its maximum potential. This would serve both to free human resources for industrialization and to provide enough foodstuffs to feed the increased urban populations. A rapid increase in agricultural output can further assist development aspirations by providing additional goods to allay the inflationary pressures that generally accompany developmental-credit expansion.

In apparent recognition of these factors, at least three Latin American republics have enacted real-property-tax laws with penalty rates for uncultivated lands. In Sao Paulo, a Brazilian state, effective April 14, 1961, the land "tax is doubled if at least 70 percent of a particular property is not being used productively . . . On the other hand, the tax is reduced if a farm is being reasonably cultivated, if soil conservation practices are being employed, and if the farm workers are provided with adequate housing."[14] Similar laws have been passed in Colombia, Venezuela, and the Brazilian state of Rio Grande do Sul.

Unfortunately, a few areas still retain just the opposite kind of taxa-

[14] Ibid., p. 56.

tion. For example, in the Mexican state of Sonora, the real property tax is imposed only on agricultural land that is producing.[15] In the Mexican state of Yucatan, only land producing henequen (sisal) is subject to the land tax.[16] The incentives provided are just the opposite of those necessary for economic development. These and any similar laws should be amended as soon as possible.

Some countries may wish to consider still a third system of agricultural-land taxation. This system would base land-tax rates on a potential productivity basis (as is common in much of Asia and Europe), rather than on a capital value basis. In countries with insufficient competition in land sales to suggest a true market value, where there are only a limited number of sales in any one year and/or where individual sales may not reflect true market transactions, it may be no more difficult to determine a meaningful productivity classification than it is a meaningful sales value. Productivity ratings range from detailed scientific soil classifications (based on such factors as the "soil profile" or soil layers, thickness of the top soil, texture, structure, moisture-holding capacity, organic content, degree of erosion, salinity) to quite limited classifications (based on such easily recognized criteria as ease of cultivation or irrigation).[17] Under this system of land taxation, the agricultural land with the greatest potential would be subject to the highest tax rate.

Productivity classifications may be superior to sales values as a tax base because graduated taxes imposed on the productivity potential of the land should encourage the landowner to make the most efficient possible use of his land, or to sell it to someone who would. (In countries where the landowner is not typically the land cultivator, it may be necessary to concurrently impose rent controls to deter the owner's shifting any increased property tax to the tenant, and thereby decreasing the possibility of attaining the most efficient land use.) This system of agricultural-land taxation is essentially equivalent to an income tax. The major difference is that the tax base is potential income rather than realized income. If the tax rates were high enough, it could substitute for the income tax on agricultural ventures. This could result in serious inequities, however, in years of crop failures or in years of low

[15] Harvard Law School International Program in Taxation, *World Tax Series: Taxation in Mexico*, pp. 67–68.

[16] *Ibid.*, p. 68.

[17] For a more detailed discussion of this interesting topic see Wald, *Taxation of Agricultural Land*, pp. 188–199.

prices. Consequently it seems preferable to try to strengthen the personal income-tax system and to use agricultural-land taxation, based on the productivity potential, as an interim, supplementary tax only.

Whatever system of land taxation is adopted in Latin America, the laws should include provisions for a review committee to handle charges of inequitable treatment. Ideally, the membership of this committee would include knowledgeable local landowners as well as fiscal officers, and possibly agronomists.

Whether or not any one of these progressive land-tax systems can be successfully implemented in the near future in Latin America remains to be seen. Early reports are not too encouraging. The Colombian revision—providing a system of land-tax incentives and deterrents—was part of a 1957 decree. As of February 1960 no penalties provided by the new law had been imposed. Thomas Carroll, a regional officer for land tenure and settlement in the Food and Agriculture Organization's Santiago office, attributes this to the lack of effective enforcement machinery.[18]

Similar attempts in other developing countries have also met with stiff political opposition. Turkey's State Planning Organization recommended a land tax with progressive rates based on the total value of the land owned by an individual or family. The Turkish Cabinet approved all other aspects of the recommended development plan, but rejected this tax scheme. As a result, top Planning Organization officials are resigning in protest. Mr. Nicholas Kaldor, a well-known economist, summarizes the problem this way:[19] "In countries where a powerful landowning class exists, the prospects for effective land taxation do not appear more promising than the prospects for land reform."

A slightly more optimistic future could be predicted for progressive land taxation on basis of the Australian experience. Nevertheless, Richard Bird, a student of that experience, warns:[20]

the difficulties encountered, even by Australia with its reliable civil service, in dealing with the administrative complexities and legal technicalities necessary to guard against avoidance, would seem to indicate that such a tax would

[18] Thomas F. Carroll, "The Land Reform Issue in Latin America," in Albert O. Hirschman (ed.), *Latin American Issues: Essays and Comments*, p. 193.

[19] Nicholas Kaldor, "Will Underdeveloped Countries Learn to Tax?" p. 414.

[20] Richard M. Bird, "A National Tax on the Unimproved Value of Land: The Australian Experience, 1910–1952," *National Tax Journal*, XIII (December 1960), 392.

be beyond the administrative capability of an underdeveloped country. A progressively graduated tax with an exemption is thus far from a simple panacea for all the economic evils of a country's land system.

Revenue Considerations

Countries considering a system of progressive land taxation for non-fiscal purposes should understand that the more successful their tax system is, the less revenue it will produce. A system designed to break-up large landholdings generally taxes large estates at relatively high tax rates and exempts holdings of the "ideal" size (or less). Therefore, when the ultimate objective has been fully realized, this tax system would produce no tax revenue. This fact need not be considered a disadvantage, however, since the attainment of such a utopian state would imply the capacity for more desirable forms of taxation anyway.

Another aspect of land-tax revenues poses a more immediate problem. That problem is the determination of the level of government that should have the jurisdiction over land taxation. It can be argued that the central government is best equipped in most underdeveloped countries to provide the manpower and equipment for necessary surveys, assessor training, soil classification, and legal registry. Greater uniformity in assessed values, in tax rates, and in enforcement is also probable when the central government retains tax jurisdiction.

On the other hand, the real-property tax is one of relatively few taxes that can be a major revenue producer for state and municipal governments. Since real property is virtually impossible to conceal, or to transport to another locale, and since the situs of the property automatically determines the local government's jurisdiction in other matters, Mexico, Brazil, and Argentina limit the real-property tax to the state or province level only. In Bolivia, both the central and provincial governments impose the property tax. In other Latin American nations having a property tax, it is imposed by the central government only.

In testimony before a subcommittee of the Joint Economic Committee of the U.S. Congress, three experts strongly urged that property-tax revenues collected in Latin America, in conjunction with Alliance-for-Progress reforms, be utilized by the local governments to support facilities basic to local development. Schools, roads, public-welfare, and community-developed projects were cited as most deserving of increased local government support. Although there is no logical reason that these functional activities could not be supported or conducted by the central government, these experts emphasized their belief that increased local organization is an essential ingredient in the economic development aspirations of Latin America. Professor Raymond J. Penn, a University of Wisconsin agricultural economist, made his point in these words:[21]

It seems to me that the real heart of the property tax in the United States was that it forced us to have a school board and other units of local government. The property tax was collected, but a school board had to decide on the amount and had to plan what they were going to spend the money for. One of the important features of a real-estate tax, then, can be that it encourages local organization that does not generally exist in Latin America.

Professor William Sprague Barnes indicated his approval of an expanded, autonomous, *municipio* level of government. He also agreed that the property tax should constitute its major source of revenue. He further contended that this would minimize the opposition to the property tax:[22]

I have encountered again and again in my own experience in working with tax people in Latin America, an attitude toward paying taxes [,] making a sacrifice without seeing the benefit, the notion that the national government swallows it up. This attitude would be changed by having a local source of revenue as the basis for local improvements.

The author concurs in the opinion that some increase in the activity of the local level of government is desirable in most countries of Latin America, and that the property-tax revenues might well be fully allocated to this level of government. However, in the interest of uniformity and expediency, the author believes that responsibility for establishing real-property-tax rates, for assessing market values (or productivity potential), and for surveying the land, should be retained by the central government. Countries already having an *effective* real-property tax imposed by a lower level of government would, of course, be an exception to this general rule. Finally, the author would emphasize that expenditures on such important governmental functions as education, highways, and welfare services should *not* be restricted to the revenues collected from the real-property tax, or any other single tax.

[21] Joint Economic Committee, *Hearings*, 87th Congress, 2nd Session, p. 36.
[22] *Ibid.*

SUMMARY

Wealth-based taxes are not strangers to the Latin American republics. Currently, however, these taxes are not productive of much revenue. The participants at the second Alliance-sponsored tax conference agreed that a net-wealth tax on real estate and financial assets would be a valuable addition to their present tax systems. But because of administrative difficulties, the participants admitted that the implementation of their suggestion may have to be delayed in many countries.

Although death and gift taxes may be both difficult to administer and productive of little revenue, they should be retained and strengthened in the Latin American tax systems in the immediate future. Repealing these taxes, as Mexico did in late 1961, permits relatively large quantities of wealth accumulation to remain untaxed. This is most inequitable to the ordinary income earner. Death and gift taxes can also assist in redistributing the existing wealth, an explicit goal of the Alliance for Progress.

One of the greatest untapped sources of tax capacity in Latin America is the tax on real property. Most of these countries retain a hoary selection of real-property-tax laws imposing very low, proportional rates, on greatly underassessed property values. Although land taxation is less desirable than a net-wealth tax, it has some administrative advantages that recommend it for more immediate consideration, at least as a transitional tax.

The traditional real-property tax in Latin America is based on capital value. Because many of the land registers are incomplete, and the assessed values grossly understated, the first steps in improving the real-property tax in most of these countries must consist of (1) making a complete and accurate survey of land ownership, and recording the same in a public record; and (2) bringing assessed values up to current market values. After making these improvements, some of the Latin American republics may wish to change from their present proportional real-property tax rates to progressive tax rates.

Land taxes with progressive rate structures based upon the aggregate value of the property actually of constructively owned by an individual or a family may serve to encourage the breaking-up of large estates. Land taxes with progressive rate structures based upon a scientifically determined productivity potential may serve to encourage an increase in agricultural productivity. Land taxes imposed at proportional rates, but providing penalty rates for land not utilized in any given year, or for land utilized in an inefficient manner, may also serve to encourage an increase in agricultural productivity. The breaking-up of large estates is an important nontax objective of the land-reform programs in most Latin American countries. Increased agricultural productivity is essential to the attainment of the economic objectives stipulated in the Alliance for Progress. Consequently, any of these alternative land-tax systems can be recommended to the Latin American republics whenever their administrative capacity is sufficient to the challenge.

The public revenues realized through real-property taxation might be used to increase the financial autonomy and the functional responsibilities of the local levels of government. If these tax revenues are retained at the local level, and spent for such obviously beneficial projects as improved education, highways, and public welfare, perhaps the political opposition to increased real-property taxation can be kept to a minimum. However, in the interest of uniformity and expediency, it may well be necessary for most of these countries to give the central level of government the final authority to set the tax rates, assess market values (or productivity potentials), and survey the land.

6. Other Taxes

Although agitation for greater reliance on direct taxation is growing in many of the Latin American republics, the majority of these countries still rely heavily on indirect taxes for most of their revenues. The historical explanation of this fact is undoubtedly the sizable revenues provided by, and the relative ease of administering, indirect taxes. Indeed, in countries with a low literacy rate, poor or nonexistent financial records, inadequate government administration, and an antitax mentality, indirect taxation may be the only real alternative to no taxation at all. In short, until the institutional setting is significantly altered, and the national income increased and distributed more equally, many countries must continue to rely on indirect taxes for an important part of their tax revenues.

The primary purpose of this chapter is to consider briefly the sales, excise, import, and export taxes, as they are utilized in Latin America. Administrative ease is only one of many important criteria in the determination of good tax policy. Therefore, the attention in this chapter is focused on possible reform measures that would minimize the conflict between a heavy reliance on indirect taxes and the objectives of the Alliance for Progress.

The chapter ends with mention of some miscellaneous taxes that simply did not fit well into other sections of this monograph. They have little in common and would not be mentioned here except for the fact that the Latin American republics might either (a) be well-advised to consider the discontinuation of their present use; or (b) want to consider their implementation in the future. Individually, none of these miscellaneous taxes are of major significance.

SALES TAXES

In addition to the claimed administrative advantage, some economists support relatively heavy sales taxation in the underdeveloped countries on the grounds that it discourages consumption and encourages investment. They point out that sales taxes have a minimum effect on the incentives to work, save, and invest, since only that part of income that is consumed is subject to tax. And, as noted in Chapter II, increased capital formation is widely recognized to be a fundamental objective of an underdeveloped country. Ideally, most of these economists would prefer a progressive expenditures tax to the sales tax, but because of the administrative complexities, they may accept the latter alternative as a satisfactory substitute for the developing country.[1]

Other individuals support sales taxation on the grounds that (1) it evokes less hostile political reaction than does an income tax providing equivalent revenue; (2) it reaches persons who are able to escape income taxation by legal or illegal means; and (3) it is better than other indirect taxes because it avoids any discriminatory effects when applied on a general basis.

Opponents of sales taxation contend that the sales tax is regressive, by virtue of the fact that individuals earning a lower income must, of necessity, spend a larger portion of their income than do the recipients of a larger income. Therefore, they maintain that the sales tax is "inequitable" since it is not positively correlated with generally accepted notions of the ability to pay. The weight of this argument depends upon the validity of the assumption that the ultimate incidence of the sales tax is largely shifted to the consumer. As explained in Chapter 2, it is virtually impossible to ascertain, with any degree of certainty, the final incidence of most taxes. Nevertheless, it is highly probable that the ultimate consumer does pay a good part of the sales tax through higher prices.

Other arguments made against sales taxation include the possibility that it may have an undesirable deflationary impact on the economy. This argument presumes that the sales tax decreases consumption, and that the decreased consumption discourages additional investment, and thus perpetrates a general decline in productive activity. Others point out that if the sales tax is passed on to the consumer in the form of higher prices, it could generate still higher prices by precipitating a further cost-wage inflationary spiral. A final argument asserted in opposition to sales taxation suggests that the tax requires much duplication of the income-tax administration and that the compliance costs, while minimal for the government, are significant for the taxpayer.

[1] For a detailed analysis of the case for the expenditure-basis of taxation see Nicholas Kaldor, *An Expenditure Tax*.

Whatever the cogency of the arguments favoring and opposing sales taxation vis-à-vis other taxes, there is little reason to suspect that the sales tax could be displaced from the significant position it now holds in the tax structure of many Latin American republics. Consequently for purposes of this study, a consideration of the advantages and limitations of the alternative forms of sales taxation is of much greater moment. The fact of overwhelming importance for Alliance-prompted tax-reform efforts is that the Latin American country's sales tax tends to be a multistage tax. Argentina, Uruguay, and Venezuela are exceptions to this general rule.

There are five major alternative forms of sales taxation. They are a transactions (or turnover) tax; a sales tax imposed at the retail, wholesale, or manufacturing level; and a value-added tax. The weight of the various arguments favors the retail-sales tax. The worst of the alternatives is widely admitted to be the transactions tax. Unfortunately, it is this form of sales taxation that has been widely employed in Latin America.

In its "pure" form the transactions tax, as the name implies, is imposed on every transfer of goods and services. Generally the tax rate is uniformly applied to the sales or gross-invoice price of each transaction. Among the major disadvantages of this alternative are the following. (1) The tax is pyramided if each purchaser bases his individual mark-up on his cost price, including all previous taxes. Therefore the ultimate consumer may pay not only the tax on the final transaction, but the tax on previous transactions plus a mark-up on each of these taxes. (2) The transactions method of sales taxation severely discriminates in favor of the vertically integrated firm. That is, the single firm handling a product from its original production to its final sale has attained a significant tax advantage over the firm that purchases a partialy completed product from another firm. In a developmental setting, increased specialization often represents an important step to increased productivity, and vertical integration is not generally conducive to a high degree of specialization. (3) The transactions tax discourages increased production by increasing the cost of producer goods, as well as consumption items. Greater production is, of course, an essential aspect of economic development. And (4) the amount of the tax on different products and different consumers is highly disparate because of tax-shifting, pyramiding, differential profit margins, and the difference in the average number of transactions through which a commodity must pass prior to reaching the final sale. Such a hap-hazard distribution of taxes seldom coincides with accepted notions of tax equity.

The only "advantages" that can be cited for the transactions tax are that it produces a substantial amount of revenue due to the large tax base; it is simple to administer since it applies to every transaction alike; and it may not arouse any great opposition because the tax rates can be kept relatively low and the real burden can be effectively concealed from all parties. On closer examination, it is not so clear that these constitute any real advantage at all. Incidentally, in several Latin American countries the transactions tax rate is really quite high. For example, the average rate in Brazil is around 2.5–3.0 percent,[2] in Mexico it is 3.0 percent,[3] and in Peru it is 2.5 percent.

As between the sales tax imposed at either the retail, wholesale, or manufacturing level, the latter two alternatives have two advantages. First, there are fewer wholesale and manufacturing firms than there are retail outlets. Second, there is a tendency for these firms to maintain accounting records of higher quality than is common to the typical retail firm. These facts may well account for the use by both Argentina and Uruguay of the manufacturer-level-sales tax. A retail-sales tax can theoretically be preferred to the wholesale or manufacturing-level-sales tax because it is less likely to be pyramided; it has the widest potential tax base, both because of the higher prices and the possibility of taxing sales of services and second-hand goods; it is readily adapted to meet social and political needs (e.g., the exemption of necessities, producers' goods, or educational materials); it minimizes problems in valuing the tax base since interfirm transactions are not found at the retail-sales level; and it applies more uniformly to all consumers since the tax base is, in all cases, only the final-sales price.

A retail-sales tax that exempts such necessities as food and inexpensive clothing significantly decreases the regressivity of the sales tax. The inclusion of sales of services in the retail-sales-tax base in-

[2] In Brazil since 1934 the sales tax has been reserved to the states. The Federal District imposes the highest tax of 4%. The 8% rate imposed by the state of Amazonas cannot be considered as equivalent to that imposed by the other states because it applies to the first sale only. The average for the other states is between 2.5 and 3.0%.

[3] In Mexico seventeen states have agreed to "participate" with the federal government in sales taxation. Therefore the effective rate of sales taxation for most of Mexico consists of the combined 1.8% federal tax and the 1.2% state tax.

creases its progressivity because higher-income recipients tend to spend a relatively greater percentage of their income on services than do lower-income recipients. Therefore, a retail-sales tax, exempting a limited number of "necessities" and taxing sales of services, could be a highly recommended form of tax reform for those member nations of the Alliance for Progress that now impose the transactions-tax form of the sales tax. Such a tax would still be relatively productive and it would make the overall tax system much less regressive than the present system.

The value-added tax is the most recent addition to the alternative forms of sales taxation.[4] It eludes all the major disadvantages of the transactions tax and includes the most beneficial aspects of the single-stage sales taxes. It does, however, involve collection complications because every manufacturing and wholesaling firm, and possibly every retailing firm, becomes a potential taxpayer. Each firm must compute the value it has added to a product (this is usually interpreted as the difference between the firm's gross receipts and the cost of the commodities it purchased from others) and remit the sales tax computed on this basis. The spreading-out of the impact of the sales tax over all levels of firms may, however, make it more politically palatable than some of the alternative forms of sales taxation.

Excise Taxes

The difference between sales taxes and excise taxes is a matter of degree rather than of kind. That is, an excise tax imposed on a wide variety of articles is very similar to a sales tax allowing many exemptions. However, in most countries, including the Latin American republics, excise taxes are generally restricted to a significantly smaller number of commodities. Among the commodities most frequently subject to an excise tax in Latin America are tobacco and tobacco products, alcoholic beverages, petroleum and petroleum products, electric energy, automotive vehicles, jewelry, furs, and toilet articles.

The justification of an excise tax typically falls into one of four categories. The most common justification, expressed in conjunction with developing economies, is that an excise tax on "luxury" goods constitutes a desirable form of taxing those deemed most able to pay, at a minimum social cost. The greatest problem is, of course, determining

---

[4] The value-added tax was first introduced in France in 1954. It is now used by the U.S. state of Michigan.

what should and what should not be considered a "luxury." On a few articles—say, furs and expensive jewelry—there is nearly universal agreement; on many other items it becomes a matter of individual preference. In spite of this definitional problem, there is probably no other aspect of tax reform that attains an equivalent unanimity of expert opinion than the suggestion that the excise tax on luxury goods be increased in the developing country. The Latin American tax experts, meeting in Santiago, Chile, in late 1962, were no exception. Their discussion of a desirable reorganization of indirect taxes concluded with these words of advice:[5]

Improvement in progressivity, as well as further augmentation of yield, can also be achieved by levying more severe excise taxes on luxury goods consumed predominantly by the middle and higher income groups. Luxury items imported from abroad already bear substantial import duties in most cases, but there is no similarly heavy indirect taxation of home-produced luxury articles, which now, in some countries, account for the greater part of luxury consumption.

The second common justification expressed for certain excise taxes is that a high positive correlation exists between the consumption of the taxed commodity and the benefit derived from a given governmental activity. The most frequently cited example of this is the excise tax on petroleum and petroleum products. The consumption of gasoline is considered a good indicator of the benefits received from government highway expenditures. While it is undeniably true that many persons, other than the immediate highway-user, benefit from the mere existence of the highway, it may well be true that the immediate user does obtain the greatest direct benefit and, therefore, the excise tax can be used as an economic and convenient alternative to a direct charge for the use of the highway. Countries desirous of attaining real economic development must not, however, restrict highway expenditures to the revenues received from such excise taxes because of the critical role a good transportation system plays in the developmental process. The limited data available on the gasoline excise taxes in Latin America suggests the possibility for a substantial rate increase in some countries. For example, the gasoline tax in Venezuela is approximately 7 percent of the retail price of standard, 9.5 percent of the retail price of high

[5] *Provisional Report of the Conference on Fiscal Policy*, OAS, Santiago, Chile, December 5–14, 1962, p. 4.

octane fuel. The same tax in the U.S. averages around 30 percent of the retail price.

Excise taxation is also used to discourage the consumption of select items on social grounds. The excise taxes on alcoholic beverages and tobacco products are, of course, prime examples. Whether or not the suggested justification is the real one, or whether it is a rationalization, is not entirely clear. It is not inconceivable that the principal reason for widespread use of an excise tax on alcoholic beverages and tobacco products is the fact that the demand for these commodities is relatively inelastic. Therefore, the sale of these commodities provides a stable and substantial tax base for a revenue-seeking government. In some countries these taxes constitute up to 75 percent of the retail-sales price of the article concerned.

The fourth and last justification of excise taxation commonly mentioned is that it serves as a rationing device. This justification is most frequently cited during war periods when specific commodities become temporarily scarce but, for one reason or another, direct control of the allocation process is deemed inappropriate. A parallel situation is likely to accompany the implementation of economic development programs in the Latin American countries. The shift of resources into more basic production will likely generate numerous shortages of certain consumption goods. A well-timed and well-calculated excise tax could provide an ideal rationing device. Unfortunately, the taxing authority seldom has either the omnipotence or the omniscience to effect the proper tax-rate changes at the proper time. Consequently, the developing countries may be better advised to use the more readily reversible, direct controls to allocate goods temporarily in short supply. The choice between the two alternatives must depend upon the peculiar set of circumstances existing in each country at the time the shortages occur.

All excise taxation can be opposed on the conceptual level since it necessarily discriminates against the taxed articles. Those economists who assume that the free-market mechanism automatically provides the "best" allocation of resources invariably oppose most excise taxation. They advocate, instead, that equivalent revenues (if needed) be collected through increased income taxation.[6] This system would still permit the individual taxpayer to exercise his nontax-biased preference

[6] Henry C. Simons is one of the most outspoken critics of excise taxation. See his *Federal Tax Reform*, pp. 36–37.

and thereby guarantee the "optimum" distribution of the smaller quantity of resources remaining for private consumption. An increasing number of economists now admit that in a developmental setting, at least a temporary aberration from market dictates is often essential to the attainment of real economic development. Therefore, these individuals are generally amenable to the suggestion of increasing excise taxes on any "nonessential" items, until the development process gets well underway. The definition of "essentials," like "luxuries," is always an arbitrary process.

Countries imposing both a sales and an excise tax must be careful to avoid the imposition of an unreasonably heavy double tax on specified articles. A single-level sales tax, with a low rate and a broad tax base, would certainly be superior to the multiplicity of specific taxes that now exist on numerous articles of mass consumption in some countries. Alternatively, Mexico has avoided the double tax, except where a contrary intention is specifically mentioned, "by the rule that receipts from the first sale (by the manufacturer or producer) of articles subject to a special federal tax imposed on the production, exploitation, or on the first sale are exempt from the commercial receipts [sales] tax."[7]

Customs Duties

As noted in Chapter 3, customs duties are still the single most important source of tax revenues in several Latin American countries, especially the smaller Caribbean nations. Very little useful generalization can be made about tax-reform efforts in regard to custom duties since these taxes are frequently imposed primarily for trade control, and only secondarily for revenue reasons. Ofttimes they are closely allied to the foreign-exchange control system.

The traditional objections to export and import taxes are well known. The most important objections are that customs duties (a) disrupt the optimum pattern of world trade; (b) invite uneconomic productive practices; (c) accentuate domestic economic instability (this argument has merit only if the government expenditures are—unwisely —restricted to current tax receipts); (d) inhibit foreign investment and capital flows (by interfering with the free flow of returns on in-

[7] Harvard Law School International Program in Taxation, *World Tax Series: Taxation in Mexico*, p. 83.

vestment—a likely possibility when the customs duty is closely related to multiple exchange differentials); and (e) violate generally accepted notions of tax equity (this argument cannot be scientifically verified since it is impossible to determine the real incidence of these taxes).

Export Taxes

The extensive use of export taxation in the small economy, dominated by a heavy dependence on the export of one or two primary products, is not without benefit. A skillfully managed export tax can serve to counteract the destabilizing influence of the export-import sector. An increase in export taxes timed to coincide with an increase in world demand, and world prices, can siphon off the windfall gain that would otherwise accrue to the export sector. If the added tax revenues are used to good advantage (as in a foreign-exchange stabilization fund, or a financing capital imports necessary to diversify the domestic economy) they may even be superior to more general taxes that are less easily adjusted upward or downward with change in the domestic economy. Authority to modify the export tax is commonly delegated to the executive branch of the government and is, therefore, amenable to rapid adjustment. Export taxes are also effective in recouping windfall gains that might otherwise accrue to exporters after a national currency devaluation.

Some countries also use the export tax as an administrative substitute for a direct tax on the branch operations of foreign firms. Although this practice is, in principle, not wholly desirable, it effectively evades the arbitrary allocation of overhead costs, and the determination of a "fair" price on all materials transferred within the firm, both of which are necessary in the computation of branch profits. It further avoids the ticklish complications of verifying expenses incurred by the branch outside the territorial boundaries of the taxing country's jurisdiction.

The export tax has some distinct advantages over alternative forms of taxation of even the domestically owned company, operating in an export-oriented, underdeveloped nation. Evasion becomes difficult by virtue of the relatively limited number of ports capable of handling international freight shipments. Smuggling can be restricted to small operations with a minimum coastal patrol. Administrative costs are minimized through the high degree of centralization of the taxing au-

thority. And standards of voluntary compliance and literacy requirements are, likewise, reduced to a minimum by the very nature of the
export tax.

Import Taxes

Import taxes are widely used in Latin America for nonrevenue purposes. Consequently, little generalization can be made on tax-reform
efforts without a detailed investigation of the trade policies of these
countries. Such an investigation is outside the scope of this project.

Suffice it to note here that the pattern for import taxes in Latin
America is closely related to the domestic production pattern. Prohibi-
tive import-tax rates are typically imposed on commodities where domestic production is deemed sufficient to satisfy the demand. Moderate
import-tax rates are common if domestic production is deemed insufficient to satisfy the existing demand. Very low or zero import-tax rates
are usually imposed on foods not domestically produced. There are, of
course, numerous exceptions to the general pattern. Extremely high
import-taxes are frequently imposed on articles of "luxury" consumption regardless of domestic production. For example, a severe tax on
heavy automobiles is typical. High import taxes are also common to the
products of those industries in which the government has determined
to encourage domestic production. Relatively high import-tax rates on
household appliances (television sets, radios, lamps), athletic equipment, toys, and cameras are also common, even when none of these are
domestically produced in sufficient quantity. The probable explanation
is the belief that these items are most widely purchased by the middle-
and upper-income groups.

Generally, the existing system of import taxation could be improved
in several of the Latin American countries. Basing the tax on a market
value—rather than on weight, or other physical basis—would make the
duty more responsive to price movements; it would also end the existing bias against cheap, heavy articles. Provisions permitting the importation of items essential to economic development duty-free should
be made an integral part of every economic development program.
More general exclusion from import taxation on all producer's goods
can be recommended whenever the foreign-exchange position of the
developing country permits. The tendency to automatically classify all
new products in the high-tariff category should be avoided. And customs officials should not be political appointees, nor should they be

paid on basis of the fines they impose, as is now common in some of the Latin American republics.

As a long-term objective, a gradual decrease in the present heavy reliance on customs taxes can be highly recommended.[8] In the interim period, the matter of primary concern must be the channeling of the export- and import-tax proceeds into the most advantageous use. Customs taxes payable in hard currencies are especially important because of the general shortage of "hard" foreign exchange. If economic development aspirations are to become economic reality, it is essential that the underdeveloped countries of Latin America use their foreign-exchange earnings judiciously. In most cases, this means that they must use them for the importation of capital goods to diversify, expand, and industrialize their domestic economy. Other countries may be justified in building up foreign exchange balances to cushion cyclical movements in their primary-goods trade pattern. The tendency to spend the hard currencies on imports of luxury consumption must be avoided by continued high import duties or by direct controls.

MISCELLANEOUS TAXES

An exhaustive study of the tax system of any country would beget, among other things, recommendations for the simultaneous deletion and addition of various taxes. Because this monograph is concerned with nineteen Latin American republics as a group, it is no more possible to suggest a comprehensive list of such additions and deletions to the existing tax systems than it is to recommend less drastic tax-reform measures for each individual country.[9] Nevertheless, the research undertaken did reveal the widespread existence of at least two taxes considered to be inconsistent with economic development ambitions.

---

[8] To the extent that these taxes are imposed on commodities sold to, or purchased from, member countries of the Latin America Free Trade Association, this recommendation should be self-enforcing. LAFTA-member countries have pledged themselves to reduce the duties on intercountry transactions to zero over a twelve-year period.

[9] The need for studies of individual countries is very great. A number of taxes that now exist must certainly have undesirable social consequences. For example, anyone named as a defendant in a Brazilian criminal action automatically pays a tax equal to 10% of the bail set. The revenue collected in this manner is used for state prison-reform programs and to improve prison conditions!

Each of these are discussed below. The chapter ends with a brief mention of the possible use of a poll or "head" tax for nonrevenue reasons.

Taxes To Be Deleted

The "excess-profits tax" and the "stamp tax" are two taxes many Latin American countries might well be advised to discontinue. The excess-profits tax is often rationalized on the nationalist sentiment that excess profits represent the exploitation of local resources. The stamp tax is an anachronism. It dates to times when the acquisition of a legal document represented one of a very limited number of contacts between the citizen and the government—therefore, one of few opportunities to impose and collect a tax.

Excess Profits Taxation

The overwhelming objection to excess-profits taxation is its involvement in an idle quest to discover what profits should be regarded as "excess." Such a concept could only have meaning in a static economy, and the developing nations of Latin America most assuredly cannot—and should not—be static. The conventional definitions of "excess profits" are wholly unrealistic. The three most common definitions are (1) all profits exceeding some arbitrary percentage of "invested capital";[10] (2) all profits exceeding the average historical profit earned in some earlier, and arbitrarily selected, period; or (3) all profits in excess of some arbitrary percentage of the current year's gross receipts.[11] The excess-profits tax imposed on this most arbitrary tax base is typically a tax with a progressive rate structure.

In an inflationary setting, as is common to many Latin American countries imposing an excess-profits tax, accounting conventions are drastically strained in the much less arduous task of computing net income. This is true because of the inappropriateness of matching *current* (inflated) revenues and *historical* costs. The matching of even

[10] The definition of "invested capital" is equally arbitrary. It is roughly considered to be the sum of paid-in capital, reserves (there is little general consensus of opinion on what should and what should not be included under this label either), and undistributed profits.

[11] For a rather complex, nonconventional definition of "excess profits," and an argument for their role in underdeveloped countries, see Benjamin Higgins, "Business Taxation and Regulation of Profits Transfers in Underdeveloped Countries," Ms.

more antiquated capital figures and current profit estimates is wholly ridiculous when used as a tax base. The resulting tax disadvantage to the older firm and to the firm established during a recession period, is generally severe and economically disruptive.

Unfortunately, the excess-profits tax can generate substantial support because it appears to eliminate a true economic surplus accruing to an impersonal giant, oft times a foreign giant! As suggested above, in most cases the surplus is much more imaginary than real. In those few cases where it is real, it may simply reflect the substantial reward for entrepreneurial and managerial skills that are in scarce supply throughout the underdeveloped nations. Alternatively, a large profit may reflect the high marginal productivity of capital possible in some areas. A high rate of return on capital investments may even be necessary because of the high degree of risk inherent in the investment. Or a high profit margin may be the reward for a high level of productivity achieved through growth.

In each of these cases, the relatively high profits serve the useful purpose of stimulating increased investment in a profitable venture. Without a strong incentive, there is little reason to suspect that the Latin American nations could ever achieve the rate of private-capital formation necessary for the realization of their economic growth ambitions, as expressed in the Alliance for Progress. Whatever degree of social control is deemed necessary can be attained through a sound system of income taxation. In short, these countries should consider the immediate repeal of their excess-profits-tax laws.

Stamp Taxes

The stamp taxes are not a major revenue producer, yet their existence does constitute an impediment to the development of a modern, complex economy. The stamp-tax law typically provides that each legal document must bear stamps issued by the level of government regulating the particular transaction. The tax base is either the number of pages or the aggregate value involved in the transaction evidenced by the legal document. Documents commonly subject to the stamp tax include loans, capital issues, security transactions, installment sales, real-estate transfers, vehicle registrations, promissory notes, and even accounting records.

Besides being administratively cumbersome and of little revenue significance, the stamp taxes can be opposed on the grounds that (a) they impose an unnecessary, additional burden on debtors in countries where interest rates are already so high they discourage investment; (b) the tax base does not represent any real taxpaying ability; (c) there is generally no relation between the stamp fee and the value of the service rendered by the government; and (d) the mere existence of the stamp tax discourages the reduction of a financial transaction to writing in just those countries where better systems of taxation must be rejected because of the absence of readily verifiable records. For all these reasons, it is believed that the countries of Latin America should repeal the tax-stamp laws still in effect.

The Poll or "Head" Tax

Governmental units sometimes use tax laws for nonrevenue reasons. The penalty systems of land taxation (to encourage better utilization of agricultural land or to break up large estates) considered in Chapter 5 are illustrative. In conjunction with the goals established in the Alliance for Progress, it is conceivable that a poll or head tax, coupled with an appropriate tax-exemption system, could have a salutary effect in Latin America.

A lump-sum tax imposed on an individual without regard to effort, wealth, or consumption, has the economic merit of not affecting incentives adversely or distorting consumption patterns. The need to pay the tax may even induce the exertion of some additional effort in the market economy. An effective exemption system, existing concurrently with a poll tax, might be used to induce other desired behavior patterns. For example, tax credits could be granted against a poll tax for attending educational classes, for receiving innoculations, for private saving, or for being employed. The objective of such a tax and tax-exemption system would, of course, be to increase the literacy rate, to improve health standards, to increase private savings, and to increase participation in the market economy.

Whether such a tax could achieve any political support is doubtful. Poll taxes are commonly opposed as highly regressive.[12] Coupling the poll tax with a generous system of exemptions based on self-improve-

[12] The poll tax attained its apex on the African continent during the period of British colonial administration. Africa is still one of the few places where poll taxes are a major revenue producer. Today, however, it has been "modernized" into a progressive tax, on the basis of an assessment made by local committees. In Nyasaland the progressive poll tax produced 25% of the total tax revenue in a recent year (see John F. Due, "The African Personal Tax," *National Tax Journal*, XV [December 1962], 385–398).

ment undertakings would serve to reduce the regressivity of the tax for those individuals willing and capable of compliance. For those unable to comply, the tax would represent an unreasonable burden and, therefore, an administrative method of exempting certain individuals (such as the very young, the very old, and the infirm) would be mandatory. At present, none of the Latin American countries are utilizing the poll tax. A few may wish to experiment with it.

SUMMARY

Indirect taxes typically provide a significant portion of the total tax revenue in the Latin American republics. The most productive indirect taxes are the sales, excise, and customs taxes. The explanation for their historically prominent position is twofold. First, these taxes are relatively easier to administer than are most direct taxes. Second, these taxes are imposed on a broad and widely diffused tax base, and therefore, they produce a relatively large revenue with minimal political opposition.

The fact that the Latin American countries have determined, in the Alliance for Progress, to increase tax revenues suggests that indirect taxes will retain a significant role in the typical Latin fiscal system for several years. It therefore becomes important that the most objectionable features of the existing indirect taxes—from an economic development standpoint—be minimized through tax-reform measures.

Relative to the sales tax, the most objectionable feature is the widespread use of a multistage transactions tax. This form of sales taxation is inconsistent with the Alliance-for-Progress tax-reform objectives because it is likely to be pyramided; it discriminates in favor of the vertically integrated firm; it increases the cost of producer goods; and it results in a haphazard distribution of the tax burden. Those Latin American countries still using a multistage sales tax should be encouraged to adopt, as part of their tax-reform efforts, one of the alternative forms of sales taxation. Either a single-stage tax imposed at the retail, wholesale, or manufacturer's level, or the value-added tax, could be a highly recommended substitute for the present system.

Relative to the excise taxes, the most objectionable feature of the present system is the multiplicity of specific taxes that now apply to selected articles of mass consumption. The total excise-plus-sales tax can represent a significant portion of the retail-sales price of any item. Excise taxes are frequently imposed at relatively high rates on commodities of "luxury" consumption, on commodities with an inelastic demand, and on commodities temporarily in short supply. The theoretical objection that this variety of taxation distorts an optimum consumption pattern has questionable merit in the developing nations since free-market allocations are frequently considered inconsistent with development aspirations anyway. Excise taxes on a few products, as on gasoline, can be justified on the grounds that the tax reasonably approximates the consumer's benefit from a particular government expenditure.

Very little useful generalization can be made about tax-reform efforts relative to customs duties because these taxes are primarily imposed for trade-control reasons, and only secondarily for revenue reasons. As a long-term objective, a gradual decrease in customs taxes can be highly recommended. In the shorter run, countries presently depending heavily upon customs taxes for public revenues must be especially careful to channel these revenues into the most advantageous uses. If they fail in this venture, there is little prospect that they will ever be capable of significantly altering their present tax systems.

Among the numerous miscellaneous taxes imposed in Latin America, the use of the excess-profits tax and of the stamp tax is particularly inconsistent with economic development ambitions. The excess-profits tax seriously inhibits private investment incentives by unduly penalizing any firm operating, for even a few years, in an inflationary setting—as most firms in Latin America must operate. The stamp tax discourages the documentation necessary to the development of a modern, complex economic system. Consequently, it is recommended that the use of these two taxes be discontinued in the near future.

7. Tax-Exemption Schemes

Paradoxical as it seems, the same countries of Latin America that are diligently seeking to discover sources for increased tax revenues are also interested in expanding tax-exemption schemes. The scope and the detailed provisions of the exemption schemes vary widely among the countries joined in the Alliance for Progress. However, the tendency is clearly toward a growing list of countries offering tax exemption as one incentive device in the economic development plan. As of January 1, 1963, Argentina, Bolivia, Brazil, British Guiana, British Honduras, Colombia, El Salvador, Guatemala, Haiti, Mexico, Paraguay, Puerto Rico, Uruguay, and Venezuela had all promulgated some form of tax exemption in conjunction with their economic development aspirations.

The purpose of this chapter is to investigate the possible economic effects of the tax-exemption schemes. These schemes often constitute an important part of a developing country's deliberate plan for economic growth. Mexico and Puerto Rico were pioneers in this area. Therefore, their systems of tax exemption will be considered in some detail in this chapter. The advantages and limitations of these schemes tend to become quite evident as the results of the early plans are analyzed.

THE ROLE OF TAX EXEMPTION IN DEVELOPMENT PLANNING

Because the self-adjusting, automatic mechanism of the market place has proven, over a rather long run, to provide many nations of the world with little more than a secular equilibrium of poverty and underemployment, an intensive interest in deliberate economic intervention has arisen. The extent of this interest was accentuated when the United States—long a verbal champion of laissez faire—made economic development planning a *quid pro quo* for financial aid in Latin America.

Most formal economic plans tend to emphasize the role of the public sector in the developmental process. Generally, the plans recognize the need for higher levels of investment, beginning with public investment in social overhead capital—*i.e.,* investment in such basic development projects as public health, education, highways, and harbors, are viewed as a precondition to further economic growth. Because these are high-cost projects, yielding little private profit, they ordinarily must be relegated to the public sector. At the same time, many of the economic development plans concede that if any sustained, material improvement in economic conditions is to be realized, other action must also be taken. It may be either increased concentration on raw materials production or a diversification of production, including industrialization. Since public resources are typically limited, this "other activity" is often temporarily, at least, assigned to the private sector.

It is exactly at this juncture in development planning that tax-exemption schemes are conceived. They are envisaged as one possible method of manipulating—albeit to a limited degree—the private sector. Typically, tax-exemption schemes are intended to encourage industrialization in a previously raw-materials-oriented economy. For proof of this apparent intention, one generally need look no further than the title of the law enacting the exemption scheme. For example, in Mexico the most important provisions are contained in the "Law for the Promotion of New or Essential Industries;" and in Puerto Rico they are part of the "Industrial Tax Exemption Act."

INDUSTRIAL-TAX EXEMPTION IN MEXICO AND IN PUERTO RICO

Tax-exemption schemes date to 1950 and earlier in both Mexico and Puerto Rico. Consequently, these plans are important both because many other countries' plans have been patterned after them, and because they have been operative long enough for the results to be analyzed. This is to suggest neither that all the other operative tax-exemption schemes existing in Latin America are highly comparable,[1] nor that all the analyses reach the same conclusions.[2]

---

[1] Indeed, many of them are highly comparable. But—as always—exceptions do exist. Two particularly notable exceptions are Panama's granting tax exemption to export industries only, and Paraguay's granting income-tax exemption to foreign-capital firms only.

[2] Typically the planning-board members strongly recommend the tax-exemption schemes whereas "outside" economists, especially public finance "experts," tend to be critical of them. Compare Mohinder S. Bhatia, "Tax Exemption in

In Mexico

Although Article 28 of the Constitution of Mexico expressly prohibits the granting of tax exemptions, the Supreme Court interprets this to mean that tax exemptions cannot be granted to a particular taxpayer. General exemptions, available to all qualifying taxpayers, are considered legal. In addition to the usual exemption extended to government enterprises, charitable, scientific, political, and cultural organizations, public and private educational institutions, and registered cooperative organizations, Mexico exempts publishers of books and periodicals serving cultural purposes. However, of much greater significance are the tax exemptions granted to enterprises engrossed in industrial production or services deemed "essential" to the economic development of Mexico.

In order to qualify as an "essential industry," a firm must either be "new" to Mexico (*i.e.*, the goods produced are new, and not merely close substitutes for existing items), or it must produce goods already produced, but produced in insufficient quantities to satisfy the domestic demand. If a firm is to qualify under the second of these criteria, the existing shortage must be both substantial and relatively permanent. These last two requirements are considered satisfied if imports equal 20 percent or more of the sum of the domestic production (net of exports) and imports in each of the last two years. In addition, the qualifying firm must have the capacity to supply at least 20 percent of the existing deficiency. Furthermore, each qualifying firm must individually add at least 10 percent of the total direct cost of producing an item. Direct costs are interpreted to include raw materials, labor, equipment, and finished or semifinished component parts.

Export firms can achieve tax-exempt status in Mexico only if 60 percent or more of their direct manufacturing costs are added in Mexico, and if the firm needs the tax exemption to be competitive in the sale of its product.[3] Firms meeting both of these criteria are also labeled "essential." The intent of this restriction is to discourage assembly operations that might attempt to avail themselves of low taxes

---

a Developing Economy," *National Tax Journal*, XIII (December 1960), 341–349; and Milton C. Taylor, *Industrial Tax-Exemption in Puerto Rico*.

[3] Guatemala has enacted an interesting variant of this notion. There the percentage of tax exemption granted varies directly with the percentage of domestic raw materials used in the production process.

and cheap labor for as long as possible and then depart, making no permanent contribution to the development of Mexico.

Tax exemption is expressly prohibited to firms engaged in metallic mineral mining or improving, petroleum production, and alcohol and tobacco production. Industries determined by competent authority, to have antisocial effects (*e.g.,* narcotics production or refinement), and industries deemed dangerous to the national security (*e.g.,* the making of armaments for export), are also ineligible for tax-exemption privileges.

The scope of the possible tax exemption in Mexico is quite comprehensive. Qualifying firms are eligible for a reduction of up to 40 percent of the Schedule II income tax; 100 percent of the federal commercial receipts (sales) tax; 60 percent of the export taxes; 100 percent of the federal stamp tax; and all import duties on necessary raw materials (if they are not produced in Mexico in sufficient quantities) and on machinery and equipment necessary to production. The distributable-profits tax can also be avoided 100 percent via the creation of reinvestment reserves. And all the states and the federal district extend exemption from selected state taxes to qualifying industries.

The period of the tax exemption varies with the classification of the new or essential industry as basic, semibasic, or secondary. Basic industries—those deemed "fundamentally important" to Mexican industry or agriculture—are exempt for ten years. Under specified conditions they may be classified of "paramount importance" and thereby attain an additional five-year exemption. Semibasic industries—those producing "vital" consumer goods, industrial tools, scientific instruments, or component parts—are exempt for seven years. They also may qualify for a five-year extension. Secondary industries—those that cannot qualify under either of the other two classifications—are exempt for up to five years. No extension is possible for firms so classified.

Specified service industries may obtain tax exemptions varying from five to ten years. The exact time period is based on the initial capital investment, the number of employees, and the productive capacity of the firm. The larger each of these quantities is, the longer the exemption period granted. Export industries are granted tax exemption on a year-to-year basis. Their exemption period cannot exceed a total of ten years.

The administrative responsibility for tax exemption rests with the Ministry of Finance, in consultation with the Ministry of the Economy. In evaluating tax-exemption applications, in addition to the legal qualifications, the ministries stress the extent the applicant uses Mexican materials, equipment, and machinery; the size of the enterprise (re capital structure and productive capacity); its technical efficiency and research potential; the extent and quality of labor it employs; and any possible social benefit or detriment resulting from the operation. Tax-exemption privileges granted may be terminated or suspended in the event of abuse, or if profits indicate that no real need for further exemption exists.

In summary, the major tax-exemption scheme in Mexico clearly favors the large-scale industrial firm. Tax exemption is more likely to be granted to the industry producing commodities that will satisfy domestic demand than to industries producing primarily for export. The extent of the possible exemption is significant both in terms of the number of taxes involved, and in terms of the time period for which it is granted. Provisions have been inserted into the law to restrict the tax-exemption privilege to the needy and deserving firm.

In Puerto Rico

The industrial tax-exemption law in Puerto Rico was first enacted in 1948. Since then, it has constituted a central feature of economic development planning. The 1948 law provided tax exemption to "new" industries, as well as to existing firms that had expansion possibilities. Qualifying firms were exempt from the income, property, municipal-license, and excise taxes. A 100 percent exemption was granted to June 1959; a 75 percent exemption was granted for the year ending June 30, 1960; a 50 percent exemption for the next twelve months; and a 25 percent exemption for the year ending June 30, 1962.

In 1954 a new tax-exemption law was passed that was quite similar to the 1948 law. The definition of eligible industries was expanded somewhat in the second law. The emphasis was placed upon the need to "transform" products from raw materials into articles of commerce. One-half the maximum exemption was also granted to firms engaged in the tourist and hotel industries. Dividend payments were declared tax exempt for seven years—so long as they were paid sometime during a firm's first fifteen years of operations. Finally, the period of exemption from the property tax was made dependent upon the amount of capital invested. If the investment in a qualifying firm was less than $1 million, property-tax exemption was granted for only five years. This time period increased up to ten-year exemption for an investment in excess of $10 million.

Although both the Mexican and the Puerto Rican tax-exemption laws are relatively sweeping, there are numerous significant distinctions between the two. Among the most important differences is the apparent attitude toward qualifying industries. Puerto Rico is obviously determined to increase the role of the manufacturing sector regardless of the source or ultimate destination of the product produced. Originally she was willing to grant exempt status to even those firms engaged in simple assembly operations. Mexico clearly emphasizes the desire for increased domestic goods by withholding tax exemption from many export industries. Both countries reward economies of scale by favoring the larger producer. Mexico provides more limitations to insure that the tax exemption is not granted to firms wholly capable of operating profitably without the exemption. (The tendency to move from a liberal to a restrictive tax-exemption is not uncommon.) Undoubtedly the liberal provisions of the Puerto Rican law were influenced by her unique relation to the U.S. mainland. Puerto Rican firms and individuals can trade duty-free with the United States mainland. Consequently there is no shortage of consumer or producer goods there. They have the further advantage of remaining outside the jurisdiction of the U.S. federal income tax. This combination of factors explains in large measure the spectacular results of the exemption law, as well as some of its provisions.

THE ADVANTAGES OF TAX-EXEMPTION SCHEMES

Industrialization of a developing economy can be accomplished in one of three ways. First, it may result from the self-initiation of private entrepreneurs acting on their own accord. Second, it may result from government ownership and operation of the industrial enterprise. Or third, it may be cultivated through government inducement and assistance extended to private enterprise.[4] The necessity of rapid industrial expansion is generally considered to be too urgent to permit any continued reliance on the first of the three methods. Thus, the real choice is between the second and the third alternatives.

As previously mentioned, governments of countries in the earliest stages of development may believe that they really have only one effective alternative since it is usually imperative that they invest much of

---

[4] This last method was aptly described as a combination of "venture government and private capital" by Muñoz Marín, Governor of Puerto Rico. See Taylor, *Industrial Tax-Exemption in Puerto Rico*, p. 134.

their rather limited resources in basic development projects. These projects are considered a precondition to any further economic growth. Granting this fact does not mean, however, that tax-exemption schemes are necessarily the cheapest, most equitable, or most effective form of government inducement and assistance to private enterprise. The popular acceptance of tax exemption can probably be attributed to two facts of minor concern to academicians, but of great practical advantage to legislators. First, a tax exemption does not appear as an expenditure in the government budget and, therefore, it appears to be "free." Second, the exemption scheme is relatively self-administering, once the decision to grant or withhold the exemption privilege has been made. This, of course, endears it to anyone predisposed to a laissez-faire philosophy. The deception inherent in this kind of thinking will be discussed presently.

A tax exemption has the real advantage of assisting firms in the financially difficult years of initiating a business. Even better-established businesses can be favorably effected by the ability to retain their entire profits for business expansion. The availability of capital is especially significant in countries with a nonexistent, or poorly developed, capital market—a condition common to most developing nations. Tax exemption undeniably does increase the support of capital funds available to any profitable firm. Exemption from the property, stamp, and sales taxes may increase the supply of capital available to even nonprofitable firms. This is one of the most important, rational advantages of tax-exemption schemes in the underdeveloped country.

Tax exemption also has a purely psychological advantage in inducing new business ventures. The strength of the advantage varies widely in different countries, and within the same country at different times. The Puerto Rican experience is witness to the possible effectiveness of the psychological advantage. The unique relation between Puerto Rico and the U.S. mainland, combined with the prevalence of an "unduly-tax-burdened-businessman" attitude on the mainland, proved a potent combination in this one case. Milton Taylor, a U.S. economist who analyzed the Puerto Rican experience, summarized the psychological advantage in this way:[5]

The apparent success of tax exemption in attracting mainland capital is probably the most unique feature in the experience of Puerto Rico with this fiscal device. It is considered unique because the literature analyzing the

[5] *Ibid.*, p. 144.

problems involved in encouraging the export of capital from the more advanced countries to the underdeveloped areas usually minimizes the effectiveness of tax exemption . . . The appeal of industrial tax-exemption in Puerto Rico is largely illogical and irrational, but nevertheless appears to be dramatically seductive.

A final advantage of the tax-exemption scheme is the deliberate selectivity that can be incorporated into the exemption law. The privilege of tax exemption can be withheld from those sectors of the economy that the development planners consider to be least capable of making a significant contribution to economic growth. The sectors considered capable of contributing the most can be given the greatest privilege. The review of the Mexican system is instructive in this regard. Uruguay has "refined" the idea of privilege-selectivity to even a geographical basis. In Uruguay, anywhere between 75 percent and 90 percent of industrial profits can be exempt from income taxation. To attain exemption, the profits must be reinvested in the renovation or acquisition of equipment. The rate is 75 percent if the profit-reinvesting firm is located in the "department" of Montevideo; 80 percent if in San Jose or Canelones; and 90 percent if in some other department. As is noted in the following section, however, a limitation of most tax-exemption schemes is the practical inability to refine the selectivity criterion even further.

The Limitations of Tax-Exemption Schemes

One incontrovertible fact is that, other things being equal, tax-exemption schemes are most effective in countries with a high and comprehensive degree of taxation. In many countries of Latin America, the existing industrial-tax exemptions do little more than *equalize* the tax-favored position of nonproductive, speculative forms of investment. As demonstrated in Illustrations 1 and 2, and as explained in the attendant sections of Chapter 4, the historical tendency in Latin America has been for relatively high levels of taxation in the manufacturing and industrial sectors; relatively low levels of taxation in non-manufacturing (especially agricultural) enterprise; and virtually no taxation of speculative gains. Consequently, an appropriate increase in the taxation of nonindustrial incomes could be as effective a stimulant to increased industrialization as are the present exemption schemes.

Second, even if a country obtains the desired form of investment through a tax-exemption scheme, the plan may be self-defeating. The exemption removes a substantial sector of the economy from the tax base. If this results in an imbalance in growth and the starvation of other sectors of the economy via heavy taxation (necessary to finance the expanding governmental functions that typically accompany economic growth), the growth process itself may be stunted.

Third the effectiveness of the tax-exemption scheme varies with each possible source of capital. An increase in the aggregate amount of private-domestic capital formation does not appear to represent a probable result of tax exemption at the existing levels of national (and per capita) income. Until substantially higher levels of real income are attained, the demand for consumption goods will necessarily remain very great. Therefore, tax exemption can be effective only through the diversion of existing investment in other activities, or through increased foreign-private investment in the exempting country. As suggested earlier, the diversionary alternative might also be accomplished through increased taxation of the nonproductive forms of investment. Increased foreign-private investment is generally considered a mixed blessing. The exemption systems of some countries specifically provide that tax exemption will not be granted to foreign-capital investment. For example, El Salvador requires that at least 50 percent of a firm's capital be of "local source" if the venture is to attain tax-exempt status.

Furthermore, if the capital-exporting country taxes the income of its residents and citizens, earned anywhere in the world, the tax privilege extended by the underdeveloped nation may simply mean a higher tax paid by the creditor in his home country. Generally the capital-exporting nations do permit the deduction of foreign taxes actually paid from the domestic tax on the income earned abroad. However, in the absence of a specific, bilateral, international, tax agreement, they do not generally permit the deduction of the "saved" (via exemption) taxes from the domestic tax. At present only two Latin American countries have enacted foreign-tax-credit agreements, and only Honduras has a tax treaty with the United States.[6]

Fourth, the tax exemption is not as selective as one might wish. For example, it cannot guarantee the rate, amount, or type of investment desired. It is also difficult to determine, at the time of granting the exemption, which firm will be willing and able to contribute permanently to economic growth. There is little advantage in encouraging

[6] Joseph P. Crockett, "Tax Pattern in Latin America," *National Tax Journal,* XV (March 1962), 95.

industries that will collapse at the expiration of the tax-exemption period. Alos, the firm with the largest profit benefits most, whereas the firm most in need—*i.e.,* one operating at a loss—typically gets little or no benefit.[7] Ideally the exemption would be granted only if necessary to attract the marginal investor.

When instituting a tax-exemption plan, a country must either discriminate against existing firms or give them an "unnecessary" benefit (*i.e.,* it is unnecessary in the sense that it induced no additional investment). The usual practice is to extend tax exemption to all existing firms at the time it is extended to a new firm manufacturing the same product. This "most-favored-company" clause is both a practical and political necessity. In the absence of such a clause, it would be difficult to maintain effective competition between new and existing firms.

Fifth, the exemption system may encourage the growth of monopoly power. The *ex-ante* incentive of the tax exemption will not appear particularly large to a firm unless it anticipates a rather large, early profit. Such a firm would probably invest even in the absence of the exemption privilege. Given the privilege, such a firm may rapidly secure an incontestable monopoly position in the economy. This may be particularly true of heavy good industries with increasing returns to scale. Of course, a country may be willing to permit the development of a monopoly industry, and retain control of it in some other fashion, rather than forgo the industry completely.

Sixth, there is a tendency for tax-exemption schemes to become at least a semipermanent feature of the growing economy. Recipients begin to consider tax exemptions their rights instead of privileges. Granted in one country tax exemption tends to proliferate itself. Neighboring countries feel compelled to instigate similar programs to avoid the diversion of any additional investment from their country to another country with a more advantageous tax climate. Thus tax exemption creates many of the undesirable side effects so deplored in the "beggar-my-neighbor" trade policies. It should be emphasized that the Alliance for Progress is an area effort for economic development, and

---

[7] Taylor (*Industrial Tax-Exemption in Puerto Rico,* p. 146) points out that in 1950, in Puerto Rico, one firm of the seventy-two holding tax-exemption privileges obtained 66% of the total tax relief granted. Of course it can be argued that the purpose of the exemption is to encourage the efficient (hence profitable) firms, and to discourage the inefficient (or low-profit) ones. In this view the benefit received is proportionate to the contribution.

policies that can be advantageous to one member country, but only at the expense of a neighboring country, are inconsistent with the basic objectives of the program.

Seventh, the loss of tax revenue does constitute a cost of the exemption scheme. Nevertheless, the author believes that the revenue-loss aspects of the problem are all too frequently overemphasized. *Ex-post* computations of taxes "lost," on the basis of historical profit reports, overstate the revenue loss. A first necessary refinement would be the netting out of taxes on firms that would not have been operative in the absence of the tax exemption. Even this net figure disregards the additional tax revenue actually generated from the incremental wages and salaries paid, the sales made, and the secondary industries initiated as a result of the expansion in the industrial sector. To quantify these many direct and indirect effects of tax exemption, in terms of a real revenue loss, is virtually impossible. Even if it were possible, the results would not be particularly meaningful since the real cost is not the revenue lost but the alternatives foregone. The cost can only be measured in terms of the benefits that would have accrued from the alternative projects the government might have undertaken had they received the exempted tax revenue. Therefore, when evaluating the possibility of instituting a new tax-exemption scheme, a developing country should give primary consideration to selecting the most advantageous alternative course of action.

Finally, tax-exemption schemes are admittedly difficult to administer. Whether or not they are too difficult to justify their very existence is wholly conjectural. A poorly administered exemption system does increase the social cost of the tax system by decreasing taxpayer confidence and morale. Evaluations of the administration of operative exemption schemes yield the usual differences of opinion.[8] However, even the critics generally do not condemn the idea of tax exemption on administrative grounds alone:[9]

This "graveyard digging" in the administrative law of industrial-tax-exemption indicates that the administration of this instrument of fiscal policy

[8] For example, compare Bhatia, "Tax Exemption," p. 348, (who admits difficulty but says tax exemption is easier to administer than many other laws); Sanford A. Mosk, *Industrial Revolution in Mexico*, p. 196, (who sees administrative abuses but who sees still greater benefits); and Taylor, *Industrial Tax-Exemption in Puerto Rico*, p. 147, (who says administration of such a law is "inordinately difficult," "inconsistent," and "deleterious").

[9] Taylor, *Industrial Tax-Exemption in Puerto Rico,* p. 67.

has been considerably below a desirable standard of performance. The administrative officers, of course, are not wholly at fault; more properly, it has been "Grade C" administration of a "Grade D" statute. There is also the likelihood that many of the problems encountered are indigenous to the use of the tax-exemption device itself, and these would remain regardless of the levels of legislative and administrative efforts. These explanations, however, do not detract from the patent need for increasing the amount spent on administration, for constant and patient effort toward improvement, and for a stable, consistent, and impartial administrative policy.

CONCLUSION

Tax exemption can be a potent instrument of economic policy. It is generally more powerful, however, in influencing the character of investment than it is in increasing total investment. That is, it is especially useful in diverting resources from a less desired to a more desired use. In the present setting of many Latin American republics, the tax exemptions granted to specified industrial ventures do little more than equalize the unjustified, but time-honored, tax preference extended many forms of relatively nonproductive investment. In these countries, at the existing levels of taxation, it seems probable that a more appropriate alternative to tax exemption consists of increasing taxes on the gains from less desirable uses of resources.

Tax concessions must be used with real discretion because of the latent limitations inherent in this incentive device. The stimulation of business ventures destined to collapse at the expiration of the exemption period does little for the realization of development aspirations. The creation of vested interests, undermining of taxpayer morale, and featherbedding of select industries—all real possibilities with a poorly administered tax-exemption law—are also inimical to economic growth. The loss in tax equity is another real cost of a tax concession. Even "successful" tax exemption is not truly satisfactory if it is successful only from a myopic point of view. The advantage gained by one member country of the Alliance for Progress may be nullified by the loss of another. In short, before the underdeveloped countries become hypnotized by the "free" benefits promised them via industrial tax-exemption schemes, they should be encouraged to investigate alternative courses of action.

The stimulation of industry may indeed be necessary for the attainment of real economic growth in many countries. At least in those countries whose economic development plans postulate this, the question of primary importance is how can industry be given the greatest boost? For example, as an alternative to industrial-tax exemption, increased taxation of nonproductive investment combined with a government-financed expansion of public utility, transportation, communication, and irrigation facilities, may be equally effective in encouraging industrial development. If these facilities are already provided in satisfactory quantity and quality, then direct subsidies (grants), long-term, low-interest loans, or the underwriting of losses might also prove superior to tax exemption as incentive devices. Foreign private investment would most likely increase if political instability, currency restrictions, and expropriation dangers (real or imagined) were reduced.

All of these alternatives can be preferred to tax-exemption schemes both because they are of general benefit to virtually all residents of the country and because they bring the beneficiary's preferred position more clearly into focus. A few, restricted tax incentives might be advantageously included in a well-considered development plan. The granting of generous loss carry-back and carry-forward provisions, accelerated depreciation methods, and preferential rates for reinvested profits, are three of the most desirable possibilities. These three serve to decrease the investor's risk and/or increase the availability of investment capital at minimum social cost.

8. Tax Administration

As noted in Chapter 4, improvements in tax administration represent the most crucial form of tax reform for the immediate future in many of the Latin American republics. All too often tax-reform discussions turn immediately to the need for a new and a more progressive tax structure, ignoring the administrative inadequacies of the existing system. Individuals working with the Alliance for Progress must understand the great danger inherent in that kind of reform thinking. No tax law, however well devised, can be satisfactory in the absence of an adequate administration. Generally, the existing tax systems of Latin America would prove much less undesirable if they were properly administered. An improvement in tax administration would also probably increase revenues significantly.[1]

The term "tax administration" is a broad, generic term encompassing many individually complicated subjects. It refers to the various aspects of taxation on the operational level. The purpose of this chapter is to consider briefly those aspects of the Latin American tax administrations most frequently in need of reform. The discussion is divided into legal factors, accounting considerations, personnel problems, administrative techniques, and enforcement attitudes.

In the area of administrative techniques in particular, the Latin Americans can learn a good deal from each other. Because of the existing social institutions common to many of the countries south of the Rio Grande, early efforts for progressive taxation necessarily incorporate numerous techniques of tax administration that are quite unlike those adopted in most economically advanced nations. Perhaps no effort could be more rewarding to the underdeveloped countries as a

[1] For example, on attaining power in Argentina the Frondizi regime eliminated selected export and import taxes and was still able to increase tax revenues in 1960 by 54%. The increased revenue is seemingly attributable to better enforcement efforts alone.

group than the promotion of research into this area of tax administration, and the eventual establishment of a common-knowledge pool, in the form of a technical tax library, specifically applied to the problems of taxation in developing countries.

LEGAL FACTORS

The most important legal aspect of administrative tax reforms is the need for a written summarization of the multiplicity of existing tax laws. The codification, into a single law, of the most important revenue provisions would, of course, be extremely beneficial to an improved tax administration. However, even a separate codification of each of the many laws, and the collection of a written compilation of existing decrees, interpretations, and opinions, into some formal system of tax regulations, would prove very helpful. In conjunction with the work of codifying the tax laws, these countries should also simplify their existing tax systems by consolidating the multiple taxes imposed on an essentially identical tax base, and by abandoning other revenue laws of only minor significance. Without such a simplification, and the reduction of tax laws to writing, self-compliance can never be a real possibility.

In the preparation of tax codes and tax regulations, particular care should be taken to explicitly define many tax terms. The following terms, common to the income tax, are illustrative of those widely used in Latin America and elsewhere with less than uniform meaning: "taxable income," "income source," "gross revenue (or income)," "net revenue (or income)," "abatement," "allowance," "credit," "deduction," "exclusion," and "exemption." Agency efforts to achieve a uniformity of terminology among all the Latin American republics would be highly desirable.

Once the tax laws are codified and simplified, they should be publicized. Simply written instructions should be made available to every taxpayer. The printed instructions and publicity programs need, of course, to be provided at public expense. Magazines and newspapers, radio and television, high schools and colleges, and business and labor groups should all be used as sounding boards for the revised tax system. In no other manner can these governments convince the public that they are entering into a new era of taxation. Corrective administrative action and general publicity programs need to be followed immediately by effective compliance efforts. Taxpayers need to be made to appreciate the essential role of taxes in their own economic development aspirations.

It is equally imperative that the reformed tax system of Latin America include free or very inexpensive litigation procedures. Taxes can no longer be used for political or personal reasons if they are to play a central role in economic development. The adjudication of tax matters has also to be accomplished with a minimum of delay.

A final consideration of the legal aspects of tax administration to be mentioned here concerns international tax agreements. If Latin America is to grow as an area, many legal problems in international taxation will necessarily need to be solved. Among the most important are the determination of tax jurisdiction over foreign-source income. The verification of deductible expenses incurred outside the taxing country, and the deductibility of foreign taxes, are two other important problems. The proper handling of "excused" taxes is yet another stumbling block in successful international taxation. The definitions of nationality, citizenship, residence, and domicile are also important. Multilateral action has never become popular in this important area. In its absence, increased legal activity in attaining bilateral tax agreements becomes mandatory.[2]

ACCOUNTING CONSIDERATIONS

Accounting is related to successful tax administration in at least two ways. First, the use of net income as a tax base presupposes the existence of reasonably reliable and verifiable accounting records, maintained on the basis of some generally accepted principles and applied on a consistent basis.[3] Second, the availability of "registered" accountants (whose competence has been verified) can promote a higher degree of

[2] The first international tax agreement was between Belgium and France, dated August 12, 1843. This and other international tax agreements have been collected by the United Nations in *International Tax Agreements*.

[3] This does not mean that "net income" must be defined identically for tax and for accounting purposes. It does, however, mean that the two measures must be sufficiently similar that records maintained for managerial purposes can in large part be used for tax matters, and that any differences between the two are readily reconcilable. In Brazil, the starting point for the determination of taxable income actually is accounting or book profits. In that kind of system it is, of course, particularly important that generally accepted accounting standards exist. See Harvard Law School International Program in Taxation, *World Tax Series: Taxation in Brazil*, p. 55.

taxpayer compliance and can facilitate the administrative proceedings inevitably enveloped in any comprehensive tax system.[4]

In many of the Latin American countries, accounting principles or standards and accounting techniques are legislated as part of the Commercial Code. This tendency is generally undesirable since new and superior methods of accounting are constantly evolving; and even generally accepted accounting principles change with the passage of time. The codification of these accounting principles and practices makes them unduly brittle.[5] In a few countries, in the total absence of an accounting profession and, therefore, of generally accepted accounting principles, the legislation of minimum accounting standards and techniques may be necessary during the earliest stages of development. With economic growth, however, professionally developed standards and techniques should be accepted for most tax purposes. For example, the adoption of the accrual method of accounting, and the use of fiscal years, other-than-straight-line depreciation, and bad-debt estimates should be acceptable accounting for income-tax purposes in all but the least developed countries.

The development of a corps of professional accountants may also promote a higher degree of taxpayer compliance and may simplify the government's administrative task. The objectives can be achieved if the government requires that private business firms have independent, qualified accountants verify the accuracy of the financial statements and/or tax returns the firms' private accountants prepare. In order reasonably to assure itself of the absence of undue collusion between the taxpayer and the independent accountant, the government should re-

[4] It is conceivable that this function could be adequately handled by members of the legal profession. If so, however, they would have to have a much greater appreciation of accounting conventions than is normal for most lawyers. Even when both professions are well developed, successful taxation requires a specially educated bar.

[5] Even the relatively "developed" countries of Brazil, Chile, Colombia, Mexico, and Venezuela legislate some accounting requirements. Ofttimes compliance with these obsolete legal provisions unnecessarily requires the maintenance of two sets of records. For example, the Commercial Code of Brazil, dating to 1850, requires businessmen to maintain a journal, cash-sales register, sales-tax-stamp register, register of customers' signed accounts, inventory register, purchase register, and a press-copy letter book, all duly-authenticated by tax stamps. The press-copy letter book is "a file of all letters sent out by the taxpayer together with the invoices, statements of account, and other data which accompanied those letters" (see Harvard Law School International Program in Taxation, *Taxation in Brazil*, pp. 113–114).

tain the right to certify or register the qualified accountant, as well as to impose a fine on him for fraudulently certifying the accuracy of a financial report.[6]

In 1960, Mexico passed what could be considered model legislation in this area. The new law provides that all taxpayers with an annual income exceeding 10 million pesos ($800,640) must employ certified public accountants to approve their balance sheet, tax return and so forth.[7] All such returns are not subject to further audit by the government, except by way of spot checks. If the CPA is related to the taxpayer, or if they are financially associated, the accountant's approval will be disregarded and the Federal Fiscal Auditing Bureau will conduct a separate audit. Taxpayers with income of less than 10 million pesos may also use the CPA's services, at their option, and thereby avoid a Bureau audit.

If a Bureau spot check discloses an irregularity and subsequent tax evasion, the CPA's name is removed from the approved register. When warranted, the attorney general may further institute criminal action against the accountant. Professional societies are also notified of the government action so that they may suspend the accountant's membership.

In recognition of the salutary effect that a well-established accounting profession can have on the tax administration, the governments of the developing countries would be well advised to (1) recruit highly

[6] For example, in Chile an accountant can be fined up to 20,000 pesos for certifying an inaccurate financial statement (this is a new provision, adopted in Law No. 2410, April 1962). In Brazil, the accountant is held jointly liable with the taxpayer for any incorrect or irregular financial statement (see Harvard Law School International Program in Taxation, *Taxation in Brazil*, p. 254.

[7] The CPA-audited return in Mexico includes a balance sheet; a profit-and-loss statement for this and the previous three periods, including any necessary explanatory notes; a special report stating the taxpayer's compliance with tax obligations; a statement that the audit was made in accordance with generally accepted auditing practices (appropriate to the circumstances) and that the statements comply with generally accepted accounting principles applied consistently with the preceding period; a statement of changes in capital; if a commercial or industrial firm, a cost analysis of volume related to the last three periods; a reconciliation of book and taxable income; a statement of fiscal obligations the taxpayer paid or remains liable for, including the income-tax base; a statement of changes in accounting practices; and a statement of changes in the reserves for bad debts, depreciation, *etc*. For greater detail, see the 1961 supplement to the Harvard Law School International Program in Taxation, *World Tax Series: Taxation in Mexico*, pp. 63–64.

qualified instructors and accounting students; (2) tighten requirements for registering or certifying accountants; and (3) enact regulative legislation, similar to that of Mexico.

PERSONNEL POLICIES

The historical shortcomings of many Latin American tax administrations can be attributed to poor personnel policies rather than the unavailability of competent officials. In several countries, there simply is no governmental career civil service. Far too much of government employment remains in the realm of spoils politics. Oftimes the military service provides whatever stability exists.

Tax-administration personnel are often grossly underpaid and poorly trained, and tax departments are typically understaffed. In addition to being underpaid, tax officials' salaries are not infrequently partially or wholly dependent upon the taxes or fines collected. Under such circumstances, it is difficult for the tax official to remain entirely unbiased in his work. The net result is an unnecessary lessening of public respect for the tax law. Countries that insist upon paying tax officials from such a revenue pool should, at a minimum, make the pool a general source of funds for all personnel associated in any way with tax administration, and should disassociate any particular contribution to the pool from any particular payment from it.

Training standards for administrative personnel can be greatly increased as written tax regulations become available in the developing country. Formal training programs and workshop seminars should be immediately arranged at both high and low operational levels. Chile's newly initiated Training School for Internal Revenue Service Personnel, at both the beginning and supervisory levels, could well be duplicated by many other nations. Carefully selected top-level personnel should be sent abroad to study other countries' tax systems, do research on needed changes at home, and aid in the drafting of tax recommendations in the future. The joint U.N.-Harvard Program in International Taxation is an example of the kind of study that ought to be fostered. Because of the greater comparability of the size and complexity of the tax systems, foreign tax experts visiting the United States may wish to study state and local tax organizations, as well as the federal Internal Revenue Service operation.

Generally the staff of the revenue administration should be greatly increased in the Latin American republics.[8] This will be even more true as tax-reform measures are implemented. In addition to increasing the size of the staff, the entire staff of tax auditors, inspectors, agents, and other tax experts should be given job security (tenure) and autonomy from political interference. Their powers should also be made quite broad—especially in respect to the investigative and auditing functions —if their labors are to be successful. As Mr. Kaldor has observed, the revenue service is the logical origin for the creation of a career civil service:[9]

the experience of many countries which suffered from much the same evils in the past shows that corruption and inefficiency can be eradicated if sufficient attention is given to the creation of corps of permanent officials whose pay, status and prospects of promotion are high enough to attract the best talent, and also high enough to establish the professional standards and etiquette associated with a public service that enjoys a privileged social status. The example of the Chinese Maritime Customs has shown what the creation of a well-paid body of permanent officials could accomplish, even in a country where corruption was as deeply ingrained as it was in Imperial China. Of course no underdeveloped country has the manpower resources or the money to create a high-grade civil service overnight. But it is not sufficiently recognized that the revenue service is the "point of entry"; if they concentrated on this, they would secure the means for the rest.

AID and other agencies can be of great help to the developing nation's tax administration through the provision of technical-training assistance (both in the developing country and abroad), the provision of necessary equipment, the introduction of improved tax methods and procedures, and so on. Efforts in these functional areas seemingly

[8] The Taxpayer Investigation Department of the Venezuelan Income Tax Administration employed approximately 50 field men in 1957 (they hope to increase this to approximately 110 men soon). Because of the manpower shortage, the Maracaibo office staff members were forced to concentrate their attentions on nine large taxpayers during the year. At one time, however, they were able to "borrow" several agents from the Caracas office. They sent these men into the streets to discover taxpayers not filing returns. In a relatively short time, they "brought in about 1200 additional declarations, sometimes as many as five from one taxpayer. About one-fourth of the additional declarations arose from the investigation of persons dealing with or working for the nine large taxpayers investigated." Commission to Study the Fiscal System of Venezuela, *The Fiscal System of Venezuela*, p. 193.

[9] Nicholas Kaldor, "Will Underdeveloped Countries Learn to Tax?" *Foreign Affairs*, XLI (January 1963), 417.

would be appreciated by any country honestly seeking development, because these efforts are likely to yield immediate and appreciable results.

ADMINISTRATIVE TECHNIQUES

No aspect of taxation is ordinarily given less attention than the administrative techniques, or mundane procedures, necessary to implement even the most profound tax law. Nevertheless, no other aspect of taxation could be of greater significance to the ultimate success or failure of a tax law enacted under the social institutions common to most developing nations. The following paragraphs are intended to suggest just a few of the administrative techniques that have contributed to the early success of income taxation under less than ideal conditions. All of the techniques discussed below were drawn from an existing tax system of one of the Latin American nations. A pooling of all the experience in this vital area could contribute significantly to the success of tax-reform efforts now being considered by the Alliance-for-Progress nations.

The "Greater-Lesser" Idea

There is no more similarity between the operations of, say, a small local retail store and the giant department store of the metropolis than there is between the typical *campesino* (peasant farmer) and the *hacendado* (plantation owner) in Latin America. In recognition of these very real differences, the laws of some countries provide a different tax treatment for the "lesser" and the "greater" taxpayer, where the definition of each group is based upon the income earned.

Mexico has developed the "lesser-greater" technique rather thoroughly. There, all taxpayers reporting income under Schedules I, II, or III (commerce, industry, or agriculture) must comply with the "greater" taxpayer requirements if their annual income is 300,000 pesos ($24,019) or more, and with the "lesser" taxpayer requirements if their annual income is less than 300,000 pesos. The most important differences between the two groups can be summarized as follows:[10]

[10] The interested reader can find these differences described in much greater detail in the Harvard Law School International Program in Taxation, *Taxation in Mexico*, pp. 58–59, and in the 1961 supplement thereto, p. 4. For a description of the very complete accounting system demanded of the "greater" income taxpayers, see pp. 121–126. For similar options for income earned by professional persons (and reported in Schedule V), see pp. 189, 284–285.

Tax Requirement	"Lesser" Group	"Greater" Group
Tax Base	Gross income	Net income
Accounting	Simple cash book	A proper accounting system
Computation	From one of seven tables	Computed by taxpayer
Period	Calendar year only	Calendar or fiscal year
Return	Highly simplified form	Relatively complex form, and numerous financial statements required to support the tax return.

Distinctions of this variety can indeed be justified in most of the developing countries. As social institutions change—as illiteracy is reduced, accounting records are improved, and so on—tax distinctions should also be reduced. Generally the income limit defining the "greater" taxpayer should be set relatively high during the earliest stages of growth, and subsequently reduced until, eventually, the differences become extinct. In some cases, the "lesser" taxpayers should be given the option of choosing the "greater" taxpayer treatment.

Assumptions and Presumptions

Many taxpayers are incapable of complying with the fiscal requirements of modern tax systems. Other taxpayers willfully evade the same fiscal requirements. In any case where no return, an incorrect return, or an unsubstantiated return is filed, it is necessary for the government to estimate the taxable income. Especially in the case of willful evasion, the normal procedure calls for using whatever records are available and estimating only those figures that cannot be determined more precisely. In other cases, the government may be forced to estimate the entire taxable income. The following list includes just a few examples of the taxable-income assumptions made in various Latin American republics.

Country	Assumption
Brazil	Re agricultural income—if inadequate books are kept, the government presumes the net income reportable in Schedule G is equal to 5% of the value of the taxpayer's land, pastures, buildings, other improvements, equipment and machinery, permanent crops, and animals.
Chile	Re income of professional men—for the person practicing his profession for over two but less than five years, the government presumes an income equal to two times the annual living wage (a figure deter-

mined annually by the government); if between 5 and 10 years, 6 times the annual living wage; if between 10 and 35 years, 8 times this amount; and if over 35 years, 4 times the same figure.

Dominican Republic Re wages, salaries, and other personal emoluments— the government may presume a net taxable income equal to three times the rental paid for work space and living quarters.

Uruguay Re agricultural income—the government may presume a net taxable income of $80 per hectare (or more in some cases).

Venezuela Re international transportation companies—the government may presume a net income equal to 10 percent of the sum of gross receipts for intra-Venezuela transportation plus 50 percent of the gross receipts from service between Venezuela and any other country.

The adequacy of these and the many other assumptions made in Latin America concerning taxable income depends upon the size of the variance between the estimated and the real income. The tax administration must constantly strive to maintain as realistic an estimate as is possible, and it should change the estimating procedure whenever it is apparent that the basis of the estimate is no longer satisfactory. In general when an assumption is made for an individual earning a relatively high level of income, the assumption should be made unfavorable to the taxpayer in order to encourage him to develop a sound basis for determining his real (unassumed) taxable income. In every case, of course, the assumed method should not be used if a better basis actually exists. And once a taxpayer has complied with more formal requirements, he should never be permitted to revert to an estimated basis; or, if he does, it should be possible only at the premium of a penalty tax rate.

"Pay-As-You-Go"

A third administrative technique that aids in successful taxation, under less than ideal conditions, involves a "pay-as-you-go" approach. This may be accomplished either through periodic tax deposits or through withholding. This technique has attained its widest use (even in the well-developed countries) in connection with the withholding of taxes from wage and salary payments. In the developing nations, the withholding tax is often deemed to satisfy wholly the employees' income-tax obligation, at least as applied to the low-income earner. That is, no further payment is required of him; no refund is available to him; and no return need be filed by him. The inequity of such a system is not unduly great for persons with a relatively stable income in countries where virtually no deductions for personal expenses are accepted for tax purposes and where tax rates are kept at reasonably low levels. In order to increase the equity of the system, however, it may be advisable to permit the taxpayer to file for a tax refund whenever this system of withholding results in an overstatement of his annual tax liability by, say, 10–15 percent.

Other common pay-as-you-go schemes involve the withholding of tax on lottery payments; on dividend payments made to owners of bearer shares; and on nearly all payments to foreign companies or in-dividuals. It is also common to require commercial and industrial firms to pay an estimated tax three or four times per year, and to adjust their actual tax liability and their estimated payments in an annual return.

The "Brother's Keeper" Notion

Tax withholding is extended beyond the traditional limits in some Latin nations in what might be described as a "brother's keeper" no-tion. The basic idea is that almost any payer—not just an employer, bank, or large corporation—can be made responsible for withholding part of a payment to another to assure that the recipient pays his tax obligation. Under certain circumstances the payor may be relieved of this obligation if the payee proves to him that he was a regular taxpayer in the previous year (the proof may be a specifically prepared form or a certified copy of the last tax return).

Once again, it is in Mexico that this administrative technique can be found in its most developed form. For example, Mexican law re-quires that anyone paying a broker's commission withhold and remit directly to the government 20 percent of the gross commission unless the recipient broker proves (with his prior year's income-tax return) that he is a regular Schedule I taxpayer. Withholding is also required of anyone making a payment to a nonresident, to an "occasional" agent or commission agent, to independent professionals, and to a stock-breeder, and on any collection or payment for a third party and pay-ment for the use of capital. Generally the payor is required to notify the tax-collector's office of the transaction and to make payment via an attachment of revenue stamps. If he fails to do this, the payor may be jointly liable for the payee's tax liability on the transaction. Alternatively, the payor may be denied a tax deduction for an expense he has incurred unless he remits the tax or states the name and address of the payee who has proved his regular taxpayer status.

Automatic Data Processing

It seems almost incongruous that anyone would recommend the combination of a slow and often hoary tax administration with an amazingly fleet and efficacious automatic-data-processing (ADP) system. Nevertheless, the last two techniques discussed suggest the need for precisely that kind of union. If great numbers of individuals are going to be made responsible for the withholding from and/or reporting of income payments made to other individuals or firms, it is mandatory that these remittances and reports be rapidly credited to the recipient's "tax account." Without ADP, such a task is virtually insuperable; with ADP and a numerical taxpayer identification system, the task is only moderately difficult.

In many countries, important information for tax purposes already is available in nonrevenue departments of the government. If this information could but be collated with tax returns, a tremendous improvement in tax administration could be anticipated. For example, municipalities might prepare lists of licenses issued, property taxes paid, and property sales completed; banks might prepare lists of interest paid, currency purchased, and bonds purchased; legal departments might prepare lists of corporate charters granted, stock and bond issues approved, and building permits endorsed. The ADP system informed of these facts could rapidly collect, store, and relate information, and duplicate it in any form necessary to best implement the tax laws.

Certainly the adoption of an ADP system requires advance preparation. Technicians trained in systems analysis and computer programming become essential. Even more important is the need of an imaginative appreciation of the opportunities presented for effective tax administration. Given these prerequisites, however, automatic data processing may hold tremendous potential for the developing nation. Indeed, it may be the best possible way to solve the current revenue-administration manpower shortage. The availability of such a system would concurrently go a long way in solving the historical shortage of reliable statistics. A small national could even consider the use of a single ADP system jointly with another country.

The author was pleasantly surprised to discover that Venezuela already has employed both a numerical taxpayer-identification system and several IBM machines in its tax administration. In fact, in Venezuela, these machines are used to print all tax bills in eight copies; to calculate taxable income and tax liabilites for the simpler returns; to print names, addresses, and identifying numbers for mailing; and so on.[11] Other Latin American republics would be well advised to study this or another similar operation for possible adaptations in their own countries.

Tax Certificates

Another procedure that has proven of real benefit to tax administration in the developing country is the requiring of a "tax certificate" for any of several actions a taxpayer may wish to undertake. The procedure is very simple. The certificate is granted to any citizen or resident upon his payment of a tax obligation. A display of the certificate is, in turn, required whenever the individual might request a passport, apply for a license or permit, use a credit institution, or request a notarization.

Since 1955 Venezuela has issued just such a certificate, called a "Certificate of Solvency," through her Income Tax Administration. She requires that this certificate be displayed for most of the transactions suggested in the previous paragraph. Chile also requires a taxpayer to prove his payment of taxes before he is permitted to engage in numerous similar transactions. However, Chile has not yet devised a formal certificate to serve as proof of tax payment. Mexico has a slightly different requirement. There, public notaries and special notaries for commercial matters "are required to demand proof from the parties who execute deeds or other documents before them that they are not in arrears with their income tax obligations . . . If a party states that he is not a taxpayer, the notary must point out the penalties attaching to a false statement and must incorporate the statement in the document that he authenticates."[12] If the party informs the notary that either he owes income tax, he is not a taxpayer, or his tax liability is entirely

[11] Commission to Study the Fiscal System of Venezuela, *The Fiscal System of Venezuela*, pp. 176–190.

[12] Harvard Law School International Program in Taxation, *Taxation in Mexico*, p. 295.

satisfied through withholding, the notary can authenticate the document, but he then must notify the Ministry of Finance of these facts.

Other Techniques

There are innumerable other administrative techniques currently in use in one or more of the Latin American countries that might prove both interesting and beneficial to other countries if they were but aware of them. For example, Colombia requires that all claims for personal exemptions be supported by "certification by two honorable neighbors." The certificate must signify the number, degree of relationship, and ability of the dependent to support himself. Chile gives the "tax tipster" (one who informs the government of another's failure to comply with legal provisions) 20 percent of the delinquent tax collected plus 50 percent of the fine imposed. Another country uses private firms to make field surveys of incomes earned since private firms were able to get more information than government agencies performing similar investigations.

In short, the Latin American republics can learn a great deal from each other about how they can best implement the new tax laws they are now demanding. In many cases the operational techniques used by more economically advanced nations are nontransferable.

TAX ENFORCEMENT

The first step in effective tax enforcement is a sound detection system. The most experienced and capable men of the tax administration should be used to select, examine, and investigate those tax returns that must be processed further than a routine review. The first selection can generally be best accomplished through an office examination which, at least in the case of the numerous smaller returns, must be based upon a random selection method. Those returns that appear questionable should then be returned for a field audit that will involve direct communication with the taxpayer.

It is important that the field examiner identify the cause for noncompliance. The error attributable to ignorance should, especially during the early period of tax reform, be treated much more leniently than the error intentionally or fraudulently committed. In the first years it is also important that a limited number of clear cases of tax evasion be developed, that the maximum fines be imposed, and that wide publicity be given to the event. The compliance and deterrent effects of such action would be substantial in all of Latin America. Not too long ago a businessman made history in Chile by being brought before the courts for tax evasion. Because it was the first action of its kind ever taken, it has had a profound effect there.[13]

Latin Americans have historically eschewed tax enforcement. In most countries, what penalties exist are restricted to economic sanctions; prison terms are simply not deemed an appropriate penalty for tax evasion. A recent change in this attitude is detectible. In Mexico and Brazil it is now possible for a taxpayer to be imprisoned for a willful or fraudulent alteration of tax information. In Chile (since April 1962), a citizen can now be imprisoned for the failure to comply within fifteen days, with the Director General's notice to present a tax return. In many other countries, similar changes presumably will not be forthcoming for some time, and probably will not be enforced for even a longer time.[14] It is important, therefore, that economic sanctions be adequate to fit the crime and yet enforce the law.

Fines can generally be made appropriate for such lesser fiscal violations as the failure to file a return within the alloted time, for maintaining inadequate records, or for failure to withhold tax. For more serious offenses, such as the falsification of information or the refusal to obey tax officials, relatively heavy penalties are essential. In order to minimize political interference, it is best if the penalties imposed permit a minimum of administrative leeway. Each county must determine a proper but effective penalty system that will be acceptable to the majority of its citizens. All penalties should be as simple as possible and publicized to the maximum extent. They must never be used for political purposes. Penalties that effectively relieve the taxpayer of his right to conduct business generally, as is accomplished through a "Certificate of Solvency" requirement, have been found very effective.

[13] As reported by Teodoro Moscoso, the U.S. Latin American Area Administrator, "Progress Report on the Alliance for Progress," *New York Times Magazine*, August 12, 1962, p. 60.

[14] Israel has recently experienced the problems of tax enforcement. Even after a major publicity campaign, the lower courts were reluctant to enforce penalties imposed for evasion of the newly revised tax system. However, after several decisions were reversed by the higher courts, and serious penalties were imposed, the lower courts and the general public finally accepted both the tax laws and the enforcement procedures.

SUMMARY

Since no tax law, regardless of how well it is devised, can operate satisfactorily in the absence of a good administrative system, it is imperative that the developing nations direct a large part of their first efforts in tax reform to administrative problems. The major problems in tax administration differ notably between the underdeveloped and the developed nations. In many developing nations, including several in Latin America, a necessary first-step is the compilation of a written code of the basic tax law, and the related decrees and regulations. The multiplicity of the existing tax laws should be simplified and the revised regulations should be made available to both tax administrators and the general public.

Another step necessary in most of these countries involves the upgrading of the operating personnel. First, their selection should be based on ability; their position should be made secure; and their pay and social position should be increased to a level befitting the importance of the work they perform. After the training programs are improved, the personnel should be given greater authority and be freed of political intervention. Improvements in equipment, even to the addition of automatic-data-processing systems, may be a requisite to attaining the level of proficiency needed in the revenue departments.

As a concurrent effort in upgrading the revenue service, it is mandatory that the Latin American nations publicize their new tax laws and tax systems so that the taxpayer might appreciate the nature and extent of his fiscal responsibility. The necessity of the tax system to economic development aspirations needs also to be explained. Appropriate penalties need to be imposed upon those who fail to comply with the tax law. Publicity of the penalties imposed for willful tax evasion should be widespread. Any corruption and fraud existing within the tax system should be exposed and eradicated immediately. In order to gain maximum self-compliance, a reasonable share of the increased tax revenues might be devoted to public projects clearly of benefit to the local community.

The social institutions existing within the Latin American nations are typically more comparable to each other than they are to those institutions existing within the economically advanced nations of Western Europe and North America. Consequently, the tax techniques necessary to implement the progressive tax systems now demanded by the developing nations can best be adopted from the experience of those similarly situated countries that have already imposed progressive taxes successfully. In this important area of tax administration, the Latin American countries can learn a great deal from each other. The experience of Brazil, Chile, Colombia, and Mexico is particularly instructive. The tax techniques described in this chapter are illustrative of what can be done to make progressive taxation successful under less-than-ideal conditions.

9. Findings and Recommendations

The aspirations of approximately 200 million Latin Americans, scattered over 8 million square miles, are succinctly asserted in the Alliance for Progress. The realization of these aspirations depends partially upon the availability of external financial and technical assistance. Of much greater import, however, is the necessity that these people and their governments consummate numerous and far-reaching reforms of institutions that have inhibited economic development for centuries.

In the Alliance for Progress, the United States promises to make available to the Latin American republics marginal financial assistance to the extent of $20 billion, over a ten-year period. The international agencies and the more economically developed nations are expected to stand ready to provide necessary technical assistance. The crucial question is, therefore, whether or not the Latin American nations are able and willing to make the far-reaching reforms demanded of them. In an apparent effort to assure positive action on this front, the formation of an economic development plan, the initiation of tax-reform efforts, and similar endeavors have been made the *quid pro quo* for external financial assistance.

Consequently, a decisive factor in the proper administration of the Alliance for Progress concerns the form and the extent of the action necessary to satisfy this prerequisite to the granting of external financial aid. Relative to tax reform in particular, a great diversity of opinion exists. The typical sentiment in this country seems to be that great strides in tax reforms are essential to the success of the Alliance program and that it is incumbent upon the United States to withhold the granting of external financial aid until the reforms are well under way. The following words of Stephen Raushenbush, an administrator with a background of first-hand knowledge of the Latin American situation, are illustrative:[1]

If the United States stands firm, as it should, on the Punta del Este agreement, and insists upon tax reform, not simply in legislative form but in practice, and makes the reason for withholding its funds public and clear, then these responsible men may prevail over the others, and heavier taxes may be imposed. If it does not stand firm, then United States money will simply be taking the place of deserting local money, and the Alliance will not achieve its goals.

The Latin Americans, on the other hand, stress the undeniable fact that social institutions, including tax systems, are deeply rooted and that it is unrealistic to assume that reform efforts can be implemented either immediately or even within a single decade. The words of Roberto de Oliveira Campos, the Brazilian Ambassador to the United States, are typical of this sentiment:[2]

A vigilant attitude of policing and reproach to underdeveloped countries for their shortcomings in the implementation of plans and programs, often ignores political realities and presupposes, on the part of the developing countries, a degree of rationality that they could have only if they were not underdeveloped socially and institutionally. Holding back aid because of the non-existence of the so-called prerequisites would thus be self-defeating, impairing the possibility of the attainment of the very objectives at which we aim.

In the opinion of this author, an intermediate position is defensible. The enactment of a poorly studied or of a hurriedly drafted tax code would not constitute the type of permanent reform the Alliance seeks to induce. Indeed, the very determination of and drafting of a truly sound tax system is contingent upon the execution of an intensive and time-consuming country-study. In most of the Latin American republics, studies of this variety are not—or at least were not at the time the Charter of Punta del Este was signed—in existence or even contemplated. The continuing need for them can hardly be overestimated.

On the other hand, the urgency of the growing demands for economic betterment, human dignity, and political freedom is so great that

---

[1] Stephen Raushenbush, *The Challenge to the Alliance for Progress,* pamphlet, p. 51.

[2] From a speech by Ambassador Roberto de Oliveira Campos to the National Conference on International Economic and Social Development held at the Palmer House, Chicago, Illinois, July 19, 1962.

the implementation of the Alliance program cannot await the fruition of such detailed studies. The objective of this monograph is, therefore, to suggest some practical guidelines for tax-reform efforts in the interim period. It is an attempt to harmonize tax policy with economic development goals, within the realistic constraints of the existing social institutions of Latin America.

Some form of tax reform is essential. If the external financial aid provided in the Alliance were primarily employed to accomplish social change (or as it is alternately labeled, "the reform-redistribution-welfare complex"), there would be little reason to anticipate any long-run improvement in Latin American conditions. A lasting basis for improvement can, in the opinion of this author, only be achieved if the external aid is in large part devoted to economic development, including industrialization. Therefore the social change of necessity remains to be serviced largely by local currency. In most countries this, in turn, means that taxes must be increased. The findings stated below establish the basis for the tax-reform configuration recommended in the closing pages of this project.

FINDINGS

The most important findings of this monograph can be divided into five broad categories. The first category concerns findings relative to the tax-reform objectives associated with the Alliance for Progress. The second category concerns findings relative to the aggregate fiscal systems as they currently exist in the Latin American republics. The third category concerns findings relative to the individual taxes. The other two categories concern tax-exemption schemes and tax administration.

Tax-Reform Objectives

The generally-accepted objectives for tax-reform efforts initiated in conjunction with the Alliance for Progress can be restated as follows:

1. An increase in tax revenues in order that more resources be made available for increased capital formation;

2. An improvement in tax equity, which is defined as a more progressive tax system, or as "demanding more from those who have most";

3. The provision of incentives to encourage the improved use of

land, to promote saving and the investment of capital, and to facilitate industrial expansion.

The first two of the three stated objectives are clearly judged of paramount importance by both the framers of the Alliance and those assigned the task of implementing it. A review of the existing fiscal scene suggests that in many of the Latin American countries a very real potential exists for attaining these objectives.

Existing Tax Systems

In recent years the ratio of tax revenues to gross national product, for the Latin American nations as a group, is estimated to be somewhere between 10 and 12 percent. Although there are many valid reasons to justify a relatively low ratio in the developing nations, some potential for increased tax revenues remains. In the more economically advanced countries the same ratio is typically between 25 and 35 percent.

The best available estimates suggest that for Latin America as a whole, 20–25 percent of the tax revenues come from income taxes; 70–75 percent from sales, excise, import, and export taxes; and 0–10 percent from property and other taxes. Statistics for individual countries deviate significantly from these average figures. In some of the larger and more diversified economies, income taxes already account for between 30 and 40 percent of total tax revenues.

Tax collection is predominantly a function of the central-level government in Latin America. With the notable exception of three countries, what tax revenues are received by state and local governments are in large measure obtained through tax-sharing devices. Whereas this fact serves advantageously to increase the uniformity of taxation and to decrease the administrative costs, the prevalence of an antitax mentality, the slow development of community initiative, and the sparseness af administrative ability have also been attributed to it.

Particular Taxes

Most of the taxes known to mankind are utilized in one or more of the Latin American nations. Since the creation of a more progressive tax system is considered a primary objective of Alliance-prompted tax reforms, the findings related to income and wealth taxes are particularly significant. The findings relative to the sales and other indirect taxes are also important because so many of these nations derive a major part of their revenues in this manner. The following statement of findings deliberately emphasizes those aspects of the prevailing taxes that are least desirable from the standpoint of economic development and, therefore, most amenable to recommended revision in the Alliance-for-Progress setting.

Income Taxes

Every member nation of the Alliance already imposes some form of income taxation. This is fortunate since no really suitable alternative to income taxation exists; high-income earners typically purchase many things not easily taxed—*e.g.,* foreign travel, domestic service, antiques, and so forth. Consequently, if a more progressive tax system is to become reality, primary attention needs to be focused on the major weaknesses of the existing income taxes. The following seven findings relative to the income tax would appear to be of prime concern:

1. A tendency toward income-tax proliferation is apparent; *i.e.,* several presumably separate taxes are imposed upon an essentially identical tax base;

2. The liberal granting of exclusions and the accepted practices in business-income taxation unduly facilitate the wealthy taxpayer's efforts to evade truly progressive income taxation;

3. Capital gains and other income from relatively nonproductive forms of investment are generally excluded from income taxation;

4. Losses are frequently not deductible from other income in the computation of taxable income, and loss carry-back and carry-forward provisions are accepted only reluctantly or are completely disallowed;

5. The schedular system of income taxation is widely adopted and substantial variations in the schedular tax rate imposed on different "kinds" of income are common;

6. The effective income-tax rate imposed on business and industrial incomes frequently approaches the level of income taxation imposed upon similar operations in the most economically advanced nations of Western Europe and North America;

7. The effective income-tax rate on relatively large personal incomes is typically quite low in the Latin American republics.

These seven findings are, of course, neither equally characteristic of each income-tax system of the nineteen Latin American members of the Alliance for Progress nor wholly characteristic of any one of them. Collectively, however, they are symptomatic of the features most in need of the income-tax reformer's attention.

Wealth Taxes

Alternative forms of wealth taxation include the net-wealth, estate, inheritance, gift, and real-property taxes. Although a net-wealth tax is not being imposed by the vast majority of the Latin American nations today, the tax experts meeting jointly at the second Alliance-sponsored tax conference in December of 1962 agreed that ideally there should be a tax on the net wealth of individuals or families in addition to the income tax. Administrative complexities associated with this tax were recognized to be sufficiently great, however, that its immediate adoption was admitted to be outside the realm of possibility in many countries.

Because of the administrative complications and the relatively small revenue yield, death and gift taxes are often eschewed by developing countries. Nevertheless many of the Alliance-member nations formally do impose these taxes. In one of the more developed of the Latin American republics the dissatisfaction with the existing system of death taxation was so great that the inheritance tax was abolished in late 1961. Other nations retain antiquated statutes which they haphazardly enforce.

The condition of the real-property-tax laws is roughly comparable. In a growing number of these nations, however, there is an increasing awareness of the possible role of property taxes in land-reform programs. The major economic problem associated with land reform concerns the traditionally low level of productivity in the agricultural sector. The major social problem concerns the concentration of ownership in the hands of the few. Real-property taxes with progressive rate structures based on the degree of underutilization of land would seem geared to increase productivity. Real-property taxes with progressive rate structures based on the aggregate size (value) of the landholdings appear capable of contributing to the breaking up of large estates.

No real-property-tax law can be successfully implemented in Latin America, however, until several improvements are made. At present there is no complete and accurate record of land ownership in most countries; assessed valuations are notoriously understated in comparison with market values; and tax rates are distinctly on the low side. The usefulness of aerial surveys, as an aid to assessment, is a recent discovery that has not yet been more than incidentally exploited.

Other Taxes

Indirect taxes—especially sales, excise, and customs taxes—typically provide a significant portion of the total tax revenue collected by the Latin American governments. The historical explanation of this finding can be attributed to the relative ease of administering these taxes, and to the relatively small amount of political opposition they arouse. Because of the need for even larger revenues in the future, it appears improbable that the level of these taxes can be decreased in the near future. Furthermore, customs duties are ofttimes imposed primarily for trade-control reasons, and only secondarily for revenue reasons.

The distribution of the indirect taxes is virtually impossible to measure with any degree of precision. At least two separate attempts to measure statistically the progressivity of indirect taxes in Latin America led to the conclusion that some progressivity does exist up to fairly high income levels. The underlying assumptions of such a study are, of course, subject to challenge. The ability of low-income earners to remain largely outside the monetary economy, and the nearly universal acceptance of the notion that all "luxury" goods should be subject to relatively severe excise taxes in a developing nation, lend credence to the conclusions.

In the author's opinion, the finding of major significance relative to indirect taxes is the tendency of the Latin American nations to impose the transactions form of sales taxation. In several countries this multistage sales tax is imposed at substantial rates.

Tax-Exemption Schemes

At least fourteen of the nations joined in the Alliance now provide some form of tax exemption as an incentive to stimulate private industrial activity in conjunction with economic development programs. They typically provide qualifying firms with relatively broad tax exemptions for from five to ten years. Independent evaluations of those exemption schemes that have been operative for a long enough time to permit evaluations are in much less than complete accord. Planning-board members generally recommend them; external fiscal "experts" tend to deprecate them.

The fact that exemption schemes do not enter the expenditures side of the government budget increases the probability that the real cost of the exemption scheme will be underestimated. If incentive devices of this variety can be successful only from a myopic point of view, as they appear to be, then they should not be condoned as part of the Alliance-for-Progress program.

Tax Administration

The formal tax systems existing in the Latin American republics are more progressive and sophisticated than the uninformed observer is likely to surmise. Income-tax laws are operative; property-tax laws are "on the books"; and heavy excise taxes on imported articles of "luxury" consumption are not unfamiliar to millions of Latin Americans. Nevertheless, the formal existence of a pre-eminently sound tax law cannot be equated with an effective tax system. The difference lies in an inadequate administrative machine.

The inadequacy of the present tax administrations cannot be attributed to any one factor. The following findings are of principal concern:

1. Many of the basic tax laws and related decrees and regulations have neither been compiled in written form nor made generally available to either tax administrators or taxpayers;

2. Operating personnel are often political appointees and, therefore, they often are not selected on the basis of ability, trained adequately, given tenure, or paid salaries commensurate with the importance of the task assigned to them;

3. The enforcement of tax obligations is generally lax, and criminal penalties are usually believed inappropriate for tax offenses;

4. Some of the more advanced nations of Latin America have invented and implemented a host of varied techniques of tax administration that contribute significantly to their success with direct taxes under less-than-ideal conditions.

On the basis of the composite findings as stated above, the author believes it is possible to construct some general guidelines for tax-reform efforts made during the first, difficult years of the Alliance-for-Progress program. Pending the results of detailed-country tax studies, those administrators assigned the task of evaluating tax-reform efforts—as a prerequisite to approval of assistance requests—might find the following recommendations helpful.

RECOMMENDATIONS

Since no tax law, however well devised, can be effective in the absence of an adequate administrative machine—and since the tax administrations of the Latin American nations are not beyond the need for improvement—reform efforts intended to rectify administrative deficiencies should be made a universal and mandatory prerequisite to the granting of external financial aid under the Alliance for Progress. Reform actions intended to correct structural shortcomings should be encouraged on a longer-term basis.

Mandatory Tax Reforms

The precise nature of the administrative reforms that should be universally required need to vary somewhat with each applicant country. An appropriate selection from the following list of administrative recommendations could be applied to any particular case.

1. The basic tax laws should be codified and the written codes, related decrees, and regulations should be widely distributed and publicized at government expense. The various conceivable means of mass communication should be utilized to inform the taxpayer of the extent and the necessity of his fiscal obligation. Current tax rulings should also be made available to administrative personnel.

2. An applicant for financial aid should also be able to demonstrate some real improvement in tax-administration personnel policies. The institution of both low- and high-level training schools for operating personnel should be a minimum requirement of all countries. A gradual decrease in the number of political appointees, and an increase in the number of competitively selected employees in the revenue department, should remain a continuing requirement. An expansion of the revenue staff and an improvement in their remuneration could also be recommended in most countries. Pay scales ought to be divorced from tax collections made, and from fines imposed.

3. In addition, all countries desiring external financial assistance should be required to prove the presence of a fair and effective tax-enforcement system. Recent and continued action against willful tax evaders should constitute a minimum requirement. Wide publicity of the enforcement action should also be encouraged.

4. Finally, on an optional basis, the nineteen republics of Latin America should be encouraged to share their tax knowledge with each other. The sharing of the administrative techniques of successful income taxation, common to the developing nations, is of particular importance. International agencies should be encouraged to render maximum assistance in accomplishing this objective.

Desirable Tax Reforms

In addition to requiring minimum reforms of an administrative nature, aid administrators could reasonably expect each applicant country to substantiate its request for financial assistance wtih further evidence of compliance with the numerous self-help provisions of the Alliance for Progress, as stipulated in the Charter of Punta del Este, the Declaration of the Peoples of America, and the Act of Bogota. Although the following list of recommendations is by no means exhaustive, it does connote the configuration of tax-reform efforts that is conceivable within the framework of existing social institutions, and that would be consistent with the economic development aspirations common to the Latin American republics.

1. Relative to indirect taxes, the recommendation of first importance is that the multistage sales (transaction) tax be abandoned in favor of a sales tax imposed at the retail, wholesale, or manufacturers' level; or, alternatively, that a value-added tax be substituted for it.

2. Relative to wealth taxes, two recommendations can be strongly supported. First, the existing systems of inheritance and gift taxes should be strengthened—not abolished—because these taxes alone can fill a gap in the income tax system made necessary by administrative considerations. Second, real-property taxes could be drastically increased. They constitute one of the largest sources of untapped revenues in virtually all of the Latin American countries today. The ultimate success of real-property taxation depends, however, upon the ability of these countries to prepare an accurate record of property ownership and to reasonably assess market values.

3. Relative to income taxes, innumerable tax reforms could be recommended. The following list is suggestive of those corrective actions deemed of fundamental importance to the short-range future.

   a. The marginal tax rates on personal incomes should be raised significantly, especially at higher levels of income. The top marginal rate should not be excessive (say, in excess of 50–60 percent) since this often serves only to decrease cooperation, to expand the list of exemptions and exclusions, to waste time and talent in search of tax loopholes, to promote bribery and corruption, and to make inclusion of some forms of income in the tax base politically impossible.

   b. The marginal tax rates on business and industrial incomes should not generally be increased to the same degree that the rates on personal income should. This is true because the effective tax rates are already relatively high on these incomes in several of the Latin American republics. In some countries, a decrease in these tax rates might even be justified. In other countries, smaller rate increases would be appropriate. In most countries the effective tax rate should probably not exceed, say, 40 percent of the taxable income since the need for expansionary capital is so great and the market for capital funds is so limited.

c. Capital gains and other income from relatively nonproductive (speculative) forms of investment should be taxed at rates equal to those imposed upon the more productive forms of investment. The acceptance of this recommendation alone would do more to remove the growing pressures for industrial tax-exemption schemes than any possible alternative course of action. Under the prevailing system, these schemes may indeed be necessary to *equalize* the tax-favored position of speculative investments, agricultural incomes, and such. An increase in these taxes would indirectly serve as an incentive to the more productive forms of investment, and the additional revenues could be used further to encourage industrial expansion through the provision of better highways, communications systems, and irrigation projects, and improved educational opportunities. In other countries, the revenues might be used for long-term, low-interest loans—or even grants—for needy industrial enterprises.

d. The variance between the schedular tax rates on different "kinds" of income should be progressively reduced since the income tax is, after all, a tax on people, and income is simply the index chosen to measure the individual's ability to pay. Eventually it would be desirable if all schedular income-tax rates were identical.

e. The consolidation of multiple taxes imposed upon an essentially identical tax base should be strongly encouraged. This would tremendously simplify the administration of the tax laws. It would also make effective evaluation of the tax system possible. Any future adjustments deemed appropriate should then be accomplished through tax-rate changes or through modification of exclusion or exemption provisions, not through the imposition of another presumedly "new" tax.

f. Tax loopholes must be closed if income taxation is to constitute the most progressive feature of the prevailing tax system. In many of the Latin American countries this will require the imposition of a progressive complementary tax on the aggregate schedular incomes (this would be in addition to the schedular income tax). In other nations it will require a reduction in the long list of exclusions currently granted from income taxation. In yet other countries, it will require major modifications to the prevailing practices in business-income taxation.

The stage for the economic development of Latin America has been set. The ability to cope with the ubiquitous problems of tax reform may well determine the success of the entire venture. The United States has stated that it will reward handsomely, with external aid, those countries that shown signs of real progress with the admittedly difficult problems of tax reform. But the problem of judging the adequacy of reform efforts remains—and it is with this matter that the present study is concerned.

10. An Epilogue

The gestation period of a book is only slightly shorter than that of a tax law. On the other hand, the life expectancy of a tax law is significantly shorter than that of a book. Thus the author of any volume dealing with taxation in other than a purely historical perspective is beset with myriad problems of remaining current. The brief two-year span that elapsed between the research and the publication of this book proved to be no exception to the general rule. Although this study was never intended to provide a current tax survey of the nineteen signatory Latin American nations joined in the Alliance for Progress, a sufficiently large number of tax-reform efforts have been instituted in these countries to require a brief comment updating the earlier materials. The purpose of this chapter is two-fold: first, to inform the reader of some of the more significant tax-reform efforts that have been instituted very recently in Latin America; and second, to evaluate these early post-Alliance efforts in light of the criterion established in the first nine chapters.

The two primary objectives for tax-reform efforts stipulated in the Charter of Punta del Este are increasing the quantity of resources available for capital formation and increasing the equity of the pre-Alliance fiscal system. The latter objective is widely interpreted as equivalent to providing a more progressive tax structure.

THE LEVEL OF TAXATION

Because taxation represents a substantial diversion of resources from the private to the public sector of an economy, an increase in the level of taxation will ordinarily represent an increase in the capital-formation potential of a nation. A government, unlike a family unit, is at least theoretically capable of expending all its resources for investment purposes. Thus an increase in the level of taxation would be viewed generally, in the Latin American countries, as a favorable event consistent with the objectives stipulated in the Alliance for Progress.

From the most recent data available, the nations participating in the Alliance were able on the average to increase their real—that is, price-level deflated—tax collections by approximately 11 percent during the three-year period 1960 to 1963.[1] This average includes fifteen nations with increasing tax collections and three nations with decreasing tax collections. When tax collections are viewed as a percentage of gross domestic product, however, the increase in the level of taxation during the same period was only 0.1 percent. In other words, even though many of these nations were able to increase tax collections in absolute terms, they were unable to increase the *relative* proportion of resources diverted from the private to the public sectors, considering the larger gross domestic product of the latter year. On this basis only eight nations were truly successful in achieving the first tax objective of the Charter of Punta del Este. Table 10 reveals these differences in a country-by-country comparison.

Perhaps the reader should be cautioned again against attaching undue significance to the precision implied by the numbers since much of the data upon which they are based is necessarily provisional. In addition, it must be remembered that public saving, in the form of increased taxation, is only one of several alternative ways of increasing capital formation. Other efforts have been directed toward increasing private saving, controlling government expenditures, and other objectives beyond the purview of this study.

MORE PROGRESSIVE TAXATION

Reform efforts intended to accomplish the second tax objective stipulated in the Charter of Punta del Este—providing greater social equity

[1] Based upon data collected from innumerable sources by the staff of the Inter-American Development Bank and published in the Social Progress Trust Fund, *Fourth Annual Report, 1964,* p. 98. The author is deeply indebted to that staff, and to the editors of the International Bureau of Fiscal Documentation, *Annual Report, 1964,* for current information concerning the tax laws in the countries of Latin America.

TABLE 10

Indexes of Central-Government Tax Collections, 1960 to 1963, in Eighteen Latin American Countries (a)

(1960 = 100)

Country	Index of tax collections (b)	Index of tax collections as percentage of GDP(b)
Bolivia	139	122
Peru (c)	139	114
Nicaragua	128	101
Venezuela (c)	127	113
Mexico (c)	124	108
Brazil	122	107
Panama	122	98
Colombia	115	101
Chile	114	99
Costa Rica	108	101
Ecuador	108	98
El Salvador	107	86
Paraguay	107	95
Honduras	102	93
Dominican Republic	101	94
Guatemala	98	87
Uruguay (d)	91	99
Argentina	88	88
Total (e)	111	100

Source: Adapted from Social Progress Trust Fund, *Fourth Annual Report, 1964,* page 98.

Notes:

(a) The indexes were based on data in prices of 1960 converted by using implicit GDP deflators of the respective countries; in cases where such deflators were not available (countries representing about 10% of the aggregate gross product covered by the table), cost of living indexes were used.

(b) Preliminary. All figures rounded to the nearest whole percent.

(c) Based on percentages of Gross National Product.

(d) Indexes based on tax collections in 1961, at prices of 1960.

(e) Indexes based on totals in dollars of 1960, obtained by utilizing exchange rates for that year used by the Economic Commission for Latin America in *Medición del nivel de precios y poder Adquisitivo de la moneda en América Latina,* except in the cases of Argentina, Bolivia, Chile, Mexico, and Peru, which were based on estimates of the IDB.

Data for Haiti were not available.

TABLE 11

Central-Government Income-Tax Collections in Eighteen Latin American Countries, 1960 and 1963

Country	Percentage Point Increase, Income Tax to Total Tax Collections, 1960 to 1963	Increase in Income Tax Collections, 1960 to 1963(a)
Mexico	8.9	$1,909.9
El Salvador	5.6	11.0
Panama	5.1	5.0
Venezuela	4.1	613.5
Dominican Republic	3.4	4.3
Guatemala	3.2	2.1
Paraguay	2.1	71.6
Costa Rica	1.6	7.7
Bolivia	1.0	18.7
Chile	.7	32.2
Honduras	.2	.2
Uruguay	.1(c)	(13.8)
Nicaragua	–0–	5.5
Ecuador	(1.0)	1.1
Colombia	(2.1)	110.5
Argentina	(2.8)	(7.0)(b)
Peru	(3.3)	600.0
Brazil	(4.8)	6.1(b)
Total (d)	0.4	U.S. $ 288.3

Source: Adapted from Social Progress Trust Fund, *Fourth Annual Report, 1964,* page 100.

Notes:

(a) Tax collection increase in millions of national currency units in 1960 prices. The 1963 data is, in most cases, preliminary. All data were converted to prices of 1960 using implicit GDP deflators of the respective countries; in cases where such deflators were not available (in countries representing about 10 per cent of the aggregate gross product covered by the table), cost of living indexes were used.

(b) In billions of national currency units in 1960 prices.

(c) Increase from 1961 to 1963; data for both years were deflated to 1960 prices.

(d) The totals in dollars of 1960 were obtained by utilizing exchange rates for that year used by the Economic Commission for Latin America in *Medición del Nivel de precios y poder adquisitivo de la moneda en América Latina,* except in the cases of Argentina, Bolivia, Chile, Mexico, and Peru, which were based on estimates of the IDB.

Data for Haiti were not available.

through a more progressive tax structure—are relatively easy to identify. Unfortunately, however, measuring the degree to which the objective is being attained is much more difficult. Most of the first reform actions designed to provide a more progressive tax structure took the form of either increased income-tax rates or additional tax on non-essential purchases. Less frequent reforms, directed to the same end objective, are included in revisions to the' inheritance, gift, and other taxes.

Income Taxes

Between 1960 and 1963 income-tax collections (in 1960 dollars) increased in Latin America from $2,357 million to $2,645 million.[2] During these three years only two countries, Argentina and Uruguay, reported a decrease in the absolute quantity of income-tax collections; sixteen countries reported an increase. On the other hand, five countries reported a decrease in the relative contribution of income-tax collections between the safe years (a measure of the change in relative contribution is obtained by comparing income-tax collections to total central-government tax collections for two different time periods). For the Latin American countries as a group the relative contribution of income taxes increased only 0.4 percent between 1960 and 1963; from 35.7 percent of total tax collections in 1960 to 36.1 percent in 1963.[3] The composition of this increase is enumerated in Table 11.

One of the more encouraging aspects of the income-tax data is the fact that seven of the nine countries reporting an increase of 1 percent or more in the relative contribution made by income-tax collections between 1960 and 1963 are countries in which income taxes had been contributing less than 25 percent of total tax collections in the pre-Alliance tax structure. The experience of the other two countries reporting increases of more than 1 percent (Mexico and Venezuela) also demonstrates that income taxation can be utilized to produce truly substantial revenues as industrialization becomes a reality, even though all of the alleged preconditions to successful income taxation may not have been satisfied.

Countries increasing existing progressive income-tax rates after 1960 include El Salvador, Haiti, Honduras, Panama, Paraguay, and

---

[2] Social Progress Trust Fund, *Fourth Annual Report, 1964,* p. 100.
[3] *Ibid.*, p. 100.

Venezuela. Ecuador and the Dominican Republic instituted, in 1963 and 1964 respectively, a new supplementary tax with a progressive rate structure; this tax applies to the aggregate schedular incomes of individuals. Guatemala and Uruguay enacted progressive personal-income taxes for the first time in their histories. The Guatemalan acceptance in 1963 of a progressive, personal-income tax came after nine unsuccessful attempts in the previous ten years.

Major changes in the existing income-tax provisions were enacted in Chile and in Mexico. In mid-1963 Chile reduced the number of tax schedules to two; one for income from employment and another for all other income. The tax rate applicable to the Chilean supplemental tax on total income was tied to the annual minimum wage, with tax rates of from 10 percent on incomes up to three times the annual minimum wage to 60 percent on incomes exceeding eighty times the same figure.[4]

In December of 1964 the President of Mexico sent the Mexican Congress a proposal that introduced an entirely new income-tax system for tax years beginning after January 1, 1965. The new, global tax is mandatory for all persons with an annual taxable income in excess of 150,000 pesos ($12,000). Persons with incomes of between 72,000 and 150,000 pesos retain the option to use the former schedular tax system. The new system includes a standard deduction (equal to the lesser of 20,000 pesos or 10 percent of the net personal income after deducting personal deductions), dependency exemptions, and medical, funeral, and other expense deductions. The maximum tax rate of 35 percent is applied to all taxable incomes in excess of 300,000 pesos. The new law also provides a clear distinction between the personal- and the corporate-income taxes. Provisions to encourage the reinvestment of corporate profits were included in the new law.

In the category of unusual income-tax reforms, two changes are noteworthy. In 1963 Ecuador added to taxable income the imputed income from owner-occupied housing. For the determination of income from agricultural activities, Uruguay changed from an imputed income based on the *potential* income (assuming systematic development of

---

[4] In 1964 the annual minimum wage in Chile was set at 150.3 escudos, or $46.20 at the approximate market rate of exchange existing on December 31, 1964. Thus the minimum tax rate would be applicable to annual incomes of $138.60 or less, and the maximum tax rate would be applicable to annual incomes of $3,696 or more.

the land) to an imputed income based upon the *average productivity* determined by geographical subareas.

Taxes on Nonessentials

Increasing taxes levied on purchases of luxury or nonessential goods is widely accepted by less well developed countries as an alternative method of increasing the tax burden placed upon the wealthier members of society. The assumption is valid, of course, only in the event that: (1) the additional tax is passed on to the ultimate consumer; and (2) only the wealthier members of the society actually elect to purchase the taxed item. A review of the items on which the taxes are often increased reveals a number of items purchased by members of all classes of most societies. For example, the excise-, sales-, or import-tax rates applicable to cigarettes or alcoholic beverages were increased in Argentina, Colombia, Costa Rica, the Dominican Republic, and Mexico, since 1960.

Motor vehicles and gasoline are perhaps second only to cigarettes and alcoholic beverages as the commodities most frequently subject to increased luxury taxes. Still other nonessential commodities subject to increased indirect taxes include television sets and washing machines (in Costa Rica); imported beans, potatoes, garlic, fresh, frozen, or refrigerated meats, and poultry (in the Dominican Republic); bottled water (in Mexico); airline tickets (in Haiti); and automobile lubricants (in Argentina). Incidentally the Venezuelan tax on lottery prizes also was nearly doubled in 1961.

Increased import duties have been effected in Argentina, Bolivia, Panama, Paraguay, and Peru. Honduras also increased by 5 percent her export tax on silver. A general 3 percent sales tax, excluding the final sale of consumer goods and commodities subject to special excise taxes, was established in Honduras in late 1963.

Increases in the inheritance- and gift-tax rates are much more likely than the previously noted changes to increase the progressivity of a prevailing tax system. Countries in Latin America that increased the inheritance- and gift-tax rates since 1960 include Chile, Colombia, Ecuador, Honduras, Nicaragua, and Venezuela. In most of these countries it is still common practice to increase the tax rate both as the size of the inheritance increases and as the remoteness of the relationship between the devisor and the devisee is extended.

The potential usefulness of real-property taxation has also been significantly advanced during the past four years in Bolivia, Chile, Costa Rica, and Panama, by the completion of land surveys or land appraisals. Personnel from the Organization of American States, the Economic Commission for Latin America, and the Agency for International Development have provided invaluable assistance in completing these tasks. In addition, the government of Nicaragua has created a subdivision of its General Revenue Service to assess real and personal property for tax purposes.

In order to increase land productivity, the taxes on idle or poorly utilized lands have been increased in Argentina, Brazil, Costa Rica, and Guatemala. Colombia and Peru have forced owners to declare reasonable real-property values for tax purposes by retaining the right to expropriate land at a price at least partially dependent upon the tax valuation declared by the owner.

In summary, because the ultimate incidence of the varied taxes discused here cannot be determined with any degree of accuracy, and because many of the taxed items are purchased, owned, or utilized by members of all classes of Latin American society, the conclusion that these tax changes have necessarily increased the progressivity of the pre-Alliance tax systems does not appear justified. The changes in the inheritance, gift, and real-property taxes, however, appear to constitute steps in the direction dictated by the terms of the Charter of Punta del Este.

OTHER TAX-RELATED REFORM EFFORTS

A primary conclusion of this study, stated in Chapter 9, is that improved administrative practices might well be accepted as the most appropriate form of tax-reform efforts in the early years of the Alliance Era. The author was encouraged to discover that by 1965 the activity in the administrative-reform area was most promising.

Administrative Reforms

In September 1965 the United States' Internal Revenue Service, in cooperation with the Agency for International Development, had tax teams in fourteen Latin American countries to assist these countries in the administrative aspects of taxation.[5] Detailed country studies to provide a sound basis for additional tax-reform efforts had been initiated in Argentina, Nicaragua, Paraguay, and Peru. At the same time, Bolivia, Chile, Costa Rica, the Dominican Republic, Ecuador, Mexico, and Paraguay had undertaken substantial efforts to improve tax collections and to curb tax evasion. Specific techniques adopted to achieve these results include the creation of a Federal Tax Register (in Mexico); the centralization of collection procedures (in Ecuador, El Salvador, and Paraguay); the initiation or extension of withholding taxes (in Argentina, Colombia, Costa Rica, Guatemala, and Panama); the utilization of a certificate of fiscal clearances as a prerequisite to any of several quasi-legal acts (in Nicaragua); the application of electronic data-processing techniques to tax matters (in Bolivia, El Salvador, and Guatemala); the initiation of penalties for late payments (in Argentina, Guatemala, and Panama); and the creation of new training schools for revenue-service personnel (in the Dominican Republic and El Salvador). The establishment of a Tax Education Department in the Dominican Republic to acquaint the taxpayer with his fiscal duties, responsibilities, and privileges is a particularly appropriate form of administrative tax-reform effort.

Tax-Exemption Schemes

The tendency to expand tax exemptions as a method of encouraging industralization continued during the first four years of the Alliance program. The details of the exemption schemes varied widely in each of the different countries. Selected industries were offered a total or partial exemption from income taxation in Argentina, Colombia, and Ecuador. The Dominican Republic exempted certain foreign-exchange-saving firms from customs duties and from other taxes on machines and raw materials. On the other hand, Costa Rica instituted a review of firms already receiving tax exemption under provisions of the Industrial Promotion Act to ascertain that only firms actually producing import substitutes were receiving benefits.

Diverse provisions to encourage the reinvestment of corporate earnings were common throughout the Latin American countries. Brazil

[5] As reported in the *Austin American*, September 23, 1965, p. 18.

restricted the reinvestment exemption privileges geographically—to the less well developed area of the nation. Honduras now gives industries of "basic importance" a higher depreciation rate and a special deduction which is related to the cost of new machinery purchases. Argentina recently exempted new industries from the documentary stamp tax for a period of from five to ten years; she also gives the new firm certain privileges in hiring foreign technicians.

Earmarking Revenues and Proliferation of Taxes

The practice of earmarking selected tax receipts also retains its earlier popularity in Latin America. Unfortunately, the earmarking practice is all to often associated with the proliferation of an already complex tax structure. For example, Brazil has a new 1 percent payroll tax earmarked for a massive housing program; Ecuador earmarks 30 percent of her export tax on bananas to a new National Highway Fund; some special excise taxes imposed in Haiti in 1963 are scheduled to finance the National Economic Development Plan; Chile and Mexico added special taxes to help finance higher education; Paraguay now has a tax on the exploitation of forests by private firms which is earmarked to fund a development of forestry in the Rural Welfare Institute; Colombia has an additional tax on corporate income to help finance low-cost housing; and Uruguay earmarked certain 1961 tax increases for her Public Works Fund.

Other recent tax-reform efforts intended to reduce the widespread proliferation of previous taxes can be strongly endorsed. In 1961 and 1962 Argentina and Uruguay each eliminated a number of low-yielding, administratively difficult taxes while increasing other more productive taxes. Ecuador consolidated 93 taxes imposed by local levels of government into three taxes based upon the export price of bananas (21.4 percent), cacao (10 percent), and coffee (9.5 percent). Ecuador further abolished some 760 municipal taxes on agricultural items; consolidated the sales tax at a national level; consolidated numerous taxes on beer, liquors, and sugar; and codified the remaining stamp taxes into a single law. Haiti similarly consolidated all previous taxes on coffee exports into a single tax, while Nicaragua reduced the number of transactions subject to the stamp tax from 230 to 50. The latter country also codified numerous administrative provisions into a single General Tax Law.

Other Tax Reforms

Although the Latin American countries remain reluctant to tax capital gains, positive action was achieved in three countries. Argentina increased the previous capital-gains-tax rate from 5 to 10 percent but at the same time increased the exemption from capital-gains taxation from 50,000 to 100,000 pesos (from approximately $330 to $660). Beginning in 1965 Chile, for the first time in history, applied a capital-gains tax to profits arising from selected transactions involving personal property, mining rights, copyrights, and patents. Colombia began imposing a capital-gains tax on real-estate profits in 1961.

Argentina was the only Latin American country to abandon the excess-profits tax during the period 1960–1964.

SUMMARY

Although the tax reform in any country is inevitably beset with multitudinous political and practical difficulties, the Latin American nations have instituted manifold changes in their pre-Alliance fiscal systems in an attempt to achieve the goals enumerated in the Charter of Punta del Este. Four and one-half years is far too short a period to permit anyone to evaluate accurately the significance of these changes. In fact, many of the tax reforms are so recent that the statistics that will eventually reflect the importance of the revisions are not yet even compiled. Perhaps the greatest danger is that some persons will expect the impossible in the tax-reform area. Fortunately, the administrators of the Social Progress Trust Fund well appreciate this danger. In their latest annual report to the Inter-American Development Bank they state:[6]

In view of the well known weaknesses in fiscal systems and the natural resistance to change on the part of those affected, who have a considerable political influence, reforms in the tax, budget, planning and administrative fields require long range programs involving many years of study, education, debate and dedicated effort by the legislative and executive branches of the government.

The author believes that the findings enumerated in this epilogue prove that appropriate tax-reform action has begun, and that if the leaders of the Latin American society continue to strive diligently to-

---

[6] Social Progress Trust Fund, *Fourth Annual Report, 1964*, p. 97.

ward those goals to which they pledged themselves, they will eventually succeed in this unparalleled venture. It is hoped that this study may provide them with some little assistance in evaluating the infinite array of tax proposals which they are currently considering.

APPENDIX 1

Resolutions of the United Nations Economic Commission for Latin America (ECLA) and the Inter-American Economic and Social Council (IA-ECOSOC) of the Organization of American States (OAS) Relative to the OAS/ECLA/IDB Taxation Program

1. *ECLA resolution adopted on 13 May 1961*
186 (IX). Fiscal Policy

The Economic Commission for Latin America

Taking note with satisfaction of the preparatory work carried out by the Secretariat, the Organization of American States and the Inter-American Development Bank, in co-operation with the Harvard University Law School International Program in Taxation, with regard to proposals for a long-range program for studying the bases for a reform of tax systems with a view to using them as instruments of fiscal and economic policy,

Considering the need of the Latin American States for resources wherewith to undertake, as a matter of urgency, intensive capital formation in the basic sectors of the economy,

Bearing in mind that the tax system may be a valuable instrument of co-operation in a policy designed to promote the more equitable distribution of income and to facilitate the financing of economic development programs,

Considering that such a system may be conducive to a more efficient use of the land, such as will increase its productivity,

Decides:

1. To request Governments to give their support to the studies which are being developed by the sponsoring agencies in connection with the tax reform and fiscal policy program, and in particular, to collaborate to the fullest extent possible with the experts who will be appointed to carry out the work of study and research on the tax systems in force in the Latin American countries;

2. To request the Secretariat that the above-mentioned tax program make express provision for the need to improve tax administration and yields, as well as to study the bases for a tax system which will mitigate the external vulnerability and inelasticity of these systems, and will serve as an

instrument of policy which may promote, in combination with others, the improvement of income distribution and land use and, in short, may constitute a valuable adjunct to economic development programs;

3. To request Governments that they facilitate the attendance of national experts at the two conferences which are being organized under the above-mentioned program, one to be held in October 1961 on tax administration, and the other in April 1962 on fiscal policy.

2. *IA-ECOSOC resolution approved on 17 August 1961*
A.3 Taxation Program

Whereas:

Satisfactory progress has been achieved by the Pan American Union, the Economic Commission for Latin America, and the Inter-American Development Bank, in co-operation with the Harvard University Law School International Program in Taxation in carrying out a long-range program to strengthen tax systems;

The American states need to mobilize their domestic resources in order to fulfill the principles of the Act of Botota; and

The application of sound tax policy and administration facilitates the financing of economic development and contributes to social progress through more equitable distribution of income and the encouragement of more productive use of land,

The Special Meeting of the Inter-American Economic and Social Council at the Ministerial Level

Recommends:

1. That the governments of the member states encourage participation in the program which is being developed by these sponsoring agencies.

2. That the Pan American Union assist in carrying out activities of training and research under the program developed by the sponsoring agencies.

3. That the governments of the member states facilitate attendance of national experts at the two conferences which are being organized under the program, the first on tax administration to be held in Buenos Aires in October 1961, and the second on tax policy, to be held in Santiago in 1962.

4. That the governments, through their Ministries of Finance or other appropriate government departments, co-operate in preparing working papers for these conferences, by providing basic data and fiscal statistics.

APPENDIX 2

Joint Program on Taxation of the Organization of American States and the United Nations Economic Commission for Latin America, with the Participation of the Inter-American Development Bank and the Co-operation of Harvard University[a]

A. *Introduction*

This report presents a summary of the aims and development of the Joint Program on Taxation undertaken by the Organization of American States and the United Nations Economic Commission for Latin America, with the participation of the Inter-American Development Bank and the co-operation of the Harvard University Law School. The latter, which has had long experience in this field, as a result of the International Program in Taxation, has appointed a full-time representative to co-operate with the committee in the technical aspects of its work.

The four participating institutions set up a Special Coordinating Committee to organize and direct the work of the programme. This document is a report by the Committee to the participating institutions and to the Special Meeting of the Inter-American Economic and Social Council at the Ministerial Level.[b]

The report covers the period between October 1960, when the Program started, and July 15, 1961.

The chief aim of the Program is to contribute to the strengthening of tax systems in Latin America, the improvement of fiscal administration and the training of fiscal officers. It will cover three successive aspects or phases: (1) preparation of a conference on Tax Administration, to be held at Buenos Aires, Argentina, from 11 to 19 October; (2) carrying out of the fiscal studies in several countries, by national and international experts to be

[a] The text reproduced here is that of document ES-RE. Information Doc. No. 10 of 28 July 1961 (Original: Spanish) issued at the OAS Special Meeting of the Inter-American Economic and Social Council at the Ministerial Level (Punta del Este, Uruguay, July-August 1961), minus the appendices.

[b] Document 4 of the Special Meeting of the Inter-American Economic and Social Council at the Ministerial Level, Uruguay, August 1961, *Report of the Group of Experts, Planning for Economic and Social Development for Latin America,* (Topic I of the Agenda), Note 1, p. 18.

concluded in 1961 or early 1962; (3) preparation of a meeting on Tax Policy in Latin America to be held at Santiago, Chile, in 1962 upon completion of the fiscal studies.

It is hoped that, a part from other benefits, the meetings will be particularly useful as forums in bringing together national and foreign specialists and experts on tax administration and policy. This will facilitate a comprehensive exchange of knowledge and experience which will enable them to come into contact with technical and practical developments and with the systems in force in other countries.

Moreover, the meetings and fiscal studies will help to develop an interest in recasting and modifying existing tax systems and administration in the Hemisphere, since they will provide valuable information on the present position of such systems and their problems.

Finally, the meetings and fiscal studies will, it is hoped, help to orient tax policy towards an efficient mobilization and allocation of resources in line with the policy of rapidly improving the level and distribution of *per capita* income.

They will, on the one hand, provide important guide lines for determining the best way to achieve international fiscal co-operation, particularly with respect to the training of tax officials and, on the other hand, they will be of great value in enabling countries to set definite goals for their respective reforms, on general principles of taxation and tax administration in accordance with their economic and social development programs.

It should be recognized that the reform of each country's tax system must be worked out by the country itself from plans drawn up by national institutions in the light of the country's own specific needs and circumstances.

The Committee expresses the hope, however, that the Programme will serve as a ready means of enlisting the co-operation required to facilitate a study of general principles leading to appropriate changes in the tax system.

B. *Conference on Tax Administration*

There are several basic reasons for beginning the Program with a study of the problems related to tax administration. Perhaps the main reason is that, no matter how suitable the tax laws of a country, tax revenue and the attainment of tax policy objectives will depend upon strict compliance with tax obligations by the taxpayer which, in the final analysis, depends on efficient tax administration. In this respect, much can be gained by improving the qualifications of fiscal employees. The experience in many Latin American countries gives reason to hope that the improvement of tax administration will, by preventing of fraud and evasion, lead to a substantial increase in tax collections. This is due to the fact that improved administration produces an immediate increase in tax revenues without requiring changes in fiscal legislation. An efficient administration, it should be noted, is in fact the only way in which the objectives sought through tax reforms can be achieved.

The first meeting, arrangements for which are well advanced, will be held at Buenos Aires, from 11 to 19 October 1961. Some sixty experts from the countries of the Hemisphere will take part. A monograph on each of the eight topics of the Agenda will be presented at this meeting. The monographs have already been prepared by experts of recognized international standing and authority in the field, and will be presented to the conference by the respective authors; comments on them will be made by at least two participants from different countries for the purpose of examining the application of the ideas expounded in the monographs to the problems of taxation and to present conditions in Latin America. In order to facilitate the work of all participants at this meeting, they will receive a copy of the monographs sufficiently in advance to enable them to study and analyze the papers in detail. Participants will thus be in a position to bring their personal experience to bear on the problems being debated.

As a further means of ensuring the progress of this first meeting and the practical application of the ideas to be discussed, a request has been made to all countries for valuable statistical material which will be compiled and an inter-country comparison made for presentation to the participants.

After the Conference has ended, the monographs and related papers will be published so that they may be widely circulated in all the countries of the Hemisphere.

C. *Fiscal Studies*

The second phase of the Programme consists of the preparation of detailed studies of the tax systems and deficiencies in the Latin American countries. The initial steps have been taken for studies on the first group of countries, which will be completed early in 1962. These studies will be subsequently extended to the remaining group. In order that they may be of general and specific use it is proposed to carry them out on the basis of uniform plans which will permit a comparative study of the results obtained. In short, it is hoped that, briefly, in addition to providing an analysis of the tax structure of the countries concerned, the studies will help to unravel the main problems common to all. They will thus form an efficient basis for consideration and discussion at the Conference on Tax Policy.

Experts from a considerable number of countries have been consulted, and an advisory group appointed for the purpose of determining the plan and content of these studies.

D. *Conference on Tax Policy*

The final agenda and bases of the Conference on Tax Policy cannot yet be indicated. They will be formulated in the light of the aforementioned consultations with national experts and the advisory group. However, reference can already be made to some of the fundamental problems which will undoubtedly be discussed at this meeting, *e.g.,* the inadequacy of current tax resources in most of the countries of the region in terms of adequate levels of public expenditure compatible with accelerated programmes of economic growth, the external vulnerability and the inelasticity of tax revenue and the lack of clear guidance in tax policy conducive to the promotion of increased national savings and investment and the channeling of the latter toward the sectors of the population making the greatest contribution to economic development.

The meetings on taxation and fiscal studies are not proposed as an end in themselves, but rather as a means of helping the Latin American countries to prepare for the difficult task of introducing tax reforms and improving administration. The genuine interest shown for the Programme in all the Latin American countries makes it possible to hope that the two conferences and the aforementioned studies will prove useful to countries where tax reforms are being carried out as well as those countries about to undertake them. As mentioned in the attached resolution of the ninth session of the Economic and Social Development Committee of the United Nations Economic Commission for Latin America, held last May, the governments have definitely supported the tax programme. It should be noted that the outstanding progress made to date in the programme would not have been possible without the enthusiastic and wholehearted co-operation of the numerous tax officials and experts whose help was sought.

BIBLIOGRAPHY

Public Documents

A. U.S. Government Publications

1. Congressional

Committee on Ways and Means. *Tax Revision Compendium: A Compendium of Papers on Broadening the Tax Base, Conducted by the Committee on Ways and Means, Beginning November 16, 1959.* Volumes I, II, and III. Washington, D.C.: U.S. Government Printing Office, 1959.

Joint Economic Committee. *Economic Policies and Programs in South America.* Submitted by the Subcommittee on Inter-American Economic Relationships, 87th Congress, 2nd Session, 1962. Washington, D.C.: U.S. Government Printing Office, 1962.

—. *Hearings Before the Subcommittee on Inter-American Economic Relationships of the Joint Economic Committee.* 87th Congress, 2nd Session, May 10 and 11, 1962. Washington, D.C.: U.S. Government Printing Office, 1962.

Senate Appropriations Committee. *Report on the Inter-American Social and Economic Cooperation Program and the Chilean Reconstruction and Rehabilitation Program.* Report Number 201, May 3, 1961. Washington, D.C.: U.S. Government Printing Office, 1961.

Senate Document No. 80. *Special Report on Latin America.* 87th Congress, 2nd Session, March 19, 1962. Washington, D.C.: U.S. Government Printing Office, 1962.

Senate Document No. 82. *Latin America and United States Policies: Report of Senator Mike Mansfield on a Study Mission to Latin America.* 87th Congress, 2nd Session, March 29, 1962. Washington, D.C.: U.S. Government Printing Office, 1962.

2. Department of State

"Alliance-for-Progress Projects Set for Five More Countries," *The Department of State Bulletin,* XLV (August 21, 1961), 316–317.

"American Republics Establish an Alliance for Progress," *The Department of State Bulletin,* XLV (September 11, 1961), 459–462.

Dillon, Douglas C. "Alliance for Progress: A Program for the Peoples of the Americas," *The Department of State Bulletin,* XLV (August 28, 1961), 356–360.

Fisher, Frederic R. *Tax Reform in Latin America.* Mimeographed. Washington, D.C.: Bureau of Latin American Affairs, January 24, 1962.

——. *Supplement to Tax Reform in Latin America.* Mimeographed. Washington, D.C.: Bureau of Latin American Affairs, February 20, 1962.

Kennedy, John F. "Alliance for Progress: A Program for the Peoples of the Americas," *The Department of State Bulletin,* XLV (August 28, 1961), 355–356.

——. "A Milestone in the Alliance for Progress," *The Department of State Bulletin,* XLV (December 18, 1961), 999–1000.

——. Presidential Address, *Department of State Bulletin,* XLIV (April 3, 1961), 471–478.

Tax Reform in Latin America since the Act of Bogota. A Staff Report, March, 1962. Washington, D.C.: Agency for International Development, 1962.

B. International Organizations' Publications

1. United Nations

Domestic Financing of Economic Development. New York: United Nations, Department of Economic Affairs, 1950.

Economic Survey of Latin America, 1958. New York: United Nations, Economic Commission for Latin America, 1959.

Financing of Economic Development: International Tax Problems. New York: United Nations, Economic and Social Council, 1956.

Foreign Private Investment in the Latin American Free-Trade Area. New York: United Nations, Department of Economic and Social Affairs, 1961.

International Tax Agreements. New York: United Nations, 1948.

Mobilization of Domestic Capital: Report and Documents of the First Working Party of Experts. Bangkok: United Nations, Economic Commission for Asia and the Far East, 1952.

Mobilization of Domestic Capital: Report and Documents of the Second Working Party of Experts. Bangkok: United Nations, Economic Commission for Asia and the Far East, 1953.

Prebisch, Raul. *The Economic Development of Latin America and Its Principal Problems.* New York: United Nations, 1950.

Statistical Yearbook, 1961. New York: United Nations, 1962.

Statistical Yearbook, 1962. New York: United Nations, 1963.

Statistical Yearbook, 1963. New York: United Nations, 1964.

Statistical Yearbook, 1964. New York: United Nations, 1965.

Taxes and Fiscal Policy in Under-Developed Countries. New York: United Nations, Technical Assistance Administration, 1954.

The Effects of Taxation on Foreign Trade and Investment. New York: United Nations, Department of Economic Affairs, 1950.

2. Organization of American States

Annual Review of Inter-American Policies and Problems in the Economic and Social Fields. Washington, D.C.: Pan American Union, 1961.

Ballesteros, Marto. SEE Union Panamericana.

Latin American Economic Integration. Washington, D.C.: Pan American Union, 1961.

Lynn, James A. SEE Union Panamericana.

Magaña, Alvaro. SEE Union Panamericana.

Planning for Economic and Social Development for Latin America. Washington, D.C.: Pan American Union, 1961.

Proceedings of the Conference on Tax Administration. (Draft Report.) Held in Buenos Aires, Argentina, October 11–19, 1961. Mimeographed. Washington, D.C.: Pan American Union, 1962.

Provisional Report of the Conference on Fiscal Policy. Held in Santiago, Chile, December 5–14, 1962. Mimeographed. Washington, D.C.: Pan American Union, 1963.

Public Opinion and the Development of Latin America. Washington, D.C.: Pan American Union, 1961.

Union Panamericana. *Reforma Tributaria para America Latina: II Problemas de politica fiscal.* Prepared under the direction of Alvaro Magaña, James A. Lynn, and Marto Ballesteros. Washington, D.C.: Secretary General, Organization of American States, 1964.

3. Other

Inter-American Development Bank. *Operations of the Social Progress Trust Fund and Measures Being Taken by Member Countries within the Spirit of the Act of Bogota and the Charter of Punta del Este* (as of July 1, 1962). Washington, D.C.: Inter-American Development Bank, July, 1962.

International Bureau of Fiscal Documentation, *Annual Report, 1964.* Muiderpoort, Sarphatistraat 124, Amsterdam, Netherlands: International Bureau of Fiscal Documentation, 1965.

Social Progress Trust Fund. *First Annual Report, 1961.* Washington, D.C.: Inter-American Development Bank, 1962.

—. *Second Annual Report, 1962.* Washington, D.C.: Inter-American Development Bank, 1963.

—. *Third Annual Report, 1963.* Washington, D.C.: Inter-American Development Bank, 1964.

—. *Fourth Annual Report, 1964.* Washington, D.C.: Inter-American Development Bank, 1965.

Villa, Hernando (Minister of Finance and Public Credit). *Reforma*

200   TAX REFORM AND THE ALLIANCE FOR PROGRESS

Tributaria: Memoria de Hacienda, Anexo III. Bogota, Colombia: Imprenta Nacional, 1959.

C. International Agreements

The Act of Bogota. Reprinted in *Department of State Bulletin,* XLIII (October 3, 1960), 537–540.

The Charter of Punta del Este. Reprinted in *Department of State Bulletin,* XLV (September 11, 1961), 464–469.

The Declaration to the Peoples of America. Reprinted in *Department of State Bulletin,* XLV (September 11, 1961), 463–464.

Supplementary Sources

A. Books

Allen, William R., and Clark Lee Allen (eds.). *Foreign Trade and Finance.* New York: The Macmillan Company, 1959.

Blum, Walter J., and Harry Kalven, Jr. *The Uneasy Case for Progressive Taxation.* Chicago: University of Chicago Press, 1953.

Butters, John Keith. *Effects of Taxation: Investments by Individuals.* Boston: Division of Research, Graduate School of Business Administration, Harvard University, 1953.

Commission to Study the Fiscal System of Venezuela. *The Fiscal System of Venezuela.* Baltimore: Johns Hopkins Press, 1959.

Deperon, Paul. *International Double Taxation.* New York: Committee on International Economic Policy, 1945.

Diamond, Walter H. *Foreign Tax and Trade Briefs.* New York: Fallon Law Book Co., 1962.

Due, John F. *Government Finance.* Homewood, Illinois: Richard D. Irwin, Inc., 1959.

Duesenberry, James S. *Income, Saving and the Theory of Consumer Behavior.* Cambridge: Harvard University Press, 1949.

Gomes de Sousa, Rubens. SEE Harvard Law School International Program in Taxation.

Gumpel, H. J. SEE Harvard Law School International Program in Taxation.

Haley, Bernard F. (ed.). *A Survey of Contemporary Economics.* Volume II. Homewood, Illinois: Richard D. Irwin, Inc., 1952.

Hansen, Alvin H. *Public Enterprise and Economic Development.* London: Routledge & Kegan Paul Ltd., 1959.

Hanson, Simon G. *Economic Development in Latin America.* Washington, D.C.: The Inter-American Affairs Press, 1951.

Harris, Seymour E. (ed.). *Economic Problems of Latin America.* New York: McGraw-Hill Book Company, Inc., 1944.

Harvard Law School International Program in Taxation. *World Tax*

Series: Taxation in Brazil. Prepared by H. J. Gumpel and Rubens Gomes de Sousa. Boston: Little, Brown and Company, 1957.

——. *World Tax Series: Taxation in Mexico.* Prepared by H. J. Gumpel and H. B. Margain. Boston: Little, Brown and Company, 1957 (1961 supplement).

Higgins, Benjamin. *Economic Development.* New York: W. W. Norton & Company, Inc., 1959.

Hirschman, Albert O. (ed.). *Latin American Issues: Essays and Comments.* New York: The Twentieth Century Fund, 1961.

——. *The Strategy of Economic Development.* New Haven: Yale University Press, 1959.

Kaldor, Nicholas. *An Expenditure Tax.* London: Allen and Unwin, 1955.

Kimmel, Lewis H. *Taxes and Economic Incentives.* Washington, D.C.: The Brookings Institution, 1950.

Kindleberger, Charles P. *Economic Development.* New York: The McGraw-Hill Book Company, Inc., 1958.

Krause, Walter. *Economic Development.* San Francisco: Wadsworth Publishing Company, Inc., 1961.

Margain, H. B. SEE Harvard Law School International Program in Taxation.

Mosk, Sanford A. *Industrial Revolution in Mexico.* Berkeley: University of California Press, 1950.

Musgrave, Richard A., and Alan T. Peacock (eds.). *Classics in the Theory of Public Finance.* New York: The Macmillan Company, 1958.

Myrdal, Gunnar. *An International Economy.* New York: Harper & Brothers Publishers, 1956.

——. *Rich Lands and Poor.* New York: Harper & Brothers Publishers, 1957.

National Bureau of Economic Research. *Problems in International Comparisons in Economic Accounts.* (Studies in Income and Wealth, Volume 20.) Princeton, New Jersey: National Bureau of Economic Research, 1957.

Nurkse, Ragnar. *Problems of Capital Formation in Underdeveloped Countries.* Oxford: Basil Blackwell, 1953.

Rolph, Earl R., and George F. Break. *Public Finance.* New York: The Ronald Press Company, 1961.

Ross, Stanford G., and John B. Christensen. *Tax Incentives for Industry in Mexico.* Cambridge: International Program in Taxation, Law School of Harvard University, 1959.

Rostow, Walt W. *The Stages of Economic Growth: A Non-Communist Manifesto.* Cambridge: Cambridge University Press, 1960.

Sanders, Thomas H. *Effects of Taxation on Executives*. Boston: Harvard University Press, 1951.

Simons, Henry C. *Federal Tax Reform*. Chicago: The University of Chicago Press, 1950.

—. *Personal Income Taxation*. Chicago: The University of Chicago Press, 1938.

Smithies, Arthur, and J. Keith Butters (eds.). *A.E.A. Readings in Fiscal Policy*. Volume II. Homewood, Illinois: Richard D. Irwin, Inc., 1955.

Stark, Harry. *Social and Economic Frontiers in Latin America*. Dubuque, Iowa: Wm. C. Brown Co., 1961.

Tax Institute. *The Limits of Taxable Capacity*. Princeton: Tax Institute, Incorporated, 1953.

Tax Institute of America. *Tax Policy on United States Investment in Latin America*. Princeton, New Jersey: Tax Institute of America, 1963.

Taylor, Milton C. *Industrial Tax-Exemption in Puerto Rico*. Madison: University of Wisconsin Press, 1957.

Wald, Haskell P. *Taxation of Agricultural Land in Underdeveloped Economies*. Cambridge: Harvard University Press, 1959.

— (ed.). *Papers and Proceedings of the Conference on Agricultural Taxation and Economic Development*. Cambridge: Harvard University Printing Office, 1954.

Wallace, Donald O. (ed.). *Argentinian Income Tax Service*. St. Petersburg, Florida: Foreign Tax Law Association, Inc., 1962.

—. *Chilean Income Tax Service*. St. Petersburg, Florida: Foreign Tax Law Association, 1962.

—. *Colombian Income Tax Service*. St. Petersburg, Florida: Foreign Tax Law Association, 1962.

—. *Peruvian Income Tax Service*. St. Petersburg, Florida: Foreign Tax Law Association, 1962.

—. *Uruguayan Income Tax Service*. St. Petersburg, Florida: Foreign Tax Law Association, 1962.

Wallich, Henry C., and John H. Adler. *Public Finance in a Developing Country*. Cambridge: Harvard University Press, 1951.

Wolf, Charles, Jr., and Sidney C. Sufrin. *Capital Formation & Foreign Investment in Underdeveloped Areas*. Syracuse: Syracuse University Press, 1958.

B. Articles

Adler, John H. "The Fiscal and Monetary Implementation of Development Programs," *The American Economic Review*, XLI, 2 (May 1952), 584–600.

"The Americas, after the Tax Evaders," *Time*, LXXVIII (October 27, 1961), 41.

"Bank Pushes Latin Progress Plan," *Businessweek* (November 11, 1961), 84–91.

Bhatia, Mohinder S. "Tax Exemption in a Developing Economy," *National Tax Journal*, XIII (December 1960), 341–349.

Bird, Richard M. "A National Tax on the Unimproved Value of Land: The Austrian Experience, 1910–1952," *National Tax Journal*, XIII (December 1960), 386–392.

Chase, Sam B., Jr. "Tax Credits for Investment Spending," *National Tax Journal*, XV (March 1962), 32–52.

Clark, Colin. "The Danger Point in Taxes," *Harper's Magazine*, CCI (December 1960), 67–69.

Crockett, Joseph P. "Tax Pattern in Latin America," *National Tax Journal*, XV (March 1962), 93–104.

Due, John F. "The African Personal Tax," *National Tax Journal*, XV (December 1962), 385–398.

Eaton, A. Kenneth. SEE National Tax Association.

Fagan, E. D. "Recent and Contemporary Theories of Progressive Taxation," *Journal of Political Economy*, XLVI (August 1938), 458–485.

Fayerweather, John. "A Principled Approach to Overseas Taxation," *Business Topics*, IX (Autumn 1961), 49–59.

Fitchett, Delbert A. "Land Taxation and Land Reform in Underdeveloped Countries: A Comment," *Economic Development and Cultural Change*, X (Part 1, 1962), 210–213.

Flores, Antonio Carrillo. SEE United Nations. *Domestic Financing of Economic Development.*

Froomkin, Joseph. "Some Problems of Tax Policy in Latin America," *National Tax Journal*, X (December 1957), 370–379.

Ganjei, Nasser D. SEE National Tax Association.

García, Desiderio. SEE United Nations. *Domestic Financing of Economic Development.*

Goode, Richard. "New System of Direct Taxation in Ceylon," *National Tax Journal*, XIII (December 1960), 329–340.

——. "Taxation of Savings and Consumption in Underdeveloped Countries," *National Tax Journal*, XIV (December 1961), 305–322.

——. SEE ALSO National Tax Association.

Harriss, C. Lowell. "Liquidity of Estates and Death Tax Liability, *Political Science Quarterly*, LXIV (December 1949), 533–559.

——. "Public Finance," in Bernard F. Haley (ed.), *A Survey of Contemporary Economics*, Volume II. Homewood, Illinois: Richard D. Irwin, Inc., 1952. Sponsored by The American Economic Association.

Jocoby, Neil H. "Taxation in Laos: Policies for a New Country with an Undeveloped Economy." *National Tax Journal*, XIV (June 1961), 145–162.

Kaldor, Nicholas. "Will Underdeveloped Countries Learn to Tax?" *Foreign Affairs*, XLI (January 1963), 410–419.

Kybal, Elba Gómez del Rey de. "Why More Taxes? Mobilizing for the Alliance," *Américas*, XIV (April 1962), 11–13.

Lindholm, Richard W. "Analysis of the Land Use and Taxation Policies of Non-Communist Underdeveloped Areas," *Economic Development and Cultural Change*, VIII (Part 3, 1960), 252–256.

—. "Taxation in Laos: Policies for a New Country with an Underdeveloped Economy—A Comment," *National Tax Journal*, XV (March 1962), 109–110.

Mora, José A. "José A. Mora on the Alliance and the Marshall Plan," *Américas*, XIV (February 1962), 2–4.

Moscoso, Teodoro. "Moscoso on the Alliance." *Américas*, XIV (September 1962), 39–40.

—. "Progress Report on the Alliance for Progress," *New York Times Magazine* (August 12, 1962), 11, 59–63.

National Tax Association. *Proceedings of the ———* Annual Conference of the National Tax Association.* Sacramento: National Tax Association, 1951–1961.

(*The 1951 Conference was the forty-fourth; annual reports were published in each of the subsequent years. The following articles are all included in the report for the year indicated:)

(1951) Goode, Richard. "Reconstruction of Foreign Tax Systems," 212–222.

(1952) Eaton, A. Kenneth. "Taxing Income in Canada," 21–31.

(1953) Goode, Richard. "Taxation and Economic Development," 225–236.

(1953) Ohl, John P. "The Capital-Exporting Countries—Income Tax Policy and Techniques," 208–224.

(1955) Ganjei, Nasser D. "Contribution of Tax Missions on Underdeveloped Countries," 208–217.

(1957) Ross, William D. "Tax Concessions and Their Effect," 216–224.

(1958) Strayer, Paul J. "Fiscal Policy for an Expanding Economy," 379–388.

(1961) Oldman, Oliver, and Elisabeth A. Owens. "The Harvard Law School International Program in Taxation," 570–585.

Nurkse, Ragnar. "International Investment To-day in the Light of Nineteenth-Century Experience," *The Economic Journal*, LXIV (December 1954), 744–758.

Ohl, John P. SEE National Tax Association.

Oldman, Oliver. SEE National Tax Association.

Owens, Elisabeth A. SEE National Tax Association.

Plaza, Galo. "Galo Plaza on the Obstacles to the Alliance," *Américas,* XIV (March 1962), 9.

Ross, William D. SEE National Tax Association.

Strayer, Paul J. SEE National Tax Association.

Sufrin, Sidney C. "A Note on Tax Exemption in a Developing Economy," *National Tax Journal.* XIV (December 1961), 400–401.

Szulc, Tad. "Selling a Revolution to Latin America," *New York Times Magazine,* (December 17, 1961), 10, 60–61.

"Tax Reform in Latin America," *Américas,* CVI (December 16, 1961), 381.

"Taxes, Land and Trade," *Américas,* XIV (January 1962), 17–18.

Taylor, Milton C. "Income Taxation in the Federation of Malaya," *National Tax Journal,* XIV (June 1961), 198–204.

Willemsen, Michael A. "The Effect upon the Rate of Private Savings of a Change from a Personal Income Tax to a Personal Expenditures Tax," *National Tax Journal,* XIV (March 1961), 98–103.

C. Pamphlets

Allocation of the Tax Burden by Income Class. New York: Tax Foundation, Inc., May, 1960.

Cantor, Manlio Dionisio Martínez. *Problemas que plantea el estudio e investigacion de los sistemas impositivos en los paises subdesarrollados.* Santiago, Chile: University of Chile, Graduate School for the Study of Latin American Economics, April 1961.

Arthur Andersen & Co. *Highlights of Taxation in Mexico for United States Businessmen.* Prepared by Nicolás Urquiza. Chicago: Arthur Andersen & Co., 1961.

Ferguson, Lloyd C. (ed.). *The Centennial Review.* East Lansing, Michigan: The Centennial Review of Arts & Science, Summer 1962.

International Chamber of Commerce, Executive Committee. *Taxation and the Developing Nations.* [Paris: n.p., 1959].

Krause, Walter. *The United States and Latin America: The Alliance for Progress Program.* Austin: Bureau of Business Research, The University of Texas, 1963.

— (ed.). *Report on Latin America.* Iowa City, Iowa: Bureau of Business and Economic Research, University of Iowa, 1961.

National Bureau of Economic Research. *The Tax Burden in Relation to National Income and Product.* (Research Aid No. 4). New York: Tax Foundation, Inc., 1957.

National Conference on International Economic and Social Development. *The Alliance for Progress: Report of the Ninth Annual Meet-*

ing of the National Conference on International Economic and Social Development, Held in Chicago, July 19–20, 1962. Washington, D. C.: 1962.

Raushenbush, Stephen. *The Challenge to the Alliance for Progress.* Washington, D.C.: Public Affairs Institute, 1962.

Urquiza, Nicolás. SEE Arthur Anderson & Co.

D. Periodicals

Reliance was placed on the following periodicals both for information as to specific points and for general background information. The issues during the period 1961–1962 were especially useful.

International Financial News Survey. Published weekly by the International Monetary Fund.

International Financial Statistics. Published monthly by the International Monetary Fund.

Latin-American Business Highlights. Published quarterly by the Chase Manhattan Bank.

Monthly Bulletin of Statistics. Published monthly by the United Nations.

The general news coverage, editorial pages, and letters to the editor in the following newspapers were also helpful.

American Statesman, Austin, Texas

The Des Moines Register, Des Moines, Iowa

The New York Times

The Wall Street Journal

E. Manuscripts

Dillon, C. Douglas, Statement by Secretary Dillon, Press Release #555, August 7, 1961.

Higgins, Benjamin. "Business Taxation and Regulation of Profits Transfers in Underdeveloped Countries." An unpublished paper included in the Wason Collection of Cornell University Library. Ithaca, New York: April 7, 1954.

"Suggestions for Fielding Tax Administration Training Missions in Several Latin American Countries." Draft Memorandum. Public Finance and Administration Unit, Economic Division, August 11, 1961. Washington, D.C.: 1961.

INDEX

accountants: in tax administration, 151–154

Act of Bogota. *See* Bogota, Act of

administration, fiscal: 18. *See also* tax administration

Africa: poll tax in, 133 n.

Agency for International Development (AID): 44, 155–156, 185

Agricultural Taxation and Economic Development, Reports of Conference on: 15

AID: 44, 155–156, 185

Alliance for Progress: origin and history of, 3–4, 6–7; master plan for, 5–6; basic documents of, 8–9, 16–19; procedures of, 9; economic implications of, 9–11; and social development, 10; nontax objective of, 111; administration of, 166–167; prerequisites for success of, 166–168; and tax reform, 16–24, 66, 173–174

Allocation of the Tax Burden by Income Class: 26 n.

Appropriations Committee, U.S. Senate: 20

Argentina: statistics for, 7(table); inflation in, 39, 40(table)

—, tax structure of: 54; income tax, 71, 90 n., 181(table), 186; tax exemptions in, 90 n., 136, 186, 187; patrimony tax, 92; business income tax, 94, 186, 188; property taxes, 116, 185; sales tax, 122; enforcement of, 149 n.; tax-collection in-

dexes for, 180(table); customs duties, 184; administration of, 186–187; capital-gains tax, 188; excess-profits tax, 188

associations, taxation of: 82

Australia: land tax in, 115–116

automatic data processing (ADP): in tax administration, 160–161

Ball, Carlos A.: 14

Barnes, William Sprague: 20, 50, 60 n., 110, 117

Bhatia, Mohinder S.: 137 n.–138 n., 146 n.

Bird, Richard: 115–116

Blum, Walter J.: 28

Bogota, Act of: 9, 12; nature of, 4–5, 16–17

Bolivia: tax structure of, 51; tax earmarking in, 60–61; land assessment in, 111 n.; land tax in, 116, 185; tax exemptions in, 136; tax-collection indexes for, 180(table); income tax in, 181(table); customs duties in, 184; tax-administration reforms for, 186

Brazil: statistics for, 7(table); compulsory debt financing in, 34; inflation in, 39, 40(table)

—, tax structure of: 54, 54(table); income tax, 40, 68, 69–70, 71, 74, 75(table), 77, 78–79, 83, 89–90, 91, 92, 94, 151 n., 157, 181(table); tax deductions in, 40, 85; tax sharing in, 58, 59; state and local taxes, 60;